crazy about
pies

crazy about
pies

Irresistible Pies for Every Sweet Occasion

Krystina Castella

STERLING
New York

STERLING
New York

An Imprint of Sterling Publishing
387 Park Avenue South
New York, NY 10016

STERLING and the distinctive Sterling logo are registered trademarks of Sterling Publishing Co., Inc.

© 2012 by Krystina Castella
Photography by Teri Lyn Fisher
Designed by Rachel Maloney

ISBN 978-1-4027-9883-2

Library of Congress Cataloging-in-Publication Data

Castella, Krystina.
  Crazy about pies : more than 150 sweet & savory recipes for every occasion / Krystina Castella.
    pages cm
  Includes index.
  ISBN 978-1-4027-9883-2
  1. Pies. I. Title.
  TX773.C349 2012
  641.86'52--dc23
                            2012024830

Distributed in Canada by Sterling Publishing
c/o Canadian Manda Group, 165 Dufferin Street
Toronto, Ontario, Canada M6K 3H6
Distributed in the United Kingdom by GMC Distribution Services
Castle Place, 166 High Street, Lewes, East Sussex, England BN7 1XU
Distributed in Australia by Capricorn Link (Australia) Pty. Ltd.
P.O. Box 704, Windsor, NSW 2756, Australia

For information about custom editions, special sales, and premium and corporate purchases,
please contact Sterling Special Sales at 800-805-5489 or specialsales@sterlingpublishing.com.

Manufactured in China

2 4 6 8 10 9 7 5 3 1

www.sterlingpublishing.com

For my baby boy, Sequoia—
Welcome to the world, "Cutie Pie"

Acknowledgments

Thank you to everyone whose help has crafted this book:

Jennifer Williams, editor

Teri Lyn Fisher, photographer

Jennifer Park, food stylist

Jennifer Farley, baking assistant

Barbara Clark, project editor

Rachel Maloney, design director

Elizabeth Mihaltse, cover art director

Jason Chow, cover designer

Contents

America's Favorite Uplifting Food

For me, the most exciting way to travel is on foot. My husband and I are both professors, and we spend our summer vacations backpacking for weeks at a time deep in the woods. We walk all day, snack on dried fruit and nuts, cook our meals on a camp stove, and eat tons of pie. So how is it that we come to eat so much pie?

Every week or so, we return to civilization and visit a small town to replenish our supplies. At every juncture, we may or may not find cookies, chocolate, ice cream, or cakes—but there is *always* homemade pie. All I can think about a day or two before we arrive is, "What kind of pie will they have?" In some towns, we'll find creamy pies piled high with meringue or fresh whipped cream; in other towns, we'll find flaky pies made from tart fresh apples or super-sweet cherries. If we are really lucky, we'll find a savory main-event pie filled with tender meats and vegetables. This is because no other food says "welcome" better than pie.

You don't need to be a hiker to get a slice of this American treat. Road trips offer the best opportunity to taste regional pies. While driving

through the Northwest, you might find blueberry or marionberry pie; in the Southwest, a tamale pie; in the upper Midwest, a cherry pie; in the lower Midwest, a coconut cream pie; in the Northeast, apple pie; and the South, Key lime pie. In every town, you'll find a truck stop, a bakery, or café where a waitress calls you Hon and where a hand-painted sign invites you in with the words WE HAVE PIE! There is always a unique character inside who labored over the crust and filling just so it could be shared with you, a total stranger. And if you time your trip right, you'll find hundreds of county fairs offering tastings, bake-offs, pie-eating contests, and many opportunities to get your face completely covered with pie.

As much as I love to eat sweet and savory pies, there are as many reasons why I love to bake them. No food says "home" more than pie. Some people relax by drinking a martini by the pool, picking strawberries fresh from the field, or hosting a glamorous dinner party. I, on the other hand, prefer the comforting hominess of baking a pie. As far as I'm concerned, selecting the ingredients of the season from my garden or from farmers markets and baking them into a pie is the best way to spend an evening or weekend morning. Hanging out in the kitchen, rolling out a crust, and smelling the aroma of apples or peaches as it fills the air is pure paradise.

Everyone has his or her own interpretation of the definition of "pie." So how do I define it? A pie is either a sweet or savory filling encased in crust. The filling can be almost anything—chocolate, fruit, cream, custard, meat, or vegetables—but there is *always* a crust. The crust can be made with whole wheat flour, oatmeal, meringue—or something else. For example, my Shepherd's Pie (page 149) has a crust made from sweet potatoes, and my Tamale Pie (page 148) is made with a creamy cornmeal crust.

In some recipes I put crusts over and around some of my favorite ingredients, including those that aren't usually served in crust. Try wrapping a butter crust over baked apples (page 221), surrounding baked macaroni with an olive oil crust (page 146), or filling a chocolate crust with creamy crème brûlée (page 86). You will also find crusts that dress up ice cream nicely, including those made from waffle cones (page 210), coconut (page 92), and pretzels (page 235).

Savory pies often take center stage at a meal. I cannot think of a mealtime experience that is more satisfying than digging a fork into a crust filled with the hidden surprise of meat and vegetables. When the steam escapes, it feels as though you have opened a gift wrapped in pastry. Enjoy a hearty Turkey Pot Pie (page 219) covered in a blanket of crust on a cool fall day. Savory pies can also be light and refreshing. Prepare a satisfying Potato Knish (page 136) for lunch, or dip Chicken Empanadas (page 156) into a tangy Yogurt Kiwi Dipping Sauce as an appetizer.

This book also includes plenty of recipes for tarts—a form that is so similar to pie that it is difficult to define the difference. Technically, tarts are made with a butter-based or puff pastry dough that is pressed (not draped) into a shallow pan that often has fluted edges and a removable bottom. But the lineage is different. Many tarts originated in France, whereas most pies originated in the British Isles. In addition, the top of a tart is usually open, like a single-crust pie. Like pie, tarts can contain either a sweet or a savory filling. Sometimes the crust is baked and the filling is added in later, as in the Blueberry Custard Tart (page 84), but at other times the filling is baked in with the crust, as in the Chocolate Almond Tart (page 178). Since the form usually defines the difference between pies and tarts, and since many of my pie recipes break the boundaries of form by eschewing the standard 9-inch round pie pan, I won't be offended if you choose to call a tart a pie or a pie a tart. It really doesn't matter, as long it tastes good.

I experimented with recipes for many years and thought long and hard about which pies to include in this book. As part of my creative process, I thought about up-to-date baking trends, new flavor combinations, and modern lifestyles. I edited the list down and chose only the recipes to which I could attach at least one of the following labels: (1) classic and comforting, (2) infused with a fusion of flavors, (3) made in a unique size or form, or (4) artisanal and handcrafted.

COMFORTING CLASSICS

Whether the pie you're craving is an authentic made-from-scratch billowy coconut cream, a juicy cherry, a tart lemon meringue, or a warming chicken pot pie, you will find many sentimental favorites here. Some of the classic pies we grew up with and learned to love are presented in the old-fashioned way, but I've refreshed them with new toppings, spices, or crusts. For example, candied walnuts are added to a banana cream pie (page 69), cardamom infuses the pumpkin pie (page 212), and a crunchy oatmeal crust complements the strawberry pie (page 43).

Retro-style pies are also reinterpreted. Hot-water-crust Cornish Pasties (page 137) are taken out of the mine shafts of old England and brought to a sunshiny picnic lunch. With the addition of a few marzipan toppings, the 1950s-style Christmas Grasshopper Pie (page 231) becomes a new holiday favorite. Pecan Pie Bars (page 214) are prepared with a thick spicy crust for a casual Thanksgiving celebration. Cheesecake Pie with Marzipan Butterflies (page 111), a dessert that is not so much a cheesecake as a custard pie, is dressed up in a full, proper graham cracker crust, baked in a pie pan, and given the place in baking classification it deserves.

FUSION FLAVORS

These days, I can't think of anything that says American pie better than a melting pot of international flavors. So in this book, in addition to homespun American classics such as the Shaker Lemon Pie (page 201) and the Roasted Sweet Potato Marshmallow Pie (page 217), you will find pies with Mediterranean, Asian, Jewish, and Latin influences.

Italian pies—such as the Ricotta Pie (page 181), the Orange Tarts (page 229), the Pine Nut Tart (page 170), the Chocolate Fig Ricotta Tart (page 82), and the Spumoni Ice Cream Pie with Amaretti Crust (page 90)—are reinvented family recipes inspired by my Italian heritage. Phyllo pastry, used in Mediterranean and Middle Eastern desserts, inspires the Pistachio Nests (page 183) and the Fruit Rose Pies (page 174). Jewish traditions inspire the Honey-Sweetened Apple Tart (page 187), the Fried Fruit Pies (page 186), the Passover Concord Grape Pies (page 189), and the Potato Knishes (page 136)—the savory street-vendor food that I grew up with in Manhattan. British tradition inspires the Shepherd's Pie (page 149), and Blackbird Pies (page 121).

Asian flavors and practices are reflected in the Green Tea and Chocolate Ice Cream Pie with Gluten-Free Coconut Crust (page 92) and the Panda Bento Box (page 140). The Philippines inspire the sweet and savory Cheddar Coconut Pies (page 145). Latin American influences permeate the Chocolate Chili Wafer Crust (page 243), the Pineapple and Mango Empanadas (page 51), and the Guava Cream Cheese Strudel (page 64).

SIZE AND FORM MATTER

When it comes to pie, size and form do matter. The crust-to-filling ratio changes with both size and shape. Individual pies, such as the Chocolate Cream Tarts (page 72) and the Pomegranate Turnovers (page 62), have more crust than, say, a large traditional apple pie or peach pie, both of which have much more filling than crust. Size and shape also influence the presentation. Ravioli (page 152) are really just simple mini pies, but when they're served on a plate with blueberry sauce, all of a sudden you have a dinner-party showstopper. Edible "landscapes," such as the Deconstructed Cherry Pie (page 150), allow you to assemble the exact ratio of crust, filling, and cream to suit your taste—and they offer a snazzy presentation.

Individual desserts (a trend that started with cupcakes, moved on to Whoopie Pies, and is still evolving today) are also represented in this book. They allow you to offer each guest his or her own personalized treat. If each pie in a batch is different, guests can choose the one that reflects their mood or favorite flavors. The recipe for Quiches with Herb Wheat Germ Crusts (page 127) shows how to blend flavors in a single batch of filling with just a few ingredients. Portability is also a big benefit to individual pies. It isn't easy to eat a slice of traditional pie on the go or while working the crowd at a party, but when you modify the form it becomes possible to "have your pie and eat it, too." The Pie Pops (page 99) can be served as appetizers or desserts; the Rum Raisin Pudding with Piecrust Chips (page 160) and Wedding Pies (page 115) are perfect for a dessert bar or buffet.

In several recipes, I introduce the concept of sharing. (Remember? We learned about that in kindergarten!) The Blueberry Pies (page 202), the Key Lime Pies (page 196), and the Individual Deep-Dish Berry Pies (page 53) are all a little too much for one person but are perfectly sized for two people to share. And on that subject, gifts of pies are always welcome. If you're hosting a large crowd, give out tiny wrappable Truffle Pies (page 177), or give a special someone a Pie in a Jar (page 106). As a traditional Amish housewarming gift, Raisin Friendship Pie with Oatmeal Crust (page 65) says welcome in a warm and memorable way.

ARTISANAL AND HANDCRAFTED PIES

Since I was very young, I have been obsessed with experimenting in the kitchen and have been fascinated with baking and the decoration of baked goods. In addition, I have been a practicing industrial designer for more than twenty years (I design a wide variety of consumer products, such as furniture, clothing, toys, and housewares, among others). This strong foundation in art, design, and craftsmanship has taught me the skills and techniques to work with all types of materials, from wood to marzipan. I couldn't resist applying my skills to pies: after all, a filling is simply a platform on which to develop new flavors, and a crust is simply a blank canvas on which to experiment with textures, shapes, and aesthetics.

You will find that many of my recipes borrow techniques from cake and cookie decorating (which I love) and apply them to pies. For me, the kitchen is simply a playground where I can exercise my creative muscles. The Gingerbread Tarts (page 224), for example, provide an opportunity to decorate two dozen gingerbread men—in potentially two dozen different ways. You can also have a lot of fun with fondant—a very versatile material—especially in the Blackbird Pies (page 121) and the dainty Mascarpone Cream Petits Fours Pies (page 109). Marzipan butterflies adorn the girly Cheesecake Pie (page 111) and an edible bride-and-groom marzipan topper adorns a Wedding Pie (page 115).

Although decorating pies is somewhat similar to decorating cakes and cookies, there are some significant differences. For example, planning your pie decorations must be done ahead of time, because many "finishing" techniques, such as edges, vents, lattices, and other top-crust decorations, are created before the pie is baked—such as those atop the Happy Birthday Nectarine Pie (page 105) and the Chocolate Pudding Pie with Chocolate-Covered Strawberries (page 76).

But, as with cakes, decorating can also be done post-baking. Fresh fruit makes an excellent graphic decorative filling and topping—as in the Fruit Tarts with Sweet Tart Shells (page 118) and the Four-Melon Tart (page 158). Your decorations can be elegant, as in the Sweet Cherry Pie with Cream Cheese Crust (page 46), or rustic, as in the Plum Crostata (page 60). Boozing up your pies not only adds depth of flavor but also allows you to decorate them with fun drink garnishes, such as those that top the Piña Colada Cream Pies (page 162).

ABOUT THIS BOOK

When I mentioned to friends and family that I was writing a cookbook about pies, I got two reactions. The first was, "I have a favorite crust that I make over and over and fill with various fillings." I can certainly understand that: in this book, for example, there are no fewer than twenty-four recipes that use my simple and delicious Basic Butter Crust (page 242). But I've also included many other crust recipes in this book—some are fluffy, some are flaky, some are tart, and some are sweet. If you're stuck in a rut, these recipes will help jolt you out of your routine and give you some creative new ideas. Try a few and see which recipes and basic techniques you prefer, and soon you will be making consistently delicious crusts. You may have a few favorites, or you may make several batches of one particular crust, storing them in your freezer so they are ready to go when the "pie urge" strikes.

The other comment people make is one that I did not understand at first. It is, "I really find it intimidating to make piecrust." I heard this over and over. I wondered where this fear came from, and thought I must have missed that memo. "Easy as pie" is a phrase we hear all the time, but one thing is for sure—pie making, as portrayed in cookbooks, blogs, and TV, is anything but easy.

Statements such as "If you have a fear of making crusts" (as though you are supposed to), or "Crusts really take a special touch and feel to make correctly" (as though only a few people are lucky enough to have the gift), or "Practice, practice, practice is the only way to make a crust" (as if anyone has time for that) seem designed to intimidate. If these statements don't scare us enough, then there is "The best piecrusts are made from lard." No wonder people today are afraid of making pies. Remember, you heard it here first—there is nothing to fear about pies! They are not difficult to make, and, yes, you will get better at it over time, with practice, but even your first crusts will probably be pretty good, too. Lard crusts are surprisingly good, but you don't need lard to bake a successful pie.

I probably shouldn't be saying this in a pie cookbook, but I will: if you are "crazy about pies" and don't have the time or desire to make them from scratch, there is nothing wrong with making pies from high-quality store-bought crusts and/or fillings. Mass-produced crusts have been perfected so that they are foolproof, and some canned fillings have been preserved at the peak of freshness with very few additives. Frozen puff pastry and phyllo dough help the home baker achieve a professional result and eliminate the intense labor needed to prepare these delicate doughs from scratch. High-quality prepared piecrusts, sold frozen in pie pans or refrigerated in rolls, are nice to have on hand. Many store-bought graham cracker and chocolate wafer crusts are good, too. Once you test out a few brands and find ones that you like, don't be embarrassed about using them.

That being said, there are many advantages to making a crust from scratch (freshness and knowledge of the ingredients, to name a couple). But the most important advantage is that making a crust from scratch gives you the opportunity to vary the tastes and textures of a pie. For example, a cherry pie in a cream cheese crust is much tangier than, and very different from, a cherry pie in an all-butter crust and even more different from a cherry pie in a chocolate or spice crust. Each crust complements the filling in a different way, which can only be achieved through mixing your own ingredients and making your own crust. Making your own crust also allows you to experiment with new techniques and forms, from rustic slabs to crostatas to dainty lattice crusts.

Homemade fillings also offer the same options. High-quality store-bought pie fillings are nice to have stocked in your pantry if you want to whip up a quick dessert, although not all fruits and custards are available in canned or jarred form. Savory fillings are also a rarity in store-bought form. Making your own filling allows you to take advantage of a much wider variety of flavors. For example, on page 43, you can see that there are many good varieties of apple to choose from when making a classic apple pie, depending on the degree of tartness you prefer. That choice is not available in store-bought fillings. In addition, if you freeze fresh fruits or can your own homemade fillings, you can enjoy most fruit pies out of season.

I organized the recipes in this book into in five sections. In Everyday Pies you will find basic recipes for fruit, cream and custard, and ice cream pies. These pies are simple to make and are perfect for spur-of-the moment baking. Special-Occasion Pies contains recipes that help us celebrate three of the most important occasions in our lives—birthdays, weddings, and baby celebrations.

The Party Pies section includes recipe suggestions for everything from a casual weekend brunch to a formal dinner. The Holiday Pies section offers traditional pies that have become synonymous with seasonal holidays as well as new ideas that present a twist on tradition. Finally, the Crusts, Fillings, and Toppings section provides recipes for the three basic elements of pie—try mixing and matching to suit your own tastes.

To my mind, this five-part method of organization reflects how we truly *experience* pies, and to me that is the most important part of baking.

If you want to learn more about the tools, techniques, ingredients, and how-to's of pie baking, from tips on choosing the right equipment to setting up your kitchen and expanding your technical skills, take a look at the Pies in the Know section. I also offer troubleshooting solutions for the most common piecrust questions. The step-by-step techniques, recipes, and design ideas in this book are here for you to re-create in your kitchen or to use as a springboard for concepts of your own. Make your pies as simple or complex as you like. Follow the recipes exactly or experiment. Whatever approach you choose, I hope you have fun exploring all the possibilities that pies provide.

Now—bring on the pie!

Chapter 1

Pies in the Know

THE PIE MAKER'S TOOL KIT

Outfitting your kitchen for pie making is not about buying a lot of gear—it's about buying the *right* gear. High-quality, well-designed tools constructed with high-quality materials make the pie-making experience easy and enjoyable. A good rolling pin, for example, will help you work quickly and lightly—vital to making a thin, flaky crust. A good pastry blender helps cut fat into dry ingredients without melting the fat, and helps you determine when you have added enough liquid. Classic ceramic or glass bowls will keep dough cool during mixing. Pie pans made out of the correct material will make the crust brown and crispy on the bottom. Pie pans in unique shapes help you come up with ideas for creative forms and presentation. Think of your tools as your friends—cheering you on, helping you make the perfect pie.

Pie and Tart Pans

Pie pans come in all sizes, although the most common is a 9- or 10-inch round. Pie pans have angled sides (so the slices are easy to remove), whereas tart pans often have straight, fluted sides and, most of the time, a removable bottom. Pie pans can be made of heatproof glass, metal, ceramic, or porcelain. Glass disperses heat really well and allows the crust to bake evenly. Another advantage of glass is that you can see the pie as it bakes and determine how much your crust has browned.

Classic metal pie pans are available in a wider range of sizes than glass pans. When choosing metal pans, buy those that are made out of aluminum or have a nonstick surface, which won't rust as easily as stainless steel pans. If you only have thin metal pans, double them up to help create even heat flow. Acidic ingredients should not be baked in metal pans, or the ingredients may turn gray.

If presentation and display are what matters, use a ceramic or porcelain pan. The blue ceramic pan that holds the large Wedding Pie (page 115) adds a colorful, home-style touch to the dessert display and breaks up the white theme that so often dominates weddings. Ramekins also make perfect individual pie pans.

Some pie pans come with a lid, which helps to keep the pie fresh in the refrigerator and safe while you're transporting it. It is nice to have one of these on hand, because many recipes call for chilling the pie to let it set, and the lid keeps the surface of the filling from getting marred with plastic wrap before serving.

TART AND TARTLET PANS

Most tart pans have fluted edges, short sides, and removable bottoms, all of which make it really easy to form the crust and transfer the tart from the pan to a serving dish. They are available in a wide range of sizes and shapes. The most common shapes are round, square, and rectangular. Miniature tart (tartlet) pans are sold separately or "ganged up" as part of a master pan in square, round, or oval shapes. Some have removable bottoms.

CAKE PANS

Cake pans are usually deeper than pie pans, and the sides do not have as much draft (degree of angularity) as pie pans. Since they don't have draft, it is harder to remove a whole pie and its individual slices from a cake pan than from a pie pan. However, cake pans are available in many more sizes and shapes, so I still like to use them. My favorite cake pans are ones that come in specialty shapes, from very simple stars and hearts to pyramids, hexagons, and domes—not to mention pans in the shape of animals (such as fish) and seasonal objects (such as snowflakes). For example, if you want to bake a pie for the Fourth of

July in the shape of the USA, you can probably find a cake pan to fill the bill. Lining a cake pan with parchment paper, and using enough so that it overhangs on all sides, will allow you to lift the pie out of the pan by grabbing the paper and will make removal much easier.

SPRINGFORM PANS AND CAKE RINGS

Looking to get more use out of your springform pan than just cheesecake? When you bake a pie in a springform pan, it is much easier to remove than if you make it in a pie pan. A springform pan also allows you to show off the golden crust by unbuckling the clasp and removing the sides of the pan. Springform pans are available in either a round or a rounded square shape. The German Chocolate Pie (page 179) is made in a springform pan.

Cake rings have no bottom. To use them, place them on a parchment-lined baking sheet, fill with dough and filling, and bake. Cake rings are also very easy to remove so that you can expose the sides of the pie.

MUFFIN TINS

If you're planning to bake a dozen or more individual pies, bake them in a muffin tin instead of purchasing several small pans. Muffin tins, also used for cupcakes, are commonly available in mini, medium, and large sizes. Since muffin cups are usually deeper than pie pans, you can use them to bake deep-dish pies. Muffin tins can be lined with disposable paper or foil liners, or, if the tin is well greased, the pies can be baked directly in the tins.

CAST IRON SKILLET

Cast iron is a wonderful material for the even distribution of heat. They also make a great rustic presentation for serving. I use these pans over an open fire when I am camping and in the oven when I am home.

PAPER AND FOIL PANS

Disposable paper cake pan liners and foil pie pans are available in a range of sizes. Use them for pies that you need to transport to a bake sale, give as a gift, or offer as party favors. When using paper cake pan liners, always choose those that have a sturdy, corrugated bottom, and place them inside a rigid metal cake pan before baking. When using foil pans, make sure to double them up or place them in a rigid metal pie pan before baking. This helps evenly distribute the heat.

RIMMED BAKING SHEET

Rimmed baking sheets are used for making hand pies, turnovers, and pie pops, as well as slab pies and crostatas, but, when covered with parchment paper or a silicone mat, they're also used under pie pans to catch drippings while baking. If you are baking several small pies or tartlets, place the pans on baking sheets to make them easier to transfer in and out of the oven.

Dough- and Filling-Making Tools

Fortunately, making doughs and fillings doesn't require too many specialized tools, and you may already have everything on hand. Here are some suggestions for equipment that is best for pies.

CUTTERS AND STRAWS

An easy way to make decorative vents and layered crust decorations is to dig into your collection of cookie cutters, which can also be used for shaping pie pops. Bubble-tea straws are also good for puncturing small holes. Fluted pie wheels make very nice scalloped edges for lattice strips and pie edges, while a straight-edge pastry wheel or pizza cutter makes clean, straight lines.

DOUBLE BOILER

A double boiler is good for items that need to be heated very slowly or gently over low heat. Precooking fillings, melting chocolate, and blending delicate custard fillings are usually best done in a double boiler. Look for one in which the top saucepan is shallow. Fill the bottom with water close to the top, but do not let it touch the top pan. Fill the top pan with ingredients as directed in the recipe. The hot water will heat the top pan and this low heat will give you good control over cooking or melting the ingredients. You can also fashion a double boiler by placing a larger heatproof bowl over a smaller saucepan filled with simmering water. Although you can also melt chocolate in the microwave, I prefer to use a double boiler because the chocolate is heated more evenly. Actively stirring while melting ensures smoother results.

ELECTRIC MIXER

An electric mixer is the best way to beat eggs to various stages of stiffness for meringues and cream toppings, and is also the best way to cream ingredients. If you're using a handheld electric mixer, you'll notice that the beaters on older models have a post running down the middle of each beater, whereas newer mixers have convex, curved wires with open centers that allow for better movement of the fillings. Buy a handheld mixer that has a good range of power and speeds as well as both whisk-style and standard beater attachments. Handheld mixers are available in cordless and corded models.

Stand mixers aren't used as often in pie making as they are for cookie dough, bread dough, and cake batter. But if you're in the market for a stand mixer, you already know that its main advantage is that you don't need to hold the bowl steady as you mix; it locks in place. Stand mixers also come with many different attachments—for whisking, kneading dough, and making ice cream.

FOOD PROCESSOR OR BLENDER

My favorite tool for making piecrusts is my food processor. I pulse it to blend the fat and dry ingredients to the consistency of coarse meal, and then drizzle the liquid through the feed tube to form the dough into a ball. I also use my food processor to grind nuts for crusts and fillings and to blend sauces. A blender can sometimes be used instead of a food processor to whip or purée.

KITCHEN SHEARS

These specialized scissors are used to trim the excess overhanging dough from the bottom and top crusts. Paring knives can also be used.

MEASURING CUPS

To achieve the most accurate measurements, use glass cups with spouts for liquids, and plastic or metal cups with handles for dry ingredients. The latter are usually sold in sets (typically ¼, ⅓, ½, and 1 cup) and are best used for dry, powdery ingredients, such as flour and sugar, and dense ingredients, such as peanut butter, shortening, and jam. Spoon the dry ingredients into cups (do not scoop), then remove any excess ingredients by running a knife over the top of the cup to level the contents.

MEASURING SPOONS

Use a graduated set of measuring spoons for both liquid and dry ingredients. Avoid tabletop flatware; it rarely is designed for exact measurements.

MIXING BOWLS

The most important thing to keep in mind when making pie dough is to keep the ingredients cold. Glass, ceramic, and metal bowls will hold a chilled bowl's cold temperature better than plastic.

PASTRY BLENDER

Many experienced bakers work the fat into the flour with their fingertips so they get the feel of the dough and know when it is just right. If you don't feel like digging your fingers into the goo, however, a pastry blender also helps you feel the dough's consistency. This tool has several parallel U-shaped wires that are attached to a handle. It is used to cut the fat (butter, shortening, or lard) into the flour until the mixture forms pea-size crumbs, usually about the size of coarsely ground meal, a critical step when making a tender crust by hand. To use the pastry blender, press down and rotate both the tool and the bowl with a slight twist. You can also use two butter knives (one in each hand) to cut in the fat into the flour by starting in a "crossed swords" position and moving the knives away from each other, cutting the fat into little pieces in the process.

PASTRY BRUSH

A pastry brush is used to brush egg washes and glazes onto the tops of piecrusts, and can come in handy for other kitchen duties as well. Invest in a tightly woven natural-boar-bristle brush. It is best to have two—one for tasks involving dry ingredients, such as brushing off flour, and one for tasks involving wet ingredients. You can also use basting brushes for pie-making purposes. Silicone brushes are designed to hold liquids for easy coating; they are also odor-resistant and easy to clean.

PLASTIC WRAP AND WAX PAPER

Use plastic wrap whenever you want to retain moisture; for example, when you put dough in the refrigerator or freezer to chill. For quick kitchen cleanup, roll out dough between two sheets of plastic wrap or wax paper rather than directly on a floured surface. This also avoids the need to keep adding more flour to your work surface as you roll. For 9-inch pies, cut the wax paper or plastic wrap to 12 inches square. Don't place anything wrapped in plastic wrap in the oven.

RASPS, ZESTERS, AND GRATERS

Used to remove the zest from citrus fruits, a rasp, zester, or grater allows you to remove only the thin outer layer of the peel and not the bitter white pith. These tools are also used to grate fresh spices, such as nutmeg and ginger. A box grater can be used for coarsely grating large ingredients, such as a squash, but many of them have a side with fine zesters as well.

ROLLING PIN

A rolling pin is the most important tool for making piecrusts. My favorite is a two-handled heavy marble rolling pin. The weight makes it much easier to roll out a very thin crust. It also stays cool, which is crucial when working with dough. When I want to get the thickness just right, however, I use a long wooden pin with tapered edges and no handles, which makes it easier to feel the dough. Wooden dowels, about 1½ to 2 inches in diameter, can also be used as rolling pins. The advantage of using a long tapered rolling pin or a long wooden dowel is that you can use them with thickness guides for a perfect crust every time (see page 9).

ROLLING SURFACE

A flat, cool, clean kitchen countertop dusted with flour works fine for rolling out dough that will be transferred to a pie pan immediately. Or, because they stay cool, you can also buy a granite or marble slab and use it for rolling out dough. The dough can be rolled directly on the surface or between two pieces of plastic wrap or wax paper. When you want to chill the dough before cutting it or transferring it to a pie pan, roll it out on a cutting board, cover with plastic wrap, and place it in the refrigerator or freezer.

RULER

An 18-inch ruler is good to have on hand for measuring rolled-out dough—use it to make sure the crust will fit in the pan before baking. A ruler also helps you to cut even lattice strips and to space decorations evenly over the top of a pie.

SIFTERS AND SIEVES

Sifting dry ingredients such as flour and confectioners' sugar gets rid of lumps that can cause clumps in your pie dough or topping. It is always best to sift flour before measuring, although it is no secret that most people skip this step and only sift occasionally. The amounts of flour called for in this book reflect the quantity after sifting—if you don't sift, keep in mind that your results may be slightly different from what you intended. If you don't have a sifter, you can use a handheld sieve. Small sifters are good for dusting pies with confectioners' sugar or cocoa powder. Sieves are also used to strain seeds and pulp from smooth fillings.

SPATULAS AND WOODEN SPOONS

Stock your tool kit with flexible silicone spatulas and wooden spoons of different sizes to use for gently folding, scraping the bowl, and smoothing meringue, cream, and ice cream pie tops. A 10-inch offset spatula with a very thin, flexible blade is good to have on hand to help release the piecrust from the work surface. Don't wait until you have finished rolling out the crust to use it; release the dough from the surface throughout the process of rolling.

WIRE WHISKS

Used to combine dry and liquid ingredients and to mix custards while thickening, whisks can also be used to whip heavy cream, but usually an electric mixer is quicker. If you hate to sift, wire whisks are the next best way to smooth out lumps while mixing dry ingredients. A large 12-inch whisk (measured from top to bottom, including the handle), 2½ inches in diameter at its widest part, will work really well.

Baking Tools

BAKING STONE

Used to give pizza and bread a wonderful crust, baking stones can

CRUSTS WITH CONSISTENT THICKNESS

The secret to making crusts with consistent thickness is to use a thickness guide. To make a guide, buy two 1/8-inch-thick wooden strips at a hardware store. They should be an inch or two wide and as long as the depth of your countertop. Place them on the counter, on either side of the mound of dough. They should be spaced apart at a distance equivalent to the desired diameter of your crust plus two inches on either side. For example, if you are making a 13-inch round crust, the guides should be spaced 17 inches apart. Set the pin on top of the strips and roll out the dough, rotating the dough until it is even with the top of the strips and has reached the desired diameter. You can also buy rolling pin rings in various sizes—1/8 inch, 1/4 inch, etc.—which raise the pins off the surface of the dough to the desired height. Buy these at the same time as you buy your pin to make sure they fit.

also be used to transfer heat to the bottom crust of your pie. If you find your crust does not cook evenly or brown on the bottom, preheat a baking stone and place the pie pan on it. Crostatas can be baked directly on the stone, too—just dust it with cornmeal before baking.

COOLING RACKS

Cooling racks are gridded metal racks with feet that allow air to circulate around the entire pie so it cools evenly. Because the crust continues to brown in the hot pan after you take the pie out of the oven, cooling racks also ensure that the crust stays evenly browned all over. And because most pies are served in the pan, a cooling rack ensures that the entire pan is cool before you put it on the table. Tarts baked in pans with removable bottoms can be taken out of the pan after the crust has cooled slightly (about 10 to 15 minutes after being removed from the oven). Then they can be placed on cooling racks to cool completely. Stainless steel racks are the best. If you have a small kitchen and will be baking multiple pies at a time, look for stackable cooling racks.

EDGE SHIELD

Shields protect the edges of your crust from burning during baking. You can make a shield from aluminum foil, or purchase a silicone or metal shield. Measure your pan before your purchase to make sure it fits. Also, when shaping the crust, make sure it isn't too big to fit under the shield.

OVENS AND THERMOMETERS

I have found that temperatures of ovens are not exact, and that every oven measures heat differently. This is why I measure temperature with an oven thermometer that I keep inside the oven. When I preheat the oven, I place it in the center of the oven, double-check it for accuracy, and make adjustments as needed. The weather, time of day, and altitude can also affect oven temperature. Know your oven's hot and cool spots and always provide adequate circulation around the pie by using the center rack and leaving several inches of space around the pan.

PARCHMENT PAPER, ALUMINUM FOIL, SILICONE MATS

Lining your crusts with parchment paper or foil encourages even blind-baking and makes it easy to remove weights (see page 10). I also line baking sheets when I prepare turnovers and pie pops. I prefer to use parchment because it does not absorb heat. Aluminum foil makes it easier to press the bottom crust into the pie pan, and conforms better to the shape of the pan, but it absorbs more heat. A silicone mat is a reusable nonstick surface used to line a baking sheet. It can also be used to roll out your dough.

PIE BIRDS

If you have never heard of pie birds, visit eBay and you will see that there are collectors out there who will pay a lot of money for antique and vintage examples of this whimsical but useful tool. Pie birds are fun to use as well as functional, and add a homey, nostalgic touch when part of the presentation. From a practical point of view, inserting a pie bird in the center of a double-crusted pie helps liquids evaporate. The hollow center vents steam and moisture out of the bird's mouth, so the moisture, especially from fruit fillings, does not build up under the top crust.

TIMER

Baking times are always going to be inexact. They will depend on the moisture in your ingredients, how many pans are in the oven at the same time, and how accurate your oven's temperature is. Buy a kitchen timer but carry it around the house with you when you are baking. You don't want to be too far away to hear the timer on your stove or oven beep!

WEIGHTS

Metal, ceramic, or clay pie weights are used when blind-baking (see page 32). Lining the crust and weighting it helps the crust retain its shape and keeps it from shrinking or puffing. Dry beans and rice can also be used as weights. I reuse the same beans and rice over and over. Fill the shell with weights until they reach ¼ inch from the top; this will prevent the sides of the crust from slipping down into the pan.

THE PIE DECORATOR'S TOOL KIT

Decorating pies is very different from decorating cakes. For one thing, pies can be decorated before they are baked by shaping, cutting, or embossing the dough. Like cakes, however, pies can also be decorated after they are baked by topping them with cream, marzipan, or fondant decorations. Here are my suggestions for a well-stocked pie-decorating kit.

CUTTERS AND STAMPS

In addition to being used for cutting vents and layering crusts, pastry cutters can also be used for cutting dough, marzipan, or fondant for decorations. Dip the cutter in confectioners' sugar or flour if it sticks to marzipan or fondant. Pastry cutters can also be used to press outlines into the crust, which can be filled with sugar or other topping ingredients. Cookie stamps are a great way to press patterns into crusts, marzipan, gum paste, or fondant. If you can't find cookie stamps you like, you can use the rubber stamps available in stationery stores, which provide many more options. You can also have your own rubber stamps custom-made by a local office supply store.

FOOD COLORING

Liquid, gel, or powdered food coloring can be added to crusts, fillings, fondant—you name it—to create almost any color in the rainbow. Liquid food coloring is available at most grocery stores, and is best used with white or light fillings or decorations. To create light colors, add a few drops; to make deep colors, add several drops. Gel and paste food colorings are highly concentrated; you need only a little bit to create dark or bright colors.

ICING SPATULAS

A flexible offset icing spatula with a thin edge makes meringues, whipped cream, and fillings much easier to apply. I also use this tool when shaping the cream and meringue. Choose a stainless steel spatula with a blade that is 6 or 8 inches long and has a rounded tip.

KITCHEN TORCH

Used for caramelizing crème brûlée and toasting meringue, this is a handy tool to have. It allows you to point the flame only where the heat is needed, preserving your beautiful golden crust from the heat of the broiler. It gives you much more control than if you place the pie back into the oven. The flame is fueled by means of a butane canister. Choose a compact torch with an adjustable flame.

PASTRY BAGS

Pastry bags are cone-shaped bags used to extrude—or pipe—garnishes such as whipped cream and meringue through a shaped tip. A coupler holds the tip to the bag. They are made out of reusable or disposable materials such as plastic, canvas, parchment paper, or nylon. Bigger is better: 10-inch and 12-inch bags are the most common, but as you learn to control the bags you may want to get larger ones. It is nice to have several pastry bags at your disposal, so you can use several different colors or fillings on a single pie without stopping to refill.

A mechanical pastry bag has a stainless steel or silicone barrel to hold the frosting or icing and usually comes with a number of interchangeable tips. Many people find mechanical bags easier to control than a conventional pastry bag. To use one, place the cream in the barrel and crank the handle to press the mixture to the tip.

You can also use homemade tools, such as recycled squirt bottles and airtight plastic bags with a corner cut off, to pipe decorations.

PASTRY TIPS

Pastry tips are sold in sets and individually. Large tips are good for thick mixtures like meringue and pastry dough; small tips are good for delicate writing, and medium-size tips are best for borders. Round tips extrude a smooth line and are used to outline shapes, to fill and pipe designs, for writing, beads, dots, balls, stems, vines, flower centers, lattice, or cornelli lace. Serrated tips extrude textured lines and are used to create stars, zigzags, textured borders, shells, ropes, and rosettes. To get started, you just need a few round and star-shaped tips in large, medium, and small sizes.

PIE SERVER

These triangular spatulas have an offset metal blade and make cutting and lifting pie slices easy.

SKEWERS AND TOOTHPICKS

Bamboo skewers can be used to poke holes for venting and to draw textures, indentations, and details (such as the veins of a leaf) on pie dough. Toothpicks serve the same purpose, but skewers are easier to work with because of their greater length.

STICKS

Paper lollipop sticks, basswood popsicle sticks, and coffee stirrers all make playful holders for pie pops. When inserting sticks before baking, make sure they are made of oven-safe material. When using wooden sticks, place a piece of parchment or foil on top of the sticks, or soak them in water before baking, to prevent burning. Sticks can also be inserted after baking into the seam where the top crust meets the bottom crust.

INGREDIENTS

The satisfaction that comes from making a pie from scratch is like no other—except, perhaps, if you have invented your own pie recipe. The pie-making process is very hands-on: slicing the fruits, rolling out the dough, and weaving a lattice feels really down-home and old-fashioned. Ingredients are the colors you arrange on your creative palette. Here, I explain how various ingredients will affect the flavor or texture of your crust or filling. Play around and customize the combinations to your own and loved ones' taste preferences.

Flours, Meals, and Oats

ALL-PURPOSE FLOUR

Most of the piecrust recipes in this book use unbleached all-purpose flour as the base ingredient. The high protein (gluten) levels in all-purpose flour, when mixed with water, make crusts sturdy, tender, and flaky. To achieve various textures and flavors, some crust recipes blend all-purpose flour with other flours or meals. Small amounts of flour are sometimes used as a thickener in fruit-pie fillings.

CAKE FLOUR

Delicate cake flour is rarely used to make piecrusts, with one exception: cake flour is sometimes added to puff pastry (page 251) to create a lighter dough.

WHOLE WHEAT FLOUR

Whole wheat flour, added to all-purpose flour, gives crusts an earthy flavor. Push it through a sieve to soften it up a bit before baking, since it does make a slightly tougher crust. If you find you like the flavor of whole wheat crust, try replacing a maximum of one-fourth of the all-purpose flour in a recipe with whole wheat flour. Whole wheat pastry flour can also be added to all-purpose flour in small amounts.

NUT FLOURS (ALMOND, HAZELNUT, CHESTNUT)

Gluten-free nut flours are ground from nuts after the oils are removed. Use them as a substitution for up to one-third of the all-purpose flour in a crust recipe to impart a nutty flavor and coarser texture.

CORNMEAL

Blue and yellow cornmeal add a stone-ground flavor and crunchy texture to piecrusts. Cornmeal is available in various textures from fine to coarse, although I prefer a medium grind. All can be used as a substitute for up to half the all-purpose flour in a recipe to impart the flavor of corn and a coarser texture to crusts.

RICE FLOUR

Both brown and sweet rice flour can be used for baking piecrusts. They can also be used as a thickener in fillings. Brown rice flour is higher in nutrients but is grittier in texture; sweet rice flour is smoother.

OATS

To create an oatmeal-flavored crust, it is best to use uncooked old-fashioned rolled oats, not quick-cooking or instant oats, which produce mushy results. Ground oatmeal cookies can also be used to make a crust. Oats absorb juices and add an interesting flavor when used as a thickener for fruit-pie fillings.

WHEAT GERM AND GRAHAM FLOUR

When added to the dough for both savory and sweet piecrusts, both wheat germ and graham flour produce earthy flavors. Graham flour makes crusts coarse and crunchy.

COOKIES

Cookie crusts are made from combining cookie crumbs with butter, spices, and other ingredients, such as nuts and coconut, for flavoring. Instead of rolled into a round, as most doughs are, they are pressed into the pie pan. Graham crackers, chocolate wafer cookies, and gingersnaps are the most common basic ingredients, but most cookies—including oatmeal cookies, biscotti, and amaretti—can be incorporated into a crust. Many cookies are available in gluten-free versions and can be used as the main ingredient in a flavorful gluten-free crust.

Thickeners

FLOUR

Flour is the most basic thickener in fruit pies. Fillings thickened with flour become opaque. If your pie has been cooked too long, or has been frozen and then thawed, the filling may become runny and too liquid.

INSTANT TAPIOCA

Tapioca is a starch that comes from the yucca root and thickens at a lower temperature than cornstarch. It is stable when frozen, and gives fruit fillings a glossy sheen. The recipes in this book call for instant tapioca because it is readily available. Grind it in a food processor before using it, to avoid lumps. Tapioca starch is more finely ground than instant tapioca and will give you a smoother texture.

CORNSTARCH OR CLEARJEL

Cornstarch is a common thickener in pies. It does not work well with acidic ingredients, however. One tablespoon (¼ ounce) of cornstarch thickens one cup of liquid. ClearJel is a trademarked name for a type of modified cornstarch used by commercial bakeries that is more stable than regular cornstarch. It works well with acidic ingredients, tolerates higher temperatures, and is ideal for canning pie filling.

TIPS FOR USING THICKENERS

- Before using a thickener, mix it into a paste with a little liquid from the filling so that it will dissolve more easily.
- If you are making a recipe with subtle spices, use arrowroot, which has the most unobtrusive flavor.
- For a high-gloss look, use tapioca or arrowroot; for a low-gloss finish, use cornstarch. Flour imparts an opaque finish.
- Use cornstarch with dairy-based ingredients. Use arrowroot with acidic ingredients.
- If you plan on freezing pies or fillings, use arrowroot or tapioca; cornstarch breaks down when frozen.

ARROWROOT

Gluten-free arrowroot, like tapioca and cornstarch, imparts a glossy finish to fruit fillings. It has the most unobtrusive flavor of all thickeners. Substitute two teaspoons of arrowroot for one tablespoon of cornstarch.

CEREAL AND NUTS

Cereal grains, such as oatmeal and farina, along with granola, bran cereal, and ground nuts, make good fruit pie thickeners and add flavor. If the granola or cereal you're using is made up of large pieces, chop it until it resembles oatmeal-size flakes before adding it to the mixture.

Shortenings

BUTTER

If you are like me and choose flavor over flakiness for your piecrusts, make an all-butter crust. Butter has a sweet taste that you cannot get from any other type of shortening. All the recipes in this book call for unsalted butter instead of salted butter because unsalted butter allows you to control the amount of salt in a recipe. Always use cold butter for doughs except when noted (for example, when you are using melted butter mixed with cookie crumbs to make crumb crusts). Butter is also added to fruit fillings for flavor.

VEGETABLE SHORTENING

If you are looking for a flaky crust with a mild flavor, vegetable shortening is the fat of choice. Refrigerate or freeze shortening before use. Vegetable shortening is a stable fat, so crusts made with it are easier to work with. They retain their shape well and the results are consistent.

LARD

Lard produces the flakiest crust. If you choose to use lard, don't use the processed kind, which has a chemical aftertaste, but use leaf lard. It can be purchased at butcher shops and at ethnic and farmers markets. Chill before use.

BUTTER CUBES

Butter should be cut into small cubes before it is incorporated into a crust. To cube butter, cut the stick in half lengthwise, then rotate the halves and cut them in half lengthwise again. Then cut the sticks crosswise in ¼-inch segments.

VEGETABLE, OLIVE, AND NUT OILS

Vegans and those looking for a crust with no trans fat or cholesterol use vegetable, olive, or nut oils to make their crusts. These oils should be chilled before using.

CREAM CHEESE

If you want your crust to have a somewhat tart flavor. swap some of the butter called for in the recipe for cream cheese. Mix softened cream cheese and butter together with an electric mixer, and then chill for 1 hour before using it to make dough.

Binders

LIQUIDS

Ice water, fruit juices, eggs, milk, vinegar, lemon juice, and cream bind the flour and fat together and add flavor and texture to a piecrust. These liquids should be added a little at a time to make sure the dough doesn't get too sticky (see page 36).

EGGS

Eggs add moisture (because of their high water content) and some fat (from the yolks) to make crusts tender. They also add protein, which gives the crust structure. Eggs are also the base for meringues, pastry creams, curds, and custards, and are used to make washes for the top crusts so they brown nicely. The basic rule of thumb is to use 1 teaspoon of liquid (such as milk or cream) for each egg white. Keep in mind that eggs are always easiest to separate when cold. All the recipes in this book use large eggs. If you have only medium eggs on hand, 3 medium eggs can be substituted for 2 large eggs.

Dairy Products

MILK

Whole milk is a core ingredient in custards and pastry creams. It can be brushed on piecrusts by itself or mixed with eggs to make a glaze that will brown the top. Since the fat in whole milk aids in the thickening, avoid low-fat and fat-free milk when making pies.

HEAVY CREAM

Heavy cream, sometimes sweetened with a little sugar, is used to make whipped cream, a main ingredient in cream pies. Light cream and half-and-half won't really whip to the correct consistency. Like whole milk, heavy cream can be brushed on piecrusts by itself or mixed with eggs to make a glaze that will brown the top.

SOUR CREAM AND YOGURT

Sour cream and yogurt are great for making tangy fillings. Sour cream is thicker and denser than yogurt, but yogurt has a cleaner, fresher taste.

SOY MILK

Made from ground soybeans, this protein-rich beverage can be used as a replacement for cow's milk, although it imparts a different flavor and texture.

CHEESE

When added to piecrusts, Cheddar and Parmesan cheeses add a rich flavor and a salty tang.

Sweeteners

SUGAR

In addition to sweetening, sugar absorbs liquid and makes pie fillings less runny. The sugars listed below are all processed. If you are looking to limit your sugar intake, you can reduce the amount of sugar called for in many of the recipes in this book without negatively affecting the results, especially since most fruits are naturally sweet.

There are five types of sugar commonly used in pies:

- Granulated sugar is standard white table sugar. It has a medium-grain texture and is a good all-around sugar for pie fillings.

- Superfine sugar, also known as castor sugar, has a fine-grain texture and is good for delicate meringues. Make your own by grinding granulated sugar in a food processor.

- Brown sugar is white sugar combined with molasses. It is available in both dark and light versions, depending on

SWEETENER SUBSTITUTIONS

If you want to vary the flavor of your sweeteners in a particular recipe, feel free to experiment. The suggestions below will help keep the texture and consistency of your pie consistent and predictable as you mix and match ingredients.

INGREDIENT	SUBSTITUTION	RATIO	NOTES
Brown sugar	Agave nectar	1:$\frac{2}{3}$	Use $\frac{2}{3}$ cup maple syrup for 1 cup granulated sugar and decrease other liquids in the recipe by $\frac{1}{4}$–$\frac{1}{3}$ cup.
Brown sugar	Granulated sugar	1:1	Add 4 tablespoons of molasses per cup of granulated sugar and decrease other liquids in the recipe by about 3 tablespoons.
Brown sugar	Honey and molasses	1:$\frac{3}{4}$	Use $\frac{1}{2}$ cup honey and $\frac{1}{4}$ cup molasses.
Granulated sugar	Agave nectar	1:$\frac{2}{3}$	Use $\frac{2}{3}$ cup maple syrup for 1 cup granulated sugar and decrease other liquids in the recipe by $\frac{1}{4}$–$\frac{1}{3}$ cup.
Granulated sugar	Brown sugar	1:1	
Granulated sugar	Honey	1:$\frac{7}{8}$	Use $\frac{7}{8}$ cup honey for 1 cup of granulated sugar and decrease other liquids in the recipe by about 3 tablespoons.
Granulated sugar	Maple syrup	1:$\frac{3}{4}$	Use $\frac{3}{4}$ cup maple syrup for 1 cup granulated sugar and decrease other liquids in the recipe by about 3 tablespoons.
Molasses	Honey	1:1	

how much molasses flavor you want. The two varieties can be used interchangeably if you only have one on hand. Always pack brown sugar firmly into the measuring cup to get an accurate measure.

- Confectioners' sugar, or powdered sugar, is sugar that is ground to a powder and combined with cornstarch. It may be used to sweeten piecrusts, but it is more often used in glazes to produce a silky-smooth surface.

- Crystal, or coarse, sugar has extra-large granules and is used for decorating and topping.

HONEY

All-natural honey is both a flavoring and a preservative. Clover honey is the most common type, although other varieties—such as lavender, orange blossom, etc.—are made when bees pollinate other types of flowers.

MOLASSES

Unsulfured molasses (made from mature sugar cane) can be used alone as a hearty sweetener, or in combination with sugar or other sweeteners to add a rich, rustic flavor. Unsulfured molasses—the finest quality available—is not treated with sulfites and contains healthful minerals. Molasses is what gives the Gingerbread Tarts (page 224) their distinctive flavor.

MAPLE SYRUP

A natural sweetener derived from black, red, or sugar maple trees, maple syrup is available in various grades. Grade A is light and has a mild flavor, grade B is darker and has a sharper flavor.

CORN SYRUP

Made from cornstarch, corn syrup primarily consists of glucose. It is used as a sweetener, thickener, and preservative. Light corn syrup is clear and colorless and has a light, sweet flavor. It contains small quantities of salt and vanilla. Dark corn syrup has a medium-brown color and contains refiners' syrup (a type of molasses). It has a much more assertive flavor. Both can be used interchangeably in recipes, resulting in the same texture but different flavors.

AGAVE NECTAR

Agave nectar is rapidly becoming the sweetener of choice for vegans and for those who want to lower their glycemic index. It is a good substitute for honey, maple syrup, corn syrup, granulated sugar, and brown sugar. Agave nectar has a more neutral flavor than honey or maple syrup. Like corn syrup, agave nectar will not crystallize. And, like other liquid sweeteners, agave nectar adds moisture to fillings. It is best to use agave nectar with dense fruits, such as apples and pears.

Flavorings

SALT

Salt boosts flavors—it even increases sweetness—and it also strengthens the gluten in wheat. Most of the time, I use common table

MAKING VANILLA EXTRACT

In a dark glass bottle, combine one ounce (about 8) split and chopped grade B vanilla beans and 1 cup 80-proof unflavored vodka. Seal in a glass container and let sit for 6 months in a dark place, shaking occasionally. Strain the liquid before using.

salt in crusts and fillings, but when I want to boost the salt flavor I use kosher salt or sea salt.

COFFEE

Coffee adds a delicious flavoring to crusts and fillings and provides a stay-awake jolt that many diners crave after a rich meal. It accents vanilla and chocolate pies perfectly but also goes well with fruity flavors, such as raspberry and orange, and nutty flavors, including almonds and hazelnuts. When thinking about coffee, think strength. Dissolve instant-coffee granules in a couple of tablespoons of hot water, prepare double-strength espresso for small amounts of fillings, and prepare triple-strength drip coffee for large quantities of filling. And if you don't mind a coarser texture in your crust, add finely ground espresso beans for an intense coffee flavor.

HERBS AND SPICES

Herbs and spices can be added to sweet or savory crusts to transform their flavor, or they can be added to fillings to complement the other flavors. I grow dozens of herbs in my garden, but I use rosemary, thyme, sage, and mint the most. I stock dried herbs in small jars because they lose their potency quickly.

EXTRACTS

Vanilla extract is added to many recipes, even those for chocolate fillings and crusts, to enhance the flavor. Natural almond extract and peppermint extract also are much tastier than chemically processed alternatives. Purchase pure extracts instead of imitation flavorings whenever possible. You can also make your own vanilla extract. If you prefer to use vanilla beans for a richer flavor, they can substitute for extract in custards by adding a split bean to the liquid while simmering.

COCOA POWDER AND CHOCOLATE

When it comes to pies, chocolate is used in both powdered and solid forms. There are two types of powdered chocolate—unsweetened cocoa powder and Dutch-process cocoa powder. Unsweetened cocoa powder is acidic and bitter but has a nice deep chocolate flavor. Dutch-process cocoa powder is treated with an alkali to neutralize its acids. It is used in recipes that have a more delicate flavor. Cocoa powder can be sifted before using or combined with a small amount of boiling water to make a paste. Solid forms of chocolate include unsweetened, bittersweet, semi-sweet, milk chocolate, German sweet chocolate, and white chocolate.

Nuts and Seeds

Nuts and seeds are high in fat. When they are exposed to heat during baking or toasting, they release their oils, thus intensifying their wonderful flavors—but they can also burn quickly. Mixing nuts into crusts and fillings protects them, but when they are placed on top of a pie they toast much more rapidly than the pie bakes, so they may burn. Covering the pie with foil after the nuts and seeds are slightly toasted will help prevent this. Nuts go rancid quickly, so keep them in the freezer to prevent spoiling.

Whether nuts are left whole, sliced, chopped, or ground makes a big difference in the flavor and texture of a pie—each technique exposes a different amount of surface area. The smaller the pieces of nut, the more flavor they contribute. Whole or half pieces can also

CHOCOLATE IN THE KNOW

Bittersweet chocolate generally has a stronger chocolate taste than other chocolates and contains less sugar than semisweet chocolate. The best bittersweet chocolate contains 65 percent or more chocolate liquor; the higher the percentage, the more flavorful the chocolate. Most chocolate chips are made from semisweet chocolate and usually contain less cocoa butter than bittersweet chocolate, so that they are better able to retain their shape during baking.

Milk chocolate is made with either condensed milk or a milk-and-sugar mixture. It contains less chocolate liquor than bittersweet and semisweet chocolate. The best brands have a high percentage of chocolate liquor, although the amount isn't usually indicated on the package. The quality is obvious in the flavor.

Sweet chocolate, often sold as German sweet chocolate, is sweeter than semisweet chocolate. This dark chocolate was created in 1852 by a man named Samuel German

(not, as is popularly supposed, in Germany). It is a chocolate blend that contains chocolate liquor, sugar, cocoa, flavorings, and lecithin.

Unsweetened is chocolate in its rawest form, with no sugar added. It has a strong bitter taste that is sweetened by the sugar in baked goods.

Rich and creamy white chocolate does not contain chocolate liquor, so technically it should not be classified as a chocolate. But high-quality brands of white chocolate contain many of ingredients found in other chocolates, including cocoa butter, sugar, milk solids, vanilla, and lecithin, so it is a close relative. White chocolate is very delicate, so always melt it over very low heat.

Couverture is a high-quality chocolate found in specialty stores. It is made with extra cocoa butter, which gives the chocolate a smooth finish and sheen, and is used for coating pastries.

TOASTING NUTS

You can toast nuts in the oven or in a skillet; either way, watch them closely because they can burn quickly.

To toast in the oven: Spread nuts on a baking sheet and toast at 325°F for 7–10 minutes, or until golden. Stir a few times to brown all sides.

To toast in a skillet: Set nuts in a nonstick skillet over medium heat and cook, stirring frequently, for about 5–7 minutes, or until golden. You may want to enrich their flavor by adding 2 tablespoons of butter for up to 3 cups of nuts.

be arranged in decorative patterns. When grinding nuts for fillings or crusts, a little sugar or flour should always be added to help make grinding easier and absorb the oils.

LIQUOR, LIQUEURS, SPIRITS, WINE, AND BEER

Many types of alcohol can be used to flavor fillings. My favorites are rum (light, golden, and dark) and bourbon. I also really like nut-based liqueurs, such as amaretto, and fruit-based liqueurs, such as Kirsch. Coffee-flavored and Irish cream liqueurs go well with both vanilla and chocolate pies. Champagne, wine, and beer can also be used in pies. When using wine to flavor a pie, simmer the amount called for in the recipe until it is reduced to one-fourth of its original volume, then cool to room temperature. This will concentrate the flavor.

WATER

Something as simple as water can affect the texture of piecrust. Hard water makes a hard crust. If you have hard water, filter it—or use bottled water or milk instead.

DOUGH TENDERIZERS

Vinegar and lemon juice can be used to tenderize piecrust dough. The acid in these ingredients helps keep the crust from breaking apart during rolling and keeps it from shrinking during baking. If you're using vinegar or lemon juice, use one teaspoon for each cup of flour and add a teaspoon of sugar and a pinch of salt to the flour before cutting in the fat to sweeten the bitter or tart flavor. Then decrease the other liquids in the recipe in a 1:1 ratio—that is, if you've added two teaspoons of lemon juice, decrease the other liquids in the recipe by two teaspoons. Some people insist on adding vinegar and lemon juice to all crusts. I don't think all crusts need these ingredients to be tender, but you can try it to see whether you like the results.

Fruits and Vegetables

DRIED FRUITS

Dried fruits, such as raisins, currants, and apricots, add flavor and a chewy texture to pie fillings. Dates make an especially strong binder

I love to bake with fresh fruits of the season. Strawberries are the first fruits of spring, peaches mean summer, and cranberries signal fall. I also love to create unique flavor combinations with fruits when they're out of season—there is nothing like adding cranberries to peach pies in summer or adding fall's pomegranates to an apricot pie in summer. So I stock up on fruits when they're in season and either freeze them or can them, enabling me to use them after they've disappeared from store shelves.

for gluten-free crusts. If the recipe calls for softening dried fruits, place them in hot water or liquid for 5 minutes before using.

VEGETABLES

Shredded, grated, or puréed vegetables, such as sweet potatoes, zucchini, and yams, are often used for both sweet and savory pie fillings.

BERRIES

Every part of the world has its own indigenous berries that grow wild in that particular region. Although strawberries, raspberries, and blueberries are the most common berries for pies, there are many other varieties to choose from (see the chart on page 55). All berries can either be served raw in a precooked crust or can be baked into the filling. Berries release a lot of juice when cooked, so most berry pies use thickeners. Frozen berries can be substituted for fresh berries, but keep in mind that they will be more liquid, so add more thickener and reduce some of the other liquids in the recipe so your filling won't be runny.

APPLES AND PEARS

There is no question that apple is *the* all-American pie, and most popular pie in America. Apples are available most of the year and, like other fruits, are high in pectin (a thickener), so they make great fillings. Most people peel apples and pears because of the rough skin, so always build in time for peeling when preparing the recipe. Both apples and pears come in multiple varieties with delicate flavor differences; some of the varieties are listed on pages 43 and 131.

CITRUS FRUITS

Citrus fruits, such as lemons, limes, and oranges, are often used in pies. Grapefruits, citrons, bergamots, mandarin oranges, kumquats, clementines, and tangerines are used less often but can also make great-tasting fillings.

When a citrus fruit requires both zesting and juicing, zest it first, and then squeeze the juice. To zest, use a zester or a grater with very small holes and zest only the colored part of the peel. Try not to zest any white pith. Then slice the fruit in half and extract as much juice as possible. Strain out the seeds before using.

COCONUT KNOW-HOW

How to Make Fresh Coconut Curls

Preheat the oven to 350°F. Using a hammer and an ice pick, pierce two of the black "eyes" on the top of a fresh coconut. Release the milk and save it for another use. Place the whole coconut on a baking sheet and bake for 30-40 minutes, or until the coconut begins to crack. Set it aside to cool for 1 hour. Wrap the cooled coconut in a clean kitchen towel and break it into pieces with the hammer. Remove the shell and, using a vegetable peeler, remove the dark skin. Use the peeler to shave long or short curls from the flesh. Store the curls in damp paper towels until ready to use or toast as directed below

Two Ways to Toast Coconut

1. Place fresh coconut curls (or packaged flaked coconut) on a cookie sheet and bake at 325°F for 7-10 minutes, or until golden. Stir a few times during baking.
2. Place a little butter in a skillet. Add fresh coconut curls (or packaged flaked coconut) and sauté for 5-7 minutes, or until golden.

STONE FRUITS

Fruits with a single pit are called stone fruits. Cherries, peaches, plums, and apricots are all stone fruits. Since the skins on these fruits are soft, they can be either be peeled or, if you're looking to make a quicker filling with more fiber, left on. After the pit is removed, small fruits should be halved and large fruits can be cut in wedges, or slices.

COCONUT

Coconut is a core ingredient in fillings—especially in classic coconut custard pies and coconut cream pies. It comes in many forms: fresh, dried, sweetened, unsweetened, shredded, flaked, and desiccated. Fresh coconut can be shredded with a grater or food processor for an authentic flavor. Packaged unsweetened coconut allows you to control the sugar in the recipe. Sweetened coconut is soaked in corn syrup and is therefore sweeter and moister than unsweetened coconut. Flaked and shredded coconut can be used interchangeably—only the textures are different. Flaked coconut makes a smooth pie and shredded coconut makes a coarser pie. I like to use large coconut flakes as a garnish. Desiccated coconut is usually unsweetened, dried, and very finely ground. Toasting coconut dramatically changes the flavor by bringing out the fruit's natural oils.

MELONS

I would never destroy the flavor of a fresh melon by cooking it, so I always use raw watermelon, cantaloupe, and honeydew in pies and tarts. The fruit can be peeled and sliced in wedges or shaped into balls with a melon baller, as in the Four-Melon Tart (page 158).

TROPICAL FRUITS

Pineapple, mango, papaya, guava, lychee, and passion fruit are all intolerant of frost and grow in tropical regions. Today, you can find most of these fruits in your local markets throughout the year. They can be used in just about any type of pie—fruit, cream, or custard—as either the star attraction or in a supporting role.

CANDIED FRUITS

Candied fruits are much sweeter and a bit softer than dried fruits. I stock up on them at holiday time, when they are readily available.

To candy your own fruit, see the recipe for Candied Blood Orange Currant Pie on page 230.

STORE-BOUGHT CRUSTS AND FILLINGS

The major obstacle for people who want to bake a homemade pie is the fear of making a bad crust. For some reason, piecrust appears to most people to require special skills and a lot of work, whereas fillings somehow seem doable. But even though I am an experienced baker who loves to experiment in the kitchen, I consider a pie made with store-bought crust to be better than no pie at all! Luckily, there are many good options for crust on the market, including frozen crusts, boxed piecrust mixes, and refrigerated crusts. There are many ready-to-go cookie crusts as well. Since phyllo and puff pastry can be tricky and time-consuming to make, packaged dough is often the best way to go when you're working with these ingredients.

There are also many store-bought fillings on the market. You can choose this option when you are short on time or fruits are out of season. Boxed instant pudding and custard mixes are also good to have on hand for making creamy pies. The fillings will be thinner than homemade creams or custards, so decrease the amount of milk called for on the package. To gauge the amount necessary, gradually add the milk when you are mixing and stop when the filling is thick but not too liquid. Remember that the mixture will also thicken as it chills.

I have yet to find a good premade savory pie filling on the market. But if you have a canned vegetable or meat stew that you like, it can be used as a pie filling as well. Simply strain out as much of the stew's liquid as you can, leaving only about ¼ cup, before putting the filling in the crust.

FREEZING FRUITS

It is nice to enjoy a cherry or blueberry pie in the middle of winter. Today, many fresh fruits are available all year long, but since fruits are usually tastiest and sweetest in season, frozen fruits that were picked and sold locally in season will offer better flavor than commercially packaged frozen fruits. Here are some tips for freezing your own fruits.

Dry-Freezing

Cranberries, blueberries, rhubarb, red currants, raspberries, strawberries, and blackberries can all be washed without breaking the skin and do not discolor much when exposed to air. To freeze them, scatter them on a rimmed baking sheet and cover with aluminum foil. Freeze overnight. Transfer to an airtight container or freezer bags and extract as much air as possible before storing in the freezer. Use within 6–8 months.

Syrup-Freezing

Plums, rhubarb, apricots, pineapple, mango, peaches, pears, apples, and other fruits that that are firm or have been sliced or halved can be frozen in a syrup.

To make the syrup, combine 1 cup granulated sugar with 2 cups water in a medium saucepan over low heat and stir until sugar dissolves. Let cool to room temperature.

Peel and slice 1 pound of fruit and layer it in an airtight container. Pour the cooled syrup over the fruit until it reaches ½ inch below the top of the container—room enough for the liquid to expand while freezing. Cover, label, and freeze. Use within 9–12 months.

ESSENTIAL TECHNIQUES

If five apple pies made by my baking friends were put in front of me, I could tell you who baked each pie. That is because pies reflect the personality of the baker. As you get more comfortable with pie-making techniques, you will develop way of working that suits your taste. Tweaking each recipe step a bit here or there will ultimately make *your* perfect pie.

Forming Piecrusts

BLENDING INGREDIENTS

DRY INGREDIENTS: For even measuring and tender crusts, sift dry ingredients before mixing. First sift the flour, then check other dry ingredients to see if they are lumpy and need to be sifted. Gently mix them together after all ingredients are smooth.

CUTTING IN: Cut the cold fat (butter, shortening, or lard) into small pea-sized cubes before adding it to the dry ingredients. Then "cut in" the fat with the tips of your fingers, a pastry blender, two knives, or a food processor until the mixture resembles coarse meal. When working in butter with your hands, make sure to use only your fingertips, as your palms will warm and soften the dough. Work quickly and handle the dough as little as possible (as you are working, the ingredients are warming).

ADDING LIQUIDS: Water, fruit juices, eggs, milk, vinegar, lemon juice, and cream should be added a little at a time to make sure the dough doesn't get too sticky. If it does get too sticky, you will need to add more flour, which is okay but will make a tougher crust. All liquids should be ice-cold to avoid melting the fats.

Don't worry about using all the water the recipe calls for. If the dough does not come together, add more water a teaspoon at a time. Do not overwork the dough, which will make it tough. You know the dough is done when you gently squeeze it between your fingertips and it just sticks together, forming small dry cracks.

RESTING AND CHILLING

Flatten the dough into a disk or disks and wrap in plastic wrap (if

---

MIXING DOUGH IN A FOOD PROCESSOR

Using the food processor to make piecrust dough is my method of choice, especially when I'm making several crusts at the same time. It is quick and easy once you get the hang of it, but you do need to be careful not to overwork the dough.

When you're using a food processor, the fats should be frozen instead of just chilled in the refrigerator. Fit the machine with the steel blade, place the dry ingredients in the bowl, and mix for 2–3 seconds. Add the fat and cut it into the dry ingredients by pulsing until the mixture resembles coarse meal. Sprinkle ice-cold liquid over the dough a little at a time, or drizzle it through the feed tube, and pulse again until it comes together, adding more liquid if necessary. The dough should be crumbly but not dry. If it is too dry, add a bit more water.

PIECRUST TIPS

- Keep ingredients cold. The key to a flaky crust is to keep the fat as cold as possible. Always chill fat and liquids. Hard-core bakers chill everything—the dry ingredients, the bowls, the rolling pin, and other equipment. Refrigerate the dough after every step.
- If you are touching the dough, make sure your hands are not too warm. Rinse them in cold water while working if necessary.
- Minimal and quick handling when mixing and rolling helps to achieve a tender crust.
- When using more than one fat (e.g., butter and shortening), soften them, then beat them together and chill before using,
- Use as little flour as possible when rolling out the dough, or roll it out between sheets of wax paper.
- When recommended, blind-bake the bottom crust at a high temperature to set the crust's structure.
- Vent double-crust pies to reduce moisture. Use a pie bird, make a lattice crust, cut holes in the top with cookie cutters, or prick with a fork.
- Use edge protectors or foil shields to protect the crust from heat and from becoming too browned.
- Bake pies in the bottom third of the oven on a rimmed baking sheet or baking stone.
- Let pies cool in the pan on a rack before serving.

FREE-FORM CRUSTS

For simple rustic pies, don't even bother using a pie pan. Roll out the dough as directed in the recipe, place it on a parchment paper-lined baking sheet or a baking stone covered with cornmeal, then place the filling in the center. Fold over the edges of the dough to cover part of the filling, pinch the sides to hold everything in, and bake.

WORKING WITH PHYLLO

The recipes throughout this book use country-style phyllo dough, which is thicker and sturdier than the extremely thin phyllo dough—usually used for baklava—that one commonly finds in the frozen-food section of the supermarket. Country-style phyllo is perfect for holding heavy pie fillings. Although any kind of phyllo creates a light, crispy, and flaky crust, it is very fragile and dries out quickly. Be sure to cover it with a damp kitchen towel as you're working. Brush each sheet with a generous quantity of melted butter after putting it in the pan.

directed to do so in the recipe). If the recipe calls for chilling, let the dough relax by chilling it in the refrigerator for 30 minutes to 2 hours before and after rolling it out. This makes the dough less elastic and easier to roll. After it is rolled out, set it on a cutting board or place it in the pie pan to chill. After removing the dough from the refrigerator, let it sit for 5 to 10 minutes to soften slightly before rolling.

ROLLING AND TRIMMING

When rolling out dough directly on a work surface, lightly flour the surface. When piecrust needs to be chilled after rolling, roll it out between sheets of wax paper on a cutting board to make it easier to transfer to the refrigerator. To make the dough tender and to keep its round shape, roll from the center outward, reducing pressure toward the ends of the crust. Lift the pin when you bring it back to the center. Turn the dough as you roll, brushing off excess flour with a dry brush when you are finished. Your dough should be about 2 inches wider than the pan. Do not overwork by rolling too much or by stretching. Rolling the dough between two sheets of wax paper will prevent sticking and you won't have to add more flour to the mixture. If holes or tears form in the dough, avoid rerolling by moistening the tears with water, then overlapping a small patch of dough and rolling over the patch.

Once the dough is the correct size, roll it around the rolling pin and transfer the dough to the pie pan. Gently press the dough into the bottom edges of the pan. Try not to stretch the dough as you fit it into the pan. Leave a 1-inch overhang. Using the outside edge of the rim as a guide, trim the excess dough with kitchen shears or a paring knife. Fold the dough remaining on the rim over itself, toward the inside of the pan, to create a thick raised edge. If you are blind-baking the crust, pierce the bottom with a fork. Cover with plastic wrap and chill for 30 minutes before filling.

For a double-crust pie, roll the top crust a little smaller and thinner than the bottom crust. When baking small individual pies, always make the crust extra-thin—thinner than ⅛ inch. This will give you the proper crust-to-filling ratio.

EDGES

These edge techniques can be used for both single- and double-crust pies. Some edges can be made with extra scraps of dough; others require more dough than is called for in a recipe (as indicated below).

CUTOUTS: Roll out the dough to ⅛ inch thick. With small cookie or fondant cutters, cut out enough identical shapes (such as hearts, leaves, or flowers) to fit, overlapping, around the edge of the crust. Brush egg wash or cold water on the top edge of the crust and press the cutouts on the edge, slightly overlapping them. If you want to make cutouts in a recipe that does not already call for them, increase the dough recipe by 30 percent.

BRAIDS: Roll the dough into two or three ¼-inch-diameter logs slightly longer than the circumference of the pan. Braid or twist the logs, and press them together to interlock. Moisten the top edge of the crust with water or egg wash and press the braid onto the edge. If you want to make braids in a recipe that does not already call for them, increase the dough recipe by 50 percent.

SQUARE OR TILED EDGES: After trimming the dough around the rim of the pan, as directed above, score the remaining dough at ½-inch intervals with a knife. Fold over every other piece toward the center, leaving those parts of the rim of the pan exposed.

FLUTED EDGES: For single-crust pies, after folding in the overhang to build up the crust, place your index finger on the edge, pointing diagonally inward, toward the center of the pie. Press down on the dough, into the rim. This technique will also work for double-crust pies after you have pressed the edges of the top and bottom crusts together.

POINTED EDGES: Point your index finger out from the inside of the rim. Use the index finger and thumb of your other hand to pinch the dough together into points around the tip of your finger.

SCALLOPED EDGES: Press your index finger on the outside of the built-up edge, pointing inward. Use the index finger and thumb of your other hand to pinch the dough from the inside, around your index finger.

SPOON-SCALLOPED EDGES: Press the round end of the spoon into the built-up edge of the crust.

FEATHERED EDGES: After building up the edge, cut diagonal incisions with kitchen shears.

VENTING DOUBLE-CRUST PIES

Venting is your friend when making double-crust pies. It allows the filling to cook evenly, and also allows moisture to be released, which prevents the filling from becoming too liquid. When a pie is filled with colorful ingredients, it is nice to partially vent the pie so you can see the inside.

- Use cookie cutters, a knife, or a straw to make holes in the top crust, or use a pie bird.
- Brush an egg wash onto the top crust and crimp the edges to form a tight seal between the top and bottom crusts so the juices won't bubble over.
- Mound the filling in the middle of the crust, and do not use too much.
- Consider precooking your filling ingredients in a saucepan before baking them in the crust. This will reduce the juices in the filling, lessening the amount of moisture that needs to escape.

APPLIQUÉS

To create a 3-D relief pattern or design on your pie, apply shapes that have been cut out from excess dough with cookie cutters or a knife. Attach them to the top of a double-crust pie, or to the edges of a single-crust pie, with egg wash.

CUTOUTS

Using a cookie cutter or a knife, cut holes—in the shapes of circles, grids, or radiating lines—into the top crust of your pie to create a patterned effect. The holes will also serve as steam-release valves for venting.

EMBOSSING

Use rubber stamps to emboss patterns, words, shapes, logos, characters, or whatever you can think of on the top crust of your pie. You can even have a rubber stamp custom-made at an office supply store. When embossing, press really hard into the dough, then freeze the crust a bit before baking. The texture will hold better in a frozen crust.

LATTICE CRUST

Roll out the top crust to a size slightly larger than the diameter of your pie pan. Cut the dough into strips with a knife or a pastry or pizza cutter. Lay half the strips in one direction, leaving space in between them, then lay the other half on top of them, perpendicular to the bottom strips. You can also weave the strips over and under each other to create a grid. Press the ends of the top strips into the bottom crust before crimping to seal.

GLAZING

Brush a beaten egg, egg wash, heavy cream, or milk on the top crust before baking. The fat in the glaze will give the pie a rich golden-brown color. If you leave some of the crust unglazed, you will have a nice glossy-to-matte and golden-to-light contrast.

STREUSEL, CRUMB, AND BISCUIT TOPPINGS

For simple toppings on single-crust pies, streusels, crumbs, and biscuit toppings offer a rustic, crunchy texture and flavor and a visual appeal that is homey and comforting.

CONTRASTING DOUGHS

Make two similar doughs in contrasting colors or textures—for example, a butter crust and a chocolate butter crust, or a plain crust and an herb crust. Just make sure they have similar ingredients and the same baking time. Cut out shapes in both crusts with cookie cutters and inlay the cutouts of one on top of the other to create a contrasting pattern.

DECORATIVE INGREDIENTS

Nuts, seeds, chocolate chips, dried fruits, and other ingredients with interesting shapes can be arranged on top of the filling to create a striking visual effect.

Baking

PREPARING THE PAN

Since piecrusts and tart shells contain a lot of fat, most of the time your crust won't stick to the pan if you don't grease it before you put the crust in. Crusts that are low in fat do require you to grease and flour the pan. Most of the time, though, I do butter and flour the pan just to be safe.

BLIND-BAKING (PREBAKING)

For single-crust pies, always partially bake the piecrust before filling. This will help keep the bottom crust from getting soggy. To blind-bake, preheat the oven to 400–425°F. Line the crust with parchment paper and fill it to the rim with pie weights. Bake until the crust just begins to color (7–15 minutes, depending on the crust), remove the weights and parchment, and continue baking until light golden. Seal with egg wash or jam, and bake for 2–3 minutes longer. Reduce the heat to the temperature specified in the recipe. If the pie requires a fully baked shell, continue baking it as directed.

It is possible to partially bake the bottom crust of a double-crust pie; it will just be hard get a good seal between the top and bottom crusts.

FRUIT PIE TIPS

Due to moisture loss, most fruit fillings shrink in volume during baking if they are not precooked in a saucepan. Prevent runny fillings by precooking them on a stove top and allowing them to thicken. The pie should be completely cooled and set before slicing.

If fruit cooks for too long, it will become mushy. To prevent mushy fillings, cut large vents in the top crusts. Bake pies at a high temperature for a short amount of time, then reduce the heat to finish baking.

To prevent gaps between the top crust and the fruit filling, mound the fruit higher in the center than around the edges, and cut vents in the top crust to allow the moisture to escape.

Creativity with the design of the top crust—as in the checkerboard crust on the Ginger Peach Pie (page 48)—can solve this problem.

FILLING

Fill double-crust fruit, fruit, meat, vegetable, and mince pies with a mound of filling taller than the edges in the middle, then press the filling down to reduce air pockets. This will help give the pie a full shape after cooking. Fill custard and cream pies about ¼ inch below the rim, being sure not to overfill.

BAKING

Baking pies in the bottom third of the oven will ensure that the bottom and top crusts brown evenly. Place the pan directly on the oven rack, or on a rimmed baking sheet to catch overflowing juices. You can also place the pan on a baking stone to ensure even distribution of heat. Always check your pie frequently and decide if you need to cover it with edge protectors or aluminum foil. Always remember to allow air to circulate around the pie. Baking more than one pie simultaneously could require you to increase the baking time.

HOW TO CAN PIE FILLING

Apple, blackberry, blueberry, raspberry, strawberry, rhubarb, pear, peach, and cherry pie fillings are all good candidates for canning. Before getting started, research the latest food safety guidelines online at http://www.foodsafety.gov/blog/home_canning .html. There are also many in-depth books on canning that will tell you in detail how to avoid spoilage. Below are the basic steps.

1. Prepare a syrup by combining sugar and water in a medium saucepan over low heat, stirring occasionally, until the sugar is dissolved. Use 2 cups granulated sugar to 1 quart water, plus any spices you'd like to add. Use about 2–3 pounds of fruit and 1–1½ cups of liquid for each quart jar. To prevent light fruits from darkening, use 1 teaspoon of ascorbic acid per gallon of water.

2. Sterilize canning jars, lids, and rings by boiling them in a large pot of water. Keep the jars in the water until ready to fill.

3. Wash, peel, core, and slice fruit. Place fruit in the hot canning jars, leaving about ½ inch headspace.

4. Fill jars with hot syrup, and gently remove air bubbles by running a sterile spatula around the inside rim of the jar.

5. Wipe the rim of the jar clean with a damp towel. Top with the lid, then tighten the ring until snug and place the jars on the rack of a water-bath canner. Process in a water-bath canner for 20 minutes.

6. Let sit on the countertop for 12 hours. Test the seal by pressing center of the lid. If the lid is down and will not move, the jar is sealed. Wash, dry, label, and store jars in a cool, dark place.

7. Before using, make sure the jar is firmly sealed, the top is concave, and no liquid is leaking. Make sure the filling does not spurt out or give off an unnatural order when the jar is opened. Drain the syrup and use the fruit as directed in the recipe.

Custard pies can be placed directly on the oven rack, but I recommend using a water bath. The crust won't brown as much, but the custard will cook more evenly. Choose a roasting pan that is about 2 inches larger than your pie pan. Place the pie pan in the roasting pan (without the rack), then fill the roaster with water until it comes about ½–⅔ of the way up the sides of the smaller pan. Remove the smaller pan and place the roaster in the oven. Preheat the oven with the water-filled roaster in it, then gently lower the filled pie pan into the heated water bath.

COOLING

After baking, place the pie, still in the pan, on a cooling rack. (You can also cool some blind-baked crusts this way.) Allow the air to circulate around the entire pie so it cools evenly. Pies that are baked in a water bath can be removed from the bath and cooled on the rack. Tarts baked in pans with removable bottoms can be removed from the pan after they have cooled on the rack for about 15 minutes.

SCALING PIES

The most commonly available pie pans are 9 inches in diameter; therefore, many of the recipes in this book were developed for a 9-inch pan. However, sometimes I prefer to make a 4-inch pie (to be shared by two people) or a 6-inch pie (to be shared by three people), and I find myself adjusting my recipes to fit the various sizes of pans in my kitchen. To make a larger pie than a recipe calls for, most of the time it is easiest to just double a recipe and save any extra dough or filling for later. Or you can make two pies—one small and one large—and freeze the small one for later, or offer it to a friend. To make a smaller pie than the recipe calls for, it is easiest to make the full amount of crust and filling and make and freeze a second pie with the extra. Keep in mind, though, that the smaller the pie, the more crust you'll have in relation to filling. So if you like thick crusts, use a smaller pan than the recipe calls for; if you like thin crusts, use a larger pan than the recipe calls for. This list offers the approximate volumes of filling needed for commonly available pan sizes.

12-inch pie = 6½–8 cups filling
11-inch pie = 5½–6½ cups filling
10-inch pie = 5–6 cups filling
9 inches x 1¼ inches deep = 4 cups filling
9 inches x 1½ inches deep = 5 cups filling
9 inches x 2 inches deep = 8 cups filling
8-inch pie = 3½–4 cups filling
6-inch pie = 2½–3 cups filling
4-inch pie = 1¾–2 cups filling
3½-inch pie = 1 cup filling
2-inch pie = 1½ tablespoons filling

FREEZING CRUSTS

When I make crusts, I rarely make one at a time. I make about a dozen and freeze them so they are ready to use on the spot. Once the dough is flattened into a disk and wrapped in plastic to be chilled, it can also be frozen. Vacuum-seal or place the disk in a freezer bag and squeeze to eliminate as much air as possible. Piecrusts can also be frozen after they are set into the pan. Wrap the pans filled with dough in foil and place them in heavy-duty freezer bags. The crusts will keep for 2 to 3 months.

TEN TROUBLESHOOTING SOLUTIONS FOR PIECRUST

1. The dough mixture is dry and crumbly or lumpy.

If your dough is dry and crumbly, break it up into smaller pieces, sprinkle with a few droplets of water, and toss with a fork until the dough holds together. If your dough is too lumpy, the fat needs to be worked into the flour more thoroughly. Break up the larger pieces of fat in with your fingertips and mix them into the flour.

2. The dough is too sticky.

You may have added too much water—always add water a little at a time and stop when the dough comes together. Add ½ teaspoon of flour at a time to the sticky dough, and continue mixing. Do not overmix or knead the dough. It's also possible that the fat may have softened. Always chill the fat before use, and chill the dough after you mix it. If the dough sticks to the rolling pin, rub a little flour onto the rolling pin as well as your work surface.

3. The dough cracks or tears while you're rolling it.

If the dough cracks in the center, it is too cold or dry. Moisten the tears with water, then cover with a small patch of dough and roll again. Rolling out too-cold dough sometimes causes it to crack. Let it warm a bit, but not too much. Add a little water and press the cracks together. Roll the dough just to the edge but not over it, then roll it toward the center. Trim the cracked edge with a knife. If the dough tears, it is too warm. Patch the tear and chill for a few minutes, then reroll.

4. The crust tears when being moved into the pan.

If the dough breaks apart, chill it and start over. If it tears a little, patch it in the pan by moistening the tears and pressing small pieces of dough over them.

5. The crust bubbles or loses shape during baking.

To prevent bubbles, prick the bottom of the crust with a fork before blind-baking. If you forgot to do this, you can rectify it by pricking it during baking. If your nicely fluted or decorative edge loses its shape, the dough was probably not cold enough when you placed the pie in the oven. It's also possible that the oven was not preheated properly. Next time, chill the crust before baking and double-check the oven temperature with a thermometer.

6. The crust falls down the sides during blind-baking.

If the crust falls down the sides of the pan, use more pie weights—they should fill the shell completely. The dough may be too thick and have been pulled down by its own weight; next time, roll it out thinner (about ⅛ inch). It could also have been overmixed, or too warm, or contain too little fat or too much water. To minimize these problems in the future, make sure the dough is mixed to the proper consistency, and do not overwork it while mixing or rolling out.

7. The crust does not brown.

If the top crust does not brown, brush it with an egg wash or milk, or raise the oven temperature. Vinegar or lemon juice added to the crust could also have inhibited browning. When using these acidic ingredients, add sugar or salt to the flour when mixing the dough. If the bottom crust does not brown, it might have been rolled out to an uneven thickness, or the pan or the oven might have hot spots, resulting in a lack of heat flow to the bottom. Next time, set the pie pan on a baking stone, or blind-bake the bottom crust. Brush it with an egg wash or jam before adding the filling.

8. The crust is soggy on the bottom.

If the bottom of your pie is soggy, the filling could be leaking; make sure all holes in the crust are patched. If the bottom crust is undercooked, it was probably not blind-baked properly. Next time, prebake for 7–10 minutes. The oven may not be hot enough, so you could try raising the temperature. Or possibly the pie was not cooled properly. Cool on a rack and allow air to circulate around the entire pan.

9. The edges are too brown or the crust is too tough.

Check the pie frequently as it bakes and cover it with an edge guard or aluminum foil if the crust becomes golden brown before the filling is done. If the crust is too tough, the dough has been overworked or there is not enough fat.

10. The cookie crust is too crumbly or dry.

Crumb crusts should hold their shape when pressed into the pan; if they don't, there is too much or too little moisture, or the crust was not pressed into the pan firmly enough. Always add butter a little at a time until the crumbs hold together, and press a second pie pan over the crust before baking. If the crust is too hard or dry, it was overbaked, so reduce the cooking time accordingly.

DECORATING PIES AFTER BAKING

Whipped cream and meringue can be spread with a spatula or piped with a pastry bag on top of pies after they are fully baked. If you like, toast the meringue in the oven or with a kitchen torch (see page 11).

Place fruit and nuts on top of pies and tarts in decorative patterns. Use them whole or cut into shapes for a colorful garnish.

Solid chocolate can be shredded, curled, or placed on top of the pie in chunks. Melted chocolate can be drizzled. Nuts and fruit can also be dipped into melted chocolate.

Fondant and marzipan are both "edible clays" that can be colored and shaped into ornamental garnishes, such as flowers, butterflies, and wedding toppers.

CUSTARD AND MERINGUE TIPS

Some pies require higher baking temperatures for the meringue topping than for the filling. To avoid sweats or beads on your meringue, don't put it on the pie until the filling is almost finished baking. At that point, top with meringue, then cook at 400–425°F for 4–5 minutes.

Keep a watchful eye on custard pies to make sure they do not puff up in the center (unless the recipe calls for it). Overbaking makes them crack, so it is okay if the center is not completely set when you take it out of the oven.

SERVING, GIVING, AND TRANSPORTING PIES

If you are frequently asked to bring a pie to a Thanksgiving meal or a summertime family potluck, it is probably best to invest in a pie carrier—maybe even a multitiered one. These are available at specialty stores. But if you don't have a lot of storage space and only need to transport pies once in a while, here are some tips:

- Choosing the right pie for the occasion is the first step to successful transporting. A dense pecan pie with a thick outer crust should be no problem to get to an event in one piece, but tall cream, meringue, or ice cream pies are another story.

- Pies with dense crusts are easier to transport than pies with thin, delicate crusts. Try the Cornmeal Crust (page 244); it is sturdier than phyllo or puff pastry crusts. Dense fillings, such as pumpkin, are better than loose fillings, such as chocolate cream.

- Small individual pies are easier to transport than large pies, and deep-dish small pies are the easiest of all. Place them on a rimmed baking sheet, butting up against one another, and wrap the entire sheet tightly with foil. If you like, you can place double-sided tape on the bottom of each pie pan.

- Pies baked in muffin tins can be transported in the tins and removed at the event.

- To transport standard-size pies, cover the cooked and cooled pie with an upside-down empty pie plate (or bowl for taller pies). Secure the two pans together with packing tape or aluminum foil.

- For pies that are to be reheated, check ahead to see if there is an oven at the location of the festivities. Freeze the pie for transporting, then reheat at the event.

- If you must make a whipped cream or meringue pie, bake the pie at home and prepare and add the topping at the event. Adding a little unflavored gelatin to the filling, or overbaking it a little, can help make the pie more rigid.

- Bake pies in disposable paper liners or foil pie pans so you don't need to worry about forgetting to take your plate home. Or do exactly the opposite—bake the pie in a nice pan, gift wrap the pie, and offer it to the host or hostess as a gift.

- Next time you are at the supermarket or a local bakery, ask to purchase several pie boxes that fit your pie pans. Along the same lines, you can save the packaging from a store-bought pie. Boxes are especially good when you have several pies, because you can stack them together and secure them with packing tape.

- If you find round metal cookie tins that fit your pie pans, stock up on them. Or look for unusual containers, such as bamboo steamers, which can be used for both transporting and giving.

- Place your 9-inch pie plate in a 10-inch cake pan. Cover with a cake board or plate. Attach the cake pan to the cover with packing tape, or wrap the entire assembly in aluminum foil.

- When traveling in a car in hot weather, put on the air conditioning and place the pie on the floor to prevent it from falling.

Chapter **2**

Everyday Pies

FRUIT PIES

I've developed many baked-dessert recipes over the years, and fruit pies are by far my favorite for their taste and the homey, old-fashioned warm feelings they evoke. If you are on a mission to find your favorite fruit pie, go ahead and dig in to this chapter. You'll be kept busy throughout the year, as each fruit has its own season. Many fruits can be found in several varieties—just look at the number of good pie apples (page 43) and plums (page 62) there are to choose from. In this chapter, I include recipes for fruit fillings in a variety of flavorful crusts and in a variety of sizes and shapes. As a result, the ratio of sweet fruit to flaky crust changes from pie to pie, and each pie becomes memorable for its own special and distinctive characteristics.

Classic Apple Pie

Makes one 12-inch double-crust pie

If you only make one pie a year, let this be the one. Anytime, anywhere, apple pie is always right. This pie blends Granny Smith, Braeburn, and Pink Lady apples for just the right amount of tart and sweet, but you can experiment with different varieties and combinations.

1. Preheat the oven to 450°F. Butter and flour a 12-inch pie pan. To make the filling, combine the apples and lemon juice in a large, heavy saucepan. Add both sugars, the cinnamon, ginger, and nutmeg, and stir to coat. Bring to a boil and cook

12 medium apples (4 Granny
   Smith, 4 Braeburn, and 4 Pink
   Lady), cored, peeled, and thinly
   sliced (about 7 cups)
Juice of 1 lemon
½ cup granulated sugar
½ cup firmly packed light brown
   sugar
1 teaspoon ground cinnamon
¼ teaspoon ground ginger
¼ teaspoon ground nutmeg
2 tablespoons cornstarch
¼ cup apple juice or water
Large batch (two disks, one
   slightly larger than the other)
Basic Butter Crust (page 242)
3 tablespoons cold unsalted butter,
   cut into cubes
1 large egg, beaten with 2 tablespoons sugar
¼ cup Cinnamon Sugar
   (page 258)

for 5–7 minutes, or until apples are tender.

2. In a small bowl, combine the cornstarch and apple juice and stir until dissolved. Add this to the apple mixture and continue to stir over medium heat for 5 minutes, or until the syrup is translucent and thickened. Remove from heat and let cool. If the mixture is watery, discard enough liquid to leave ¼ cup in the pan.

3. To make the bottom crust, roll out the larger disk on a floured work surface, forming a circle about ⅛ inch thick and 14 inches in diameter. Drape the dough over the pie pan, allowing the excess to hang over the rim. Brush the edge with some of the egg mixture. Prick the crust with a fork. Spoon the apple mixture into the crust. Top with butter cubes.

4. To make the top crust, roll out the smaller disk into a circle about ⅛ inch thick and 13 inches in diameter. Using a pastry wheel or a knife, cut the dough into 12 strips, each a little more than 1 inch wide. Lay half the strips over the fruit, leaving space in between. Lay the other half of the strips on top of them, placing them perpendicular to the bottom strips. You can also weave the strips in a basketweave pattern. Press the ends of the strips into the edge of the bottom crust. Fold the overhang over the rim to conceal the edges of the lattice. Seal by pressing together the top and bottom crusts with the tines of a fork. Brush the exposed crust with the remaining egg wash and sprinkle the entire pie with cinnamon sugar.

5. Bake for 15 minutes. Lower the temperature to 375°F and bake for an additional 40–50 minutes, or until the crust is golden and the juices are shiny and bubbly.

Variation

APPLE RAISIN PIE WITH CRUMBLE TOPPING: Make a medium batch of Basic Butter Crust (page 242) and prepare the pie without a top crust. Preheat the oven to 375°F. Soak ¾ cup raisins in 3 tablespoons rum for 10 minutes. Discard the rum and add the drained raisins to the apple mixture. Sprinkle

GOOD PIE APPLES

When choosing apples for your pies, texture and taste are the most important traits to consider. Apples that keep some crunch and retain their flavor after baking are best. Many people like tartness in their apple pies, so they make their pies with a single variety of tart apples. But you can mix both sweet and tart apples in the same pie to achieve the perfect balance between sweet and tart, according to your own taste. For example, Granny Smith apples have a wonderful flavor, but their crispness also makes them dry when they're baked. When they're combined with Rome or Gala apples, however, which are too soft to stand up on their own in a pie, Granny Smith apples can be an excellent choice. McIntosh and Red Delicious apples are also too soft and/or sweet to use on their own, but can be included a blended pie. Adjust the sugar in the recipe to reflect the sweetness of the apple.

BRAEBURN: Sweet and tart

CORTLAND: Juicy and slightly tart

EMPIRE: Firm-textured and slightly tart

FUJI: Sweet and crisp

GOLDEN DELICIOUS: Rich and sweet

GRANNY SMITH: Sharp, crisp, and sour

GRAVENSTEIN: Tart

HONEYCRISP: Crisp and juicy, with a honey-like sweet-tart flavor

IDARED: Tangy

JONAGOLD: Tangy-sweet

JONATHAN: Sweet-tart and spicy

MACOUN: Crisp; hints of strawberry and spice

MUTSU (A.K.A. CRISPIN): Very juicy and crisp

NORTHERN SPY: Crisp, sweet, and tart

PINK LADY: Crisp and sturdy

PIPPIN (A.K.A. NEWTOWN PIPPIN): Sweet-tart with nuances of spice and pine

WINESAP: Aromatic, with a spicy bite

with cinnamon sugar and bake for 30 minutes. Top with Crumble Topping (page 258) and bake for an additional 20–30 minutes.

Baked Strawberry Pie with Oatmeal Crust

Makes one 9-inch lattice-top pie

When strawberries are at their prime, they are so sweet and juicy that it seems sinful to ruin their natural perfection by baking them or covering them with a goopy glaze. I prefer to serve them uncooked, with just a little lemon juice, sugar, and fresh cream. On the other hand, if I've had strawberries sitting in my refrigerator for a few days and they've started to darken, or if it's the beginning or the end of the season, when strawberries tend to be tart, that's when I like to bake them in a pie—a process that brings out the strawberries' inherent

*Large batch (two disks, one
  slightly larger than the other)
  Oatmeal Crust (page 250)*
*6 cups fresh strawberries, rinsed,
  hulled, and cut in quarters*
*1 teaspoon freshly squeezed lemon
  juice*
½ cup granulated sugar
2 tablespoons instant tapioca
¼ cup granola
¼ teaspoon salt
*1 tablespoon cold unsalted butter,
  cut into cubes*

flavors and sweetness. So here are two recipes—the basic baked strawberry pie and a variation, which uses unbaked berries. Flax seed and walnuts give the oatmeal crust a nutty flavor; the granola in the filling absorbs the juices and unites the flavors of the filling and the crust.

1. To make the crust, roll out the larger disk on a floured work surface, forming a circle between ⅛ and ¼ inch thick and 12 inches in diameter. Roll out the smaller disk to a circle 11 inches in diameter. Refrigerate both disks for 30 minutes.

2. Preheat the oven to 375°F. Butter and flour a 9-inch pie pan. Gently lay the 12-inch crust into the pan, pressing it into the bottom edges and allowing the excess to hang over the rim. Fold the overhang down over the rim and decoratively crimp the edge. Cover the crust with parchment paper and fill with pie weights.

3. Bake for 10–15 minutes, or until the crust is partially baked. Cool on a rack for 10 minutes. Remove the weights and parchment.

4. To make the strawberry filling, combine the strawberries and lemon juice in a large bowl and toss to coat. Combine the sugar, tapioca, granola, and salt in a small bowl. Sprinkle over the strawberries and toss to coat. Gently toss with butter. Fill the cooled bottom crust with strawberry filling.

5. Remove the smaller crust from the refrigerator and, using a pastry wheel, pizza cutter, or sharp knife, cut the dough into nine 1-inch-wide strips. Lay five strips over the filling, and then rotate the pan 90 degrees. Weave the remaining strips one at a time over and under the first layer. Press the edges of each strip into the crimped edge of the bottom crust. Cut off any extra from the ends.

6. Bake for 40–50 minutes, or until the crust is golden and the filling is thick and bubbling. Cool on a rack for 1 hour. Serve at room temperature.

FRESH STRAWBERRY PIE: Prepare a small batch of Oatmeal Crust and blind-bake it for 15–20 minutes. Omit the lattice top. Omit the tapioca, granola, salt, and butter from the filling. Make 4 cups of Whipped Cream (page 261); spoon half of it into a pastry bag fitted with a large star-shaped tip. Pipe five stripes across the pie, stopping ½ inch from the border. Refill the bag with the remaining cream. Rotate the pan 90 degrees and pipe five stripes across the first layer, stopping ½ inch from the border. Pipe a layer of cream around the edge of the pan, closing off the edges of the stripes.

STRAWBERRY BALSAMIC PIE: Replace the lemon juice with 2 tablespoons balsamic vinegar.

Sweet Cherry Pie with Cream Cheese Crust
Makes one 9-inch double-crust pie

Don't miss out on the chance to indulge in this great American comfort pie during the few weeks in summer when cherries are at their flavor peak. Make it with fresh sweet Bing cherries, or use sour cherries and add an additional ½ cup sugar to the filling (see the variation following the recipe). The cream cheese crust is sweet and a little tart, just like the cherries. Fresh cherries release their juices when baked, so I coat the bottom crust with some of the dry ingredients to absorb the moisture, and I create large decorative vents on the top crust to allow moisture to escape. The extra-thick edge is surefire way to tighten the seal. For tips on venting double-crust pies, see page 31. To make the pie in a variety of sizes, as pictured, see Scaling Pies (page 34).

1. Preheat the oven to 450°F. Butter and flour a 9-inch pie pan.

2. To make the bottom crust, roll out one of the disks on a floured work surface, forming a circle about ⅛ inch thick and 12 inches in diameter. Drape the dough over the pie pan, pressing the dough into the bottom edge, allowing the excess to hang over the rim. Brush the edge of the crust with some of the egg white and prick the bottom with a fork.

3. To make the cherry filling, combine the flour and sugar

Crust
Large batch (two disks) Cream Cheese Crust (page 245)
1 egg white
3 tablespoons whole milk

Cherry Filling
¼ cup all-purpose flour
½ cup granulated sugar
4 cups Bing or other fresh sweet cherries, stemmed and pitted
1 tablespoon cold unsalted butter, cut into cubes

in a large bowl. Coat the bottom of the piecrust with 2 tablespoons of the mixture. Add the cherries and butter to the dry ingredients in the bowl and mix to coat.

4. Roll out the second disk into a circle about ⅛ inch thick and 12 inches in diameter. Cut patterned vents into the center with a sharp knife or cookie cutter. Save the cut-out pieces to attach later.

5. Place the top crust over the filling and fold the edge of the bottom crust inward, over the top crust. Press the edges together in a scalloped pattern (see page 30).

6. Attach the cutouts to the top crust by brushing egg white on the back of each cutout and pressing them into the top crust. Brush the entire top crust with milk and place the pie on a baking sheet. Bake for 10 minutes, then reduce the heat to 350°F and bake for additional 40–50 minutes, or until the crust is golden and the juices are shiny and bubbly. Cool on a rack.

Variations

SOUR CHERRY PIE: Replace the Bing cherries with fresh Montmorency or Morello cherries. Add ½ cup sugar to the filling mixture. If the cherries are frozen, canned, or packed in water, drain the liquid and reduce the cooking time to 30–40 minutes.

CHOCOLATE CHERRY PIE: Prepare the pie in a large batch of Chocolate Butter Crust (page 242). Melt ¼ cup bittersweet chocolate and brush on the bottom of the crust before adding the filling. Drizzle with Chocolate Icing (page 200).

Ginger Peach Pies with Cornmeal Crust

Makes one 9-inch single-crust, double-crust, or checkerboard-top pie

There are many choices to make when baking a pie. What type of crust goes best with the filling? Should it be single-crust or double? What should the topping be like? Here are three ways to encase peach filling in cornmeal crusts. The open-faced pie allows moisture to escape easily, and is decorated with a spiral of thinly sliced peaches on the top. The vented double-crust pie retains a bit more moisture

Peach Filling

½ cup granulated sugar

½ cup firmly packed light brown sugar

⅓ cup all-purpose flour

½ teaspoon ground ginger

6 large fresh peaches, pitted and thinly sliced (about 5 cups)

Crust

Small or large batch (one or two disks) Cornmeal Crust (page 244)

1 egg white, lightly beaten with 2 tablespoons whole milk

2 tablespoons cold unsalted butter, cut into cubes

2 tablespoons whole milk

1 teaspoon granulated sugar

in the filling and has more of the cornmeal-crust taste. The checkerboard pie, topped with small squares, combines the best features of the other two. The crust can be made with either yellow or blue cornmeal. Yellow is easier to find, whereas blue cornmeal has a richer taste. The peaches could be peeled or left unpeeled.

To make the filling:
Combine the sugars, flour, and ginger in a large bowl. Add the peaches and toss to coat.

To make the double-crust pie:

1. Preheat the oven to 425°F. Butter and flour a 9-inch pie pan. Prepare a large batch (two disks) of Cornmeal Crust. Roll out one disk on a floured work surface, forming a circle about ⅛ inch thick and 12 inches in diameter. Drape the dough over the pie pan, allowing the excess to hang over the rim. Brush the entire crust with half the egg mixture. Fill with peach filling and evenly distribute butter over the filling.

2. Roll out the other disk into a circle about ⅛ inch thick and 12 inches in diameter. Cut patterned vents into the center with a sharp knife or cookie cutter.

3. Place the top crust over the filling and fold the edge of the bottom crust inward, over the top crust, pressing together to seal. Create a pointed edge (see page 30). Smooth with your fingers.

4. Brush the remaining egg mixture over the edges and top. Sprinkle with sugar.

5. Bake for 15 minutes, then reduce the heat to 350°F and bake for an additional 30–40 minutes, or until the juices are bubbling and

the crust is golden. Cool on a rack for 20–30 minutes. Serve warm.

To make the single-crust pie:

1. Preheat the oven to 375°F. Butter and flour a 9-inch pie pan. Prepare a small batch of Cornmeal Crust, roll it out into a single (bottom) crust, and put it in the pie pan as instructed in step 1 above. Set aside one-fourth of the peach slices for the topping. Cut a small circle out of one of the slices and set aside.

2. Cover the crust with parchment paper and fill with pie weights. Blind-bake for 10–15 minutes, then remove from oven.

3. Fill the crust with filling, topping with the reserved peach slices. Arrange the slices in circles, starting with the outside edge and working your way toward the center. Place the peach circle in the center. Evenly distribute butter over the filling. Sprinkle with sugar.

4. Bake for 25–30 minutes, or until the crust is golden and juices are bubbly. Cool on a rack for 30 minutes. Serve at room temperature with Whipped Cream (page 261).

To make the checkerboard pie:

1. Preheat the oven to 375°F. Butter and flour a 9-inch pie pan. Working with a large batch of Cornmeal Crust, roll out one disk on a floured work surface, forming a circle about ⅛ inch thick and 12 inches in diameter. Drape the dough over the pie pan, allowing the excess to hang over the rim. Create a pointed edge (see page 30). Smooth with your fingers.

2. Cover the crust with parchment paper and fill with pie weights. Blind-bake for 10–15 minutes, then remove from the oven and fill the crust with filling. Evenly distribute butter over the filling.

3. Roll out the second disk of dough into a 5-inch square that is ⅛ inch thick. Using a pastry wheel or knife, cut the dough into 1-inch squares. Place the squares in an

offset checkerboard pattern over the filling. Sprinkle with granulated sugar. Bake for 25–30 minutes, or until the crust is golden and juices are bubbly. Cool on a rack for 20–30 minutes. Serve warm.

Variations
PEACH BASIL PIE: Replace the ginger with 2 teaspoons chopped fresh basil.
PEACH CINNAMON CRUMBLE PIE: Prepare the single-crust pie with Crumble Topping (page 258).

Pineapple and Mango Empanadas

Makes 8 hand pies

Empanadas, a.k.a. hand pies, are pretty simple to make, especially when using store-bought frozen empanada dough. Even this recipe, which features a bready, not-too-sweet yeast crust, is simple, and since you're using homemade dough you can form it into semicircles, squares, triangles, or any shape you can think of. The directions for pineapple and mango fillings are the same; only the ingredients vary. Make both fillings if you want four of each type of empanada, or double the filling recipe of your choice if you want eight of a single kind.

1. To make the dough, combine the yeast, ½ cup of the water, and sugar in a small bowl. Let sit for 8–10 minutes, until foamy.

2. Combine the flour and salt in a large bowl. With

Yeast Empanada Dough

1 packet (¼ ounce) active dry
  yeast
1¼ cups warm water
1 teaspoon granulated sugar
5½ cups all-purpose flour
1 teaspoon salt
½ cup (1 stick) cold unsalted butter, cut into cubes
2 large eggs

Pineapple Filling

1 pineapple, peeled, cored, and cut
  into small cubes
¾ cup granulated sugar
1 tablespoon cornstarch
¼ teaspoon salt
¼ teaspoon ground cinnamon

Mango Filling

3 large mangoes, peeled and cut
  into small cubes
1 cup granulated sugar
½ tablespoon cornstarch
½ cup water
¼ teaspoon ground cinnamon

Topping

Lemon Icing (page 261)

a pastry blender or your fingertips, work in the butter. Add the yeast mixture.

3. Separate one of the eggs. Beat the whole egg and the yolk (keep the egg white in reserve) with the remaining ¾ cup water. Mix into the flour mixture. Knead lightly, adding more flour if necessary, until the dough pulls away from the bowl.

4. Turn the dough out onto a floured work surface and knead for 8–10 minutes, until the dough is smooth and stretchy. Return dough to the bowl, cover with a clean kitchen towel, and leave in a warm place to rise for 2 hours, or until doubled in size.

5. To make the fillings, combine all ingredients in a medium saucepan. Cook, stirring occasionally, until the sugar has dissolved and the mixture has thickened. Remove from heat and cool for 15 minutes. Cover and refrigerate 1–2 hours.

6. Preheat the oven to 350°F. Line two baking sheets with parchment paper.

7. Knead the dough again for 30 seconds on a lightly floured surface. Divide the dough in half and roll out one batch into a 10-inch square that is ⅛ inch thick. Using a plate as a template, or roughly estimating by eye, cut out four 5-inch circles from the dough. Scoop 2–3 tablespoons of pineapple filling onto the top half of each circle and brush a little of reserved the egg white around the bottom half of the circle. Fold the bottom edge over the top and stretch the dough to elongate the circle. Press with your fingers to seal. Crimp the edges decoratively and brush the tops with the remaining egg white. Repeat with the other half of the dough and the mango filling.

8. Place the empanadas on the baking sheets and bake for 20–25 minutes, or until golden. Cool on a rack.

9. Spoon the icing into a pastry bag fitted with a small round tip. Pipe crosshatched lines on the top of each empanada.

Berry Filling

1¼ cups granulated sugar

6 tablespoons all-purpose flour

1 tablespoon grated lemon zest

6 cups fresh berries (such as blueberries, red or golden raspberries,
  and blackberries)

2 tablespoons freshly squeezed
  lemon juice

2 tablespoons cold unsalted butter,
  cut into cubes

Crust

Medium batch (two disks, one
  slightly larger than the other)
  Basic Butter Crust (page 242)
  or Chocolate Butter Crust
  (page 242)

1 large egg white beaten with 2
  tablespoons heavy cream

3 tablespoons granulated sugar

Individual Deep-Dish Berry Pies

Makes four 3½-inch deep-dish pies

While traveling on road trips around the USA, I like to stop in every region for a taste of their local berry pie. Some of the fillings I've tasted, such as those made from the blackberries and marionberries that grow wild on the roadsides of Oregon, are familiar. Others, such as the olallieberry pies that I can't resist in central and Northern California, are less well known. Others, such as the "bumbleberry" pies served at the Bumbleberry Inn in Springdale, Utah, near Zion National Park, carry a certain mystique. What is a bumbleberry? I asked. Well, I was told, bumbleberries are burple and binkel berries grow on giggle bushes! (I later found out that a bumbleberry pie is simply a pie made with mixed berries.)

When making these single-serving pies, experiment with different varieties of crusts, berries, and toppings. You could make the bottom crusts with one type of dough and the top crusts with another, or you could choose different mixtures of berries for each pie. Any way you make them, the finished pies usually provide a wide range of tartness and sweetness.

Consider the juiciness of the berries you're using when creating the lattice tops. Tightly spaced strips will hold more juice in the pie, whereas widely spaced strips will allow more moisture to escape and result in a denser filling. Twisted lattices are for the pure fun of decoration.

1. To make the filling, combine the sugar, flour, and lemon zest in a bowl. Toss the berries in lemon juice, then coat with the sugar mixture.

2. Butter and flour four 3½-inch deep-dish pie pans. Preheat the oven to 425°F. Roll out one disk of dough on a floured work surface, forming a 14-inch square that is ⅛ inch thick. Cut the square into four 7-inch circles. Fit the circles into each pan, pressing the dough into the bottom edge and allowing the excess to drape slightly over the rim. Fold the overhang inward, over the rim, and crimp decoratively. Brush the top edge of the crust with some of the egg mixture. Prick holes in the bottoms and fill with berries.
Top with butter cubes.

3. Roll out the second disk on a floured work surface, forming an 8-inch square that is ⅛ inch thick. Using a pastry wheel or a knife, cut the dough into two 4 x 8-inch rectangles. Then cut each rectangle into sixteen 4 x ½-inch lattice strips. Place 4 strips, one at a time, on each pie. Rotate the pans 90 degrees and place an additional 4 strips across each pie, perpendicular to the first layer of strips. Weave both layers of strips together. Press the ends of the strips into the edge of the bottom crust. Trim the excess. Brush the tops of the strips with the remaining egg mixture and sprinkle with sugar.

4. Bake for 20 minutes, then reduce the heat to 350°F and bake for an additional 25–30 minutes, or until the berries are bubbly and the crust is golden. Cool on a rack for 20 minutes. Serve warm with Whipped Cream (page 261) or ice cream.

BERRIES

Oh, how I love berries. I can never get enough of their subtle and intricate flavors. Spend a day berry picking in your region, or check your local farmers market for common and not-so-common varieties for your next berry pie. Stock up on fresh berries and freeze them when they are in season—they get pricey out of season.

BILBERRY: Similar to blueberries in appearance and taste

BLACKBERRY: Ranges from sweet to tart; related to raspberries

BLUEBERRY: Always sweet and juicy

BOYSENBERRY: Genetically engineered cross between raspberries, blackberries, and loganberries

BUFFALO BERRY: A large, red fruit that grows wild throughout the Great Plains

COWBERRY (A.K.A. LINGONBERRY): Tart red fruit, similar to cranberries

CRANBERRY: Tart, fresh flavor; grown in swamps and bogs

CURRANT: Small round fruit, translucent white, red, or purple in color, with a rich, tart flavor

GOOSEBERRY: Tart green or orange berries; thrives in cool areas

HUCKLEBERRY: Similar to blueberries; grows wild throughout the Pacific Northwest

JUNEBERRY: Red berries that turn blue-black on ripening; similar in size to blueberries

LOGANBERRY: Cross between a raspberry and a blackberry

MARIONBERRY: Cross between an olallieberry and a blackberry; tart and earthy, with traces of sweetness

MULBERRY: A multiple fruit—i.e., a single fruit formed from a cluster of flowers—available in red, purple, or black varieties; thrives in warm climates in the South

OLALLIEBERRY: Cross between the loganberry and youngberry

RASPBERRY: Sweet, flavorful, cold-hardy fruit available in red, black, purple, and golden varieties

SALMONBERRY: Orange or red fruit that resembles raspberries

STRAWBERRY: Ranges from quite sweet to tart; grown in many temperate regions around the world

TAYBERRY: Sweet, red fruit; a cross between a loganberry and a black raspberry

YOUNGBERRY: A cross between a blackberry and a dewberry

Variations

BERRY PIE WITH NUT BUTTER CRUMBLE: Prepare a medium batch (one disk) Basic Butter Crust, fit into a 9-inch pie pan, add the filling, and bake for 20 minutes. After reducing the heat, spoon on 2½ cups Nut Butter Crumble (page 258) and bake for an additional 25–30 minutes.

BERRY GRANOLA PIE: Prepare a medium batch (one disk) Basic Butter Crust, fit into a 9-inch pie pan, add the filling, and bake. Top the pie with 1½ cups sweet granola 15 minutes before it finishes baking.

Rhubarb Pie with Graham-Flour Crust

Makes one 9-inch double-crust pie

No wonder rhubarb makes good pies—it is the only plant that has the nickname "pie plant." It is best known for its extremely tart taste, which is why it's almost always mixed with a sweetener. Buy fresh, crisp stalks, peel the strings on the outside, and refresh the stalks by standing them in cold water for an hour before using. The crust, made with graham flour, is coarse and crunchy.

1. To make the crust, combine the butter and shortening in a medium bowl. Beat with an electric mixer until smooth. Form the mixture into a ball, wrap in plastic, and chill until firm.

2. Combine ⅓ cup all-purpose flour, water, and lemon juice in a small bowl. Mix into a paste and set aside.

3. Cut the chilled butter mixture into tablespoon-size pieces. Combine the remaining flour, graham flour, and salt in the bowl of a food processor fitted with a metal blade and pulse to mix. Add the butter mixture and pulse 4 or 5 times, or until the dry ingredients are coated. Pour in the reserved flour paste and pulse 25–30 times, or until the mixture begins to gather into a ball. If it is wet, add a bit more flour. Divide into two disks, flatten, and wrap in plastic wrap. Refrigerate for 30 minutes.

4. To make the filling, combine the sugar, cornstarch, and salt in a large bowl. Add the rhubarb and lemon juice and toss to coat.

5. Preheat the oven to 450°F. Butter and flour a 9-inch pie pan.

Graham-Flour Crust

7 tablespoons unsalted butter, at room temperature

7 tablespoons vegetable shortening, at room temperature

2 cups all-purpose flour

⅓ cup cold water

1 teaspoon freshly squeezed lemon juice

½ cup graham flour

¼ teaspoon salt

¼ cup whole milk

Rhubarb Filling

1¼ cups granulated sugar

2 tablespoons cornstarch

¼ teaspoon salt

2½ pounds rhubarb stalks, trimmed and cut into ¼–½-inch pieces (about 6–6½ cups)

1 teaspoon freshly squeezed lemon juice

2 tablespoons cold unsalted butter, cut into cubes

Roll out one disk of dough on a floured work surface, forming a circle about ⅛ inch thick and 12 inches in diameter. Drape the dough over the pie pan, pressing it into the bottom edge and allowing the excess to hang over the rim. Fold the overhang inward, over the rim, and decoratively crimp the edge. Cover the crust with parchment paper and fill with pie weights.

6. Bake for 10 minutes, or until the crust begins to brown. Cool on a rack for 10 minutes. Remove the weights and parchment and reduce the oven temperature to 350°F.

7. Roll out the second disk of dough on a floured work surface, forming a circle about ⅛ inch thick and 13 inches in diameter. Using a 1-inch round cookie cutter, cut out the circles that will form the top crust.

8. Mound the filling on the bottom crust and top with butter. Place the dough circles on top of the filling, overlapping each circle and pressing down slightly as you work. Brush the circles with milk where you want them to stick together. When all circles are on top of the pie, brush the entire surface with milk. Return the pie to the oven and bake for 35–45 minutes, or until the liquid is bubbly, the crust is golden, and the rhubarb feels soft when pierced with a knife. Cool on a rack.

Variation

STRAWBERRY RHUBARB PIE: Prepare the pie in a small batch of Lemon Graham Cracker Cookie Crust (page 248). Reduce the rhubarb to 3½ cups and add 3½ cups hulled fresh strawberry quarters and 1 additional tablespoon cornstarch to the filling.

Apricot Almond Skillet Pie

Makes one 10-inch single-crust pie

Capture the flavors of fresh apricots in this single-crust skillet pie. The even browning of the crust and consistent baking of the fruit—advantages of baking in a cast iron skillet—will impress you. The skillet also makes a nice rustic presentation. Single-crust pies with flavorful toppings are simple to make, so if you like this crunchy streusel topping, also try the Crumble Topping (page 258).

1. Preheat the oven to 375°F. Butter and flour a 10-inch cast iron skillet.

2. Roll out the chilled crust dough on a floured work surface, forming a circle about ⅛ inch thick and 14 inches in diameter. Drape the dough over the skillet, pressing it into the bottom edge and allowing the excess to hang ½ inch over the rim. Prick the crust with a fork and set aside.

Crust

*Medium batch (one disc) Nut
  Butter Crust made with almonds
  (page 243)*

Apricot Filling

¼ cup granulated sugar
½ cup firmly packed light brown
  sugar
2½ tablespoons all-purpose flour
¼ teaspoon salt
½ teaspoon ground nutmeg
20–24 fresh apricots (with skins),
  pitted and sliced (about 8 cups)

Streusel Topping

⅓ cup all-purpose flour
⅓ cup rolled oats (not instant)
⅓ cup slivered almonds
½ teaspoon ground nutmeg
¼ teaspoon salt
6 tablespoons unsalted butter, at
  room temperature
½ cup firmly packed light brown
  sugar

3. To make the filling, combine the sugars, flour, salt, and nutmeg in a large bowl. Sprinkle the piecrust with 2 tablespoons of the mixture. Add the apricots to the remaining filling mixture and toss to coat.

4. To make the streusel, combine the flour, oats, almonds, nutmeg, and salt in a medium bowl until blended; set aside.

5. Beat the butter and sugar in a medium mixing bowl with an electric mixer on medium speed until smooth and creamy. Using a wooden spoon, gradually add the flour mixture to the butter mixture until it reaches the consistency of coarse crumbs.

6. Pour the filling into the crust and form the overhang into a border; fold in the excess, rolling to form an edge around the inside rim of the skillet. Bake for 20 minutes. Sprinkle the streusel on top and bake for an additional 20–30 minutes, or until the juices are bubbling and the crust and streusel are golden. Cool in the pan on a rack for 20 minutes. Serve warm.

PIE À LA MODE

The first meaning of "à la mode" in Webster's dictionary is "fashionable, stylish," and the second is "topped with ice cream." It's no wonder: serving apple pie with ice cream has been in fashion since the late 1800s. Today, ice cream can go with any type of fruit pie—in fact, the more interesting the combination, the better. Try topping the Classic Apple Pie (page 41) with Pumpkin Ice Cream (page 257), the Deep-Dish Berry Pie (page 53) with Caramel Ice Cream (page 257), or the Ginger Peach Pie (page 48) with Green Tea Ice Cream (page 92).

Plum Crostata with Sour Cream Ice Cream

Makes 4 crostatas

Crostatas are an excellent choice when you want to create a pie for fragile fruits, such as plums, or savory fillings that get very juicy while baking. Here, I've added some whole wheat pastry flour to the dough to give this plum tart a rustic taste. When shaping the edges, remember that crostatas are meant to be informal, so there's no need to worry about creating picture-perfect edges or a perfectly even thickness. Just make sure the edges of each crust are folded far enough over the filling to hold it in while baking but not so far that the moisture has no room to escape. These crostatas are baked directly on a baking stone, so the bottoms will brown nicely. If you don't have a baking stone, use a baking sheet lined with parchment paper.

1. To make the ice cream, whisk the heavy cream, sour cream, salt, vanilla, and sugar together in a bowl until smooth. Freeze the mixture in an ice cream maker according to the manufacturer's instructions.

2. To make the pastry, combine the flours, confectioners' sugar, and salt in a bowl. With a pastry blender or your fingertips, cut in the butter until the mixture resembles coarse meal.

3. Combine the water and vanilla in a small bowl and add to the dough until it forms a ball. Add a little more water if necessary. Flatten into a disk, wrap in plastic wrap, and chill for 1 hour.

4. Dust a baking stone with cornmeal. Place the baking stone in the oven and preheat to 400°F.

5. To make the filling, gently combine the plums, brown sugar, lemon juice, vanilla, cinnamon, flour, and cornstarch in a large bowl; set aside.

6. Roll out the dough on a floured work surface into a 13-inch square that is about ⅛ inch thick. Using a knife, cut out four 6-inch circles from the dough. Use a small plate as a guide if necessary. Place the dough circles on the baking stone.

Pastry

1¾ cups all-purpose flour

½ cup whole wheat pastry flour,
   sifted

3 tablespoons confectioners' sugar

¼ teaspoon salt

¾ cup (1½ sticks) cold unsalted
   butter, cut into cubes

3 tablespoons cold water

1½ teaspoons vanilla extract

3 tablespoons cornmeal

Topping

1 large egg white, beaten

3 tablespoons firmly packed light
   brown sugar

Filling

8–10 large fresh plums (with
   skins), pitted and sliced

¼ cup firmly packed light brown
   sugar

3 tablespoons freshly squeezed
   lemon juice

½ teaspoon vanilla extract

½ teaspoon ground cinnamon

1½ tablespoons all-purpose flour

½ teaspoon cornstarch

7. Drain excess liquid from the plums, leaving about ⅛ cup, and spread the slices over the dough, leaving a 1–2-inch border on each circle. Fold the borders over the plums, pressing the dough down to hold it in place. Brush the edges with egg whites and sprinkle with brown sugar.

8. Bake for 25–30 minutes, or until the crust is golden brown and juices are bubbling. Cool for 20 minutes on a rack. Serve warm with the ice cream.

When choosing plums for baking, pick firm fruits that are not too hard or too soft. They will be easy to cut and will soften a bit during baking, but they will hold their shape and not lose much of their sweet juice. Red plums tend to be tart, with a taste a bit like green grapes. Black and purple plums tend to be sweeter, with a taste somewhat like wine.

BLACK BEAUTY: Deep purple

BLACK DIAMOND: Black skin; red flesh; small

CASSELMAN: Bright red

DAMSON (A.K.A. DAMASK): Yellow-green flesh, blue-purple skin; tart for a purple plum

FRIAR: Deep black with a small pit, so there is a lot of fruit on each plum

LARODA: Reddish-yellow flesh in a purple skin

MIRABELLE: Yellowish, small oval

PLUOT: Mottled green and maroon skin; cross between an apricot and a plum; sweeter than red plums

RED BEAUTY: Even red color

RUBY ROYAL: Mottled red skin

SANTA ROSA: Crimson-red skin and sweet-tart flavor; one-third of all plums sold are Santa Rosa plums

Variations

SOUR CREAM PLUM CROSTATA: Combine 1 cup sour cream with 1 cup sifted confectioner's sugar. Spread one-fourth of this mixture on the bottom of each crust before adding the plums.

CROSTATA DI RICOTTA: Omit the plum filling and fill the crostata with Ricotta Filling (page 82). Bake for 20–25 minutes.

Pomegranate Turnovers

Makes 9 turnovers

Although Americans have only recently started to cook with them, fresh pomegranates are common in many of the world's cuisines. Their flavor is a real standout in these turnovers. But, if you prefer, many of the other fruit fillings in this book can be encased in turnovers. Just

HOW TO SEED A WHOLE POMEGRANATE

Score the pomegranate with a knife and break it open. You will see that the seeds are separated from the peel by a yellowish-white, pulpy membrane. Fill a medium bowl with water. Place the pomegranate under the water and break it apart with your fingers. The seeds will sink and the pulp will float. Discard the skin and pulp, then drain the seeds.

Pastry

1 batch Puff Pastry (page 251), or one package (14 ounces) all-butter frozen puff pastry, thawed

2 large egg whites, beaten

¼ cup crystal sugar

Pomegranate Filling

1 cup pomegranate or apple juice

¼ cup cornstarch

½ cup firmly packed light brown sugar

½ teaspoon ground ginger

¼ teaspoon salt

1 tablespoon freshly squeezed lemon juice

2 tablespoons instant tapioca

3 cups pomegranate seeds (from about 3 or 4 large pomegranates)

cut the fruit into smaller segments than you would for pie filling. Try the Cherry Filling (page 46), the Apple Filling (page 138), the Apricot Filling (page 59), the Peach Filling (page 49), the Berry Filling (page 53), or the Rhubarb Filling (page 56).

Store-bought puff pastry makes these pies quick and easy to prepare, although if you want to attempt building the layers in the dough yourself, try the relatively simple recipe for Puff Pastry in chapter 6. Watching any type of puff pastry expand in the oven will reward your efforts.

1. Make the dough and chill until ready to use. Line two baking sheets with parchment paper.

2. In a medium saucepan over medium heat, mix the pomegranate juice, cornstarch, sugar, ginger, and salt. Stir until thickened. Remove from heat and stir in the lemon juice and tapioca. Allow the mixture to cool for 10 minutes. Fold in the seeds.

3. Roll out the dough on a floured work surface into a 15-inch square that is ⅛ inch thick. Using a pastry wheel or pizza cutter, cut the dough into nine 5-inch squares.

4. Spoon about ⅓ cup filling onto center of each pastry. Brush egg white on the edges and fold in half to make a triangle. Press and pinch the edges with your fingertips to seal tightly.

5. Place the turnovers on the baking sheets. Brush the tops with egg whites and sprinkle with crystal sugar. Chill for 20 minutes.

6. Preheat the oven to 400°F. Bake for 15 minutes, then reduce the heat to 350°F and reverse the placement of the baking sheets. Bake for an additional 10–15 minutes, or until golden brown. Cool on the baking sheets for 5 minutes, then transfer to a rack to cool for an additional 15 minutes. Serve warm or at room temperature.

Guava Filling

3–4 large fresh guavas (with
  skins), cut into ½-inch cubes
  (about 3 cups)

2½ cups water

1½ cups granulated sugar

1 teaspoon freshly squeezed lime
  juice

¼ teaspoon salt

1 teaspoon cornstarch

Pastry

½ cup (1 stick) unsalted butter,
  melted

1 pound country-style phyllo
  dough (eight 18 x 14-inch
  sheets), thawed if frozen

2 tablespoons crystal sugar

Cream Cheese Filling

1½ cups Cream Cheese Filling
  (page 255)

Guava Cream Cheese Strudel

Makes one 9 x 5-inch strudel

Yes, strudel is a proud member of the pie family. This guava-and-cream-cheese filling offers a tropical twist on the traditional apple strudel. Prepared with phyllo dough, the crust resembles classic Turkish pastry (a close relative of phyllo) more than it does the noodle-like unleavened dough used for traditional Viennese strudel (which is more difficult to make). If you can't find fresh guavas, replace the filling with 2 cups of guava jam.

1. To make the guava filling, combine the guava, 1½ cups water, sugar, lime juice, and salt in a saucepan over medium heat. Bring to a boil, reduce heat to simmer, and cook for about 15–20 minutes, stirring occasionally, until thickened. Set aside to cool.

2. Strain the mixture through a sieve to separate out the seeds. Return the mixture to the saucepan and add the remaining 1 cup water and the cornstarch. Simmer for 15–20 minutes, or until thickened further. Cool for 15 minutes, then refrigerate the mixture for 1 hour.

3. Preheat the oven to 350°F. Line a baking sheet with parchment paper.

4. Place one sheet of phyllo on the baking sheet and brush with some of the butter. Repeat with the remaining 7 sheets, leaving the top layer without butter.

5. Spoon the cream cheese filling and then the guava mixture on top, in the center of the phyllo, forming a rectangle about 9 x 5 inches and leaving a border on all sides that will completely secure the filling when folded (about 4½ inches on each side). Brush the border with butter. First fold over the short ends of the phyllo and overlap the filling, then fold over the long ends and press to seal. Brush additional butter over the outside to tighten the seal.

6. Carefully lift the strudel and turn it over, placing it seam side down. Brush the top with butter. Cut slits through the

top layers of the phyllo, through to the filling, spacing them about 2 inches apart. Sprinkle with crystal sugar.

7. Bake for 15–20 minutes, or until golden. Cool on a rack. Cut crosswise into 2½–3-inch pieces to serve.

Crust

¼ cup raisins, soaked in 3 tablespoons hot water
Large batch Oatmeal Crust (page
  250), mixed but not yet chilled
1 large egg white, beaten with 2
  tablespoons water

Sour Cream Raisin Filling

6 egg yolks
1½ cups firmly packed dark
  brown sugar
2 cups sour cream
½ cup cornstarch
½ teaspoon grated lemon zest
2 cups raisins

Raisin Friendship Pie with Oatmeal Crust

Makes one 9-inch single-crust pie

Raisin pie is traditionally served at wakes in Amish communities. Friends of the deceased bake the pies and bring them to the wake; the pies' sweetness is meant to console the mourners. Raisin pies are also known as a traditional gesture of friendship. Since they're made with a sturdy, hearty crust, they're easy to transport, and since raisins are available throughout the year, the pies can be baked whenever they're needed. Over the years, many other American communities have adopted the practice of offering a raisin pie as a token of neighborliness, or as a housewarming gift. This recipe, made with a spicy oatmeal crust, has sour cream added to the traditional filling to make it extra creamy. If you plan on bringing this to a funeral or giving it to a friend, bake it in a pretty dish and gift the whole thing—or try lining the pie pan with a paper liner so you don't have to worry about asking for your pan back.

1. Combine the ¼ cup raisins and hot water and let the fruit plump for 10 minutes. Make the crust and, before refrigerating, mix in the plumped raisins. Divide the dough in half, wrap in plastic wrap, and chill for 30 minutes. Line a 9-inch pie pan with a disposable paper liner.

2. To make the filling, beat the yolks and sugar in a large mixing bowl with an electric mixer on medium speed until light. Beat in the sour cream, cornstarch, and lemon zest. Fold in the raisins. Cover and chill until ready to use.

3. Preheat the oven to 450°F. Roll out one pastry disk on a floured work surface to form a circle about ⅛ inch thick and 13 inches in diameter. Drape the dough over the pie pan, allowing the excess to hang over the rim. Press the dough

into the bottom edges, and trim the excess to a ¼-inch overhang. Brush the edge of the crust with some of the egg white mixture. Spoon the filling into the center.

4. Remove a 2-inch ball of dough from the remaining disk and set aside. Roll out the remaining disk on a floured work surface to form a circle about ⅛ inch thick and 10 inches in diameter. Place this top crust over the filling, pressing the edge to seal. Roll the overhanging dough over the edge toward the center, and crimp decoratively.

5. Roll out the 2-inch ball to form a circle about 4 inches in diameter and ⅛ inch thick. Using a cookie cutter or a knife, cut out a house shape, about 3½ inches tall, then cut out two windows and a door from the scraps around the edges.

6. Brush some of the egg white mixture over the entire top crust. Attach the house, then brush egg white on the backs of the windows and door and attach them to the house. Brush the entire house with egg white. Cut slits in the top of the crust to vent.

7. Bake for 10 minutes, then reduce the heat to 350°F and bake for an additional 20–25 minutes, or until the top is golden. Cool on a rack and serve.

CREAM AND CUSTARD PIES

Whether your tastes slant toward the retro—as in the Banana Cream Pie and the Coconut Custard Pie—or whether you're inspired by snazzy contemporary flavor combinations, such as those in the Fig Ricotta Tart and the Plantain Cashew Custard Tart, you'll find plenty of tasty treats in this section. These pies all share one main claim to fame: the creamy richness of fresh whipped cream, eggs, or cheese, all baked to smooth perfection in a crispy crust.

Banana Cream Pie with Candied Walnuts

Makes one 9-inch single-crust pie

Candied walnuts accent the flavor of the bananas in this indulgent classic. To keep the bananas on top of the pie looking fresh, coat them with fresh lemon juice. Another alternative is to use fresh bananas in the filling and dried banana chips on the top.

Candied Walnuts

1¼ cups walnut halves

⅓ cup granulated sugar

1½ tablespoons golden rum

Crust

Small batch (one disk) Basic Butter Crust (page 242)

1. Preheat the oven to 325°F. Butter and flour a 9-inch pie pan. Line a baking sheet with parchment paper.

2. To make the candied walnuts, spread walnuts on a baking sheet and toast for 5–7 minutes, watching carefully so that they don't burn.

3. Combine sugar and rum in a medium saucepan over low heat. Cook, stirring, until the sugar begins to melt and the mixture turns brown. Add the walnuts, stirring to coat thoroughly. Remove from the heat and spread on the lined baking sheet, separating the nuts so they do not stick. Place the baking sheet on a rack and let cool completely for about 30 minutes.

4. Preheat oven to 350°F. Roll out the crust to form a circle about ⅛ inch thick and 12 inches in diameter. Drape the dough over the pie pan, allowing the excess to hang over the rim. Press the dough into the bottom edges, and trim the excess to a ¼-inch overhang. Fold the overhang over the rim and decoratively crimp the edge. Prick the bottom

Banana Filling

¼ cup cornstarch

⅛ teaspoon salt

½ cup granulated sugar

4 large egg yolks

2½ cups whole milk

2 tablespoons unsalted butter

1 teaspoon vanilla extract

6 ripe medium bananas (about 2 pounds), or 3 ripe medium bananas and ¾ cup dried banana chips

2 tablespoons freshly squeezed lemon juice

Topping

3½–4 cups Whipped Cream (page 261)

with a fork. Top the crust with parchment paper and fill with pie weights. Blind-bake for 15 minutes, or until the crust is partially baked. Remove the paper and weights and bake for additional 10–15 minutes, or until golden. Remove from the oven and cool on a rack.

5. To make the filling, combine the cornstarch, salt, and sugar in a small bowl and set aside.

6. Beat the egg yolks and milk in a medium saucepan with an electric mixer over low heat. Gradually add the cornstarch mixture, stirring continuously with a wooden spoon until the mixture comes to a boil. Reduce the heat and continue stirring for about 5 minutes, or until the mixture thickens. Remove from the heat and stir in the butter until melted. Add the vanilla. Cool for 15 minutes, then cover with plastic wrap so it touches the top of the filling and refrigerate for 1 hour.

7. Cut 3 of the bananas on the diagonal into ¼-inch slices and gently toss with about half the lemon juice. Arrange the slices in the crust in overlapping circles, then top with half the candied walnuts. Spread the cream mixture over the walnuts, pressing down to remove any air pockets.

8. Spread half the whipped cream over the filling with a spatula, creating a smooth mound. Spoon the rest of the whipped cream into a pastry bag fitted with a star-shaped tip and pipe the cream around the edges. Chill for 1 hour. When ready to serve, cut the remaining bananas on the diagonal into ¼-inch slices and gently toss with the remaining lemon juice. Top the pie with the bananas and remaining candied walnuts.

Variations

CHOCOLATE BANANA CREAM PIE: Substitute a small batch of Chocolate Chip Crust (page 247) for the Basic Butter Crust. Replace the whipped cream with the Chocolate Pastry Cream (page 256). Drizzle the top with ¼ cup melted semisweet chocolate.

CARAMEL BANANA CREAM PIE: Make ⅔ cup Caramel Topping (page 91). Pour ½ cup over the bananas in the crust and drizzle the remainder over the cream on top.

Coconut Cream Filling

2½ cups whole milk

1 cup sweetened flaked coconut

1 whole vanilla bean, split

3 large eggs

⅔ cup granulated sugar

3½ tablespoons all-purpose flour

5 tablespoons unsalted butter

Crust

Small batch Basic Butter Crust (page 242), flattened into a disk and chilled

Topping

3½–4 cups Whipped Cream (page 261)

1½ cups toasted flaked coconut (page 25)

1 cup large fresh coconut curls (page 25)

Coconut Cream Pie

Makes one 9-inch single-crust pie

A creamy classic, this pie makes the most of the many different ways that coconut can be prepared and served.

1. Butter and flour a 9-inch pie pan.

2. To make the filling, combine the milk, coconut, and vanilla bean in a medium saucepan over medium heat and simmer for 7–10 minutes, or until thickened and bubbling around the edges. Remove from heat and discard the vanilla bean.

3. Beat the eggs, sugar, and flour in a medium mixing bowl and gradually whisk in one-fourth of the hot milk mixture. Add

the egg mixture to the milk in the saucepan and whisk for about 5 minutes over low heat, until cream thickens. Remove from the heat and stir in the butter until melted. Transfer to a bowl, cover with plastic wrap touching the surface, and refrigerate for 3 hours.

4. Preheat the oven to 350°F. Roll out the crust to form a circle about ⅛ inch thick and 12 inches in diameter. Drape the dough over the pie pan, allowing the excess to hang over the rim. Press the dough into the bottom edges, and trim the excess to a ¼-inch overhang. Fold the overhang over the rim and decoratively crimp the edge. Prick the bottom with a fork. Top the crust with parchment paper and fill with pie weights. Blind-bake for 15 minutes, or until the crust is partially baked. Remove the paper and weights and bake for an additional 10–15 minutes, or until golden. Remove from the oven and cool on a rack.

5. Fill the crust with coconut cream. Top with the whipped cream, toasted coconut, and coconut curls.

Crust

Large batch (six disks) Sweet Tart Crust (page 253)

Topping

2 cups Chocolate Whipped Cream (page 261)
¼ cup chopped almonds
3 tablespoons whole almonds
2 tablespoons chocolate-covered almonds

Chocolate Almond Cream Tarts

Makes six 4-inch tarts

If you love chocolate, this is a tart for you. Vary the taste by using different types of chocolate.

1. Preheat the oven to 375°F. Butter and flour six 4-inch tartlet pans. Roll out each disk of dough on a floured work surface to form six circles, each about ¼ inch thick and 5½ inches in diameter. Fit the crusts into the pans, pressing into the bottom edges. Line the crusts with parchment paper and fill with pie weights. Blind-bake for 20 minutes. Remove the parchment paper and weights and bake for an additional 7–12 minutes, or until golden. Cool for 20 minutes in the pans on a rack, and then remove from the pans and transfer to a rack to cool completely.

Chocolate Filling

¼ cup Dutch-process cocoa
   powder

2 tablespoons cornstarch

⅛ teaspoon salt

1 cup whole milk

½ cup heavy cream

⅓ cup granulated sugar

2 large egg yolks

3 ounces dark chocolate (at least
   60% cacao), melted

¼ cup chopped almonds

1 teaspoon vanilla extract

1½ tablespoons unsalted butter,
   melted

2. To make the filling, combine the cocoa powder, cornstarch, and salt in a small bowl and set aside.

3. Heat the milk in a heavy saucepan over high heat until boiling. Remove from heat and skim off any skin that may have formed. Add ½ cup of the hot milk to the cocoa powder mixture and stir it into a paste. Transfer the rest to a double boiler.

4. Add the heavy cream, sugar, and egg yolks to the double boiler. Stir over medium-low heat until the mixture thickens and heavily coats the back of a wooden spoon, about 10 minutes. Remove from heat and stir in the chocolate, almonds, vanilla, and butter. Set aside for 10 minutes to cool.

5. Spoon the filling into the crusts, making a taller mound in the center than around the edges, and cover with plastic wrap so that it touches the filling. Chill for 2 hours.

6. Spoon the whipped cream into a pastry bag fitted with a star-shaped tip. Pipe mounds of whipped cream on the tarts. Top with chopped almonds, whole almonds, and chocolate-covered almonds.

Variation

CHOCOLATE CHERRY CREAM TARTS: Replace the chopped almonds in the filling with ½ cup chopped fresh cherries. Top with grated chocolate and whole fresh cherries.

Apricot Almond Tart with Marzipan Lattice Top
Makes one 11-inch tart

The delicate flavors of apricots and almonds are highlighted in this creamy, elegant tart. The top is made from a single sheet of marzipan with diamond-shaped cutouts, which gives the pie a lattice effect and reveals the tempting filling inside. There are several homemade components to this recipe—including the almond paste—that you can replace with store-bought ingredients if you are short on time.

1. Butter and flour an 11-inch tart pan. Fit the dough into the pan, pressing it into the bottom edges and the sides. Create an edge flush with the top rim of the pan. Prick the bottom with a fork. Top the crust with parchment paper and fill with pie weights. Refrigerate for 1 hour.

2. To make the almond paste, combine the sugar, honey, and water in a small saucepan and stir over medium heat until the sugar has dissolved. Blend the ground almonds and sugar mixture in

Crust
Large batch (one disk) Almond Sweet Tart Crust (page 254)

Almond Paste
Makes 1¼ cups
¼ cup granulated sugar
¼ cup clover honey
2 tablespoons water
¾ cup ground almonds
2 tablespoons unsalted butter, at room temperature

Filling

¼ cup apricot preserves

3½ cups Almond Pastry Cream
   (page 256), or store-bought
   almond or vanilla pudding,
   chilled for 2 hours

4 fresh apricots, halved

Topping

1¼ cups Marzipan (page 259)

1 egg white, beaten

¼ cup slivered almonds

1½ cups Almond Buttercream
   (page 260)

a food processor until the mixture forms a smooth paste. Add more honey if necessary. Cover with plastic wrap and chill for 30 minutes. When ready to use, knead in the butter.

3. Preheat the oven to 375°F. Blind-bake the crust for 25 minutes. Remove the parchment and weights and bake for an additional 7–12 minutes, or until golden. Cool for 20 minutes and then remove from the pan and transfer to a rack to cool completely.

4. Spread the apricot preserves over the crust and the almond paste over the preserves. Spread the almond pastry cream over the almond paste. Press the apricot halves, cut sides up, into the pastry cream.

5. Line a baking sheet with parchment paper. Coat a work surface with confectioners' sugar, and roll out the marzipan to form a circle about ⅛ inch thick and 11 inches in diameter. Using the tart pan as a template, cut out a circle from the marzipan. Cut diamond shapes out of the circle to create a lattice pattern; set the latticed marzipan on the prepared baking sheet. Brush the beaten egg white over all the marzipan and bake for 3–5 minutes, or until browned. Watch carefully to make sure the marzipan doesn't burn. Remove from the oven and let cool completely. (You could also brown the marzipan with a kitchen torch.)

6. Set the marzipan over the tart, allowing the halved apricots to peek through the holes in the lattice. Sprinkle with slivered almonds.

7. Spoon the Almond Buttercream into a pastry bag fitted with a large star-shaped tip. Pipe stars where the marzipan meets the crust to seal.

Variation

CHERRY ALMOND TART: Substitute cherry preserves for the apricot preserves. Replace the apricots with 1½ cups stemmed and pitted sweet fresh cherries.

Crust

Small batch Chocolate Cream
Cheese Crust (page 245), pre-
pared through step 2

Large batch Cream Cheese Crust
(page 245), prepared through
step 2

2 large egg whites, beaten

Chocolate-Covered Strawberries

4 ounces dark chocolate (at least
60% cacao), chopped

4 large fresh strawberries

Dark Chocolate Pudding Filling

7 ounces bittersweet chocolate,
chopped

¼ teaspoon salt

2½ tablespoons cornstarch

2 tablespoons Dutch-process
cocoa powder

1 large egg

2 large egg yolks

2½ cups whole milk

⅓ cup granulated sugar

2 tablespoons unsalted butter

1 teaspoon vanilla extract

Topping

1 cup Whipped Cream (page 261)

3 tablespoons dark chocolate (at
least 60% cacao) shavings

Chocolate Pudding Pie with Chocolate-Covered Strawberries

Makes one 9-inch single-crust pie

Chocolate-covered strawberries shine in the center of this chocolate pudding pie. To enhance the flavors and create contrast in the braid, the crust is made with both regular cream cheese crust and chocolate cream cheese crust. Feel free to use either one or the other if you prefer. Also, you can try varying the fruits used in this recipe. Try dipping cherries, Mandarin oranges, bananas, grapes, dried apricots, raisins, and dried pineapple in chocolate. Match your favorite pudding recipe to the fruit, or create tasty combinations of fruit flavors.

1. Make the cream cheese crusts, setting aside one-third of the plain crust and one-fourth of the chocolate crust. Wrap the two large portions of dough and two small portions of dough in plastic wrap separately. Chill for 1 hour.

2. To make the chocolate-dipped strawberries, melt the dark chocolate in a double boiler, stirring until smooth. Hold the strawberries by the stems and dip them into the melted chocolate. Place on parchment paper and let set for 30 minutes.

3. Preheat the oven to 450°F. Butter and flour a 9-inch pie pan. Line a baking sheet with parchment paper.

4. Roll out the two large crusts into two rectangles, each about 6½ inches long, 5 inches wide, and ⅛ inch thick. Fit the two crusts into the pan by draping one crust over one half of the pan and the other crust over the other half of the pan, pressing both crusts together in the center and draping the extra over the sides. Press the crusts into the bottom edge, then fold the overhang over the rim to create an edge.

5. Divide the remaining chocolate dough in half. Roll out one batch into a rectangle about ⅛ inch thick and 7 inches in diameter. Using cookie cutters, cut out three large flowers (each about 3½ inches) and five small flowers (each about 1 inch).

6. Set aside a small piece of the regular cream cheese crust and roll out the remainder into a circle about ⅛ inch thick and 3 inches in diameter. Cut out 5 dots for the centers of the flowers with the tip of a straw. Attach the small dots to the small flowers with some of the egg whites and place on the baking sheet. Bake for 10–12 minutes, or until golden.

7. Roll the remaining chocolate dough and the remaining regular dough into three logs, each about 28 inches long. Braid the logs together.

8. Brush more egg whites around the top rim of the crust and press the braid onto the edge. Prick the bottom of the crust with a fork. Line the crust with parchment paper and fill with pie weights. Bake for 35–40 minutes, or until golden. Cool on a rack.

9. To make the pudding, melt 6 ounces of the chocolate in a double boiler; set aside. Combine the salt, cornstarch, and cocoa in a small bowl; set aside. Beat the egg, yolks, and ½ cup of the milk in a medium mixing bowl with an electric mixer on medium speed for about 1 minute, or until blended and foamy.

10. Bring the remaining 2 cups milk and sugar to a boil in a heavy saucepan. Reduce the heat to medium. Add the dry ingredients and stir until blended.

11. Gradually add the egg mixture and stir for 7–10 minutes, or until the pudding thickens. Remove from the heat and add the butter and vanilla. Cool 5 minutes.

12. Pour the pudding into the piecrust. Place a piece of plastic wrap directly on the top of the pudding (to prevent a skin from forming) and chill for 4 hours to set.

13. When ready to serve, place the large chocolate flowers on top of the pudding and the chocolate-covered strawberries on top of the chocolate flowers. Spoon the whipped cream into a pastry bag fitted with a large star-shaped tip. Pipe the whipped cream into the center of the pie and cover the

entire pie with chocolate shavings. Melt the remaining 1 ounce chocolate and use it to glue the small flowers to the braided crust. Let sit for 15 minutes to harden.

Crust

2 cups crushed pistachio biscotti cookies (about 10–12 cookies)

¼ cup unsalted butter, melted

Pistachio Lemon Filling

1 cup whole pistachio nuts

1½ cups granulated sugar

3 tablespoons water

4 large egg yolks

½ teaspoon grated lemon zest

3 tablespoons freshly squeezed lemon juice

⅛ teaspoon salt

¼ cup cornstarch

1½ cups whole milk

Topping

2 cups Whipped Cream (page 261)

3 pistachio biscotti cookies, broken in half

Pistachio Pudding Pie with Biscotti Crust

Makes one 9-inch single-crust pie

Flavored with pistachio paste, this homemade pudding filling is much closer to the nut's true flavor than the bright green packaged pudding mix you can find in the supermarket (although I love that, too, for its nostalgic effect). This cookie crust is made with pistachio biscotti, but if you can't find them use your favorite biscotti as a substitute.

1. Preheat the oven to 350°F. Butter and flour a 9-inch pie pan.

2. Toss the cookie crumbs and butter in a bowl until coated. Using your hands, press the crumbs onto the bottom and up the sides of the pan. Bake for 8–10 minutes, or until the edge is golden.

3. Combine ¾ cup whole pistachio nuts, ½ cup granulated sugar, and the water in a food processor. Process until the mixture reaches the consistency of a paste; set aside.

4. Combine the eggs, remaining 1 cup sugar, lemon zest, lemon juice, and salt in a medium mixing bowl. Beat with an electric mixer on medium speed until smooth. In a separate bowl, stir the cornstarch into the milk, and then beat into the egg mixture.

5. Transfer to a double boiler set over simmering water and cook, stirring occasionally, for 8–10 minutes, or until thickened. Stir in the pistachio paste. Cool for about 10 minutes, then pour into the piecrust. Cover with plastic wrap, making sure it touches the surface of the filling, and chill for 4 hours.

6. When ready to serve, top with whipped cream, remaining pistachio nuts, and biscotti halves.

Coconut Custard Filling

3 large eggs, beaten

1 cup granulated sugar

¼ teaspoon salt

2 tablespoons all-purpose flour

½ cup whole milk

½ cup heavy cream

1 tablespoon unsalted butter, melted

1 teaspoon vanilla extract

1½ cups sweetened flaked coconut, lightly toasted (see page 25)

Crust

Medium batch (1 disk) Egg Crust (page 246)

1 large egg, beaten with 2 tablespoons whole milk

Topping

¾ cup large coconut curls, lightly toasted (see page 25)

Coconut Custard Pie

Makes one 11-inch single-crust pie

Here is my take on a traditional Southern favorite. I like to use a pie pan with a wide rim so that I can form the edge of the crust into a sunny border with radiating "arms." As the songwriter Johnny Nash said, "It's going to be a bright, bright, sunshiny day."

1. Preheat the oven to 450°F. Butter and flour an 11-inch pie pan.

2. To make the filling, combine the eggs, sugar, and salt in a large mixing bowl. Beat with an electric mixer on medium speed until blended. Add the flour, milk, cream, butter, and vanilla and mix until blended. Fold in the sweetened flaked coconut. Chill until ready to use.

3. Roll out the pastry disk on a floured work surface into a circle about ⅛ inch thick and 14 inches in diameter. Drape over the pie pan, allowing excess to hang over the rim. Press the crust into the bottom edges of the pan. Using kitchen shears or a knife, cut the excess dough flush with the rim of the pie pan. Measure the top rim of the pan from the inside to the outside and cut straight slits in the dough around the crust, spacing the slits the same distance apart as the width of the rim. This will form the dough into squares. Brush the edge of the crust with the beaten egg mixture. Fold over each square on the diagonal to create triangles, and press to seal.

4. Prick the bottom of the crust with a fork. Line with parchment paper and fill with pie weights. Blind-bake for 7–10 minutes, then remove from the oven and transfer to a rack. Reduce the oven temperature to 350°F. Prepare a water bath (see page 34) and set the water bath in the oven.

5. Spread the custard mixture into the crust, set the pan into the preheated water bath, and bake for 1 hour, or until the filling is firm in the center. Remove water bath and pie from the oven and cool in pan on a rack. Serve at room temperature, topped with large coconut curls.

Variations

GUAVA COCONUT CUSTARD PIE WITH MERINGUE TOPPING: After blind-baking the crust, spread first with Guava Filling (page 64) and then add the coconut custard filling on top. Bake as directed. After it has cooled, top with Meringue Topping (page 260).

ORANGE COCONUT CUSTARD PIE: Replace the vanilla with 1 tablespoon orange juice and 1 teaspoon grated orange zest. Top with candied orange slices (page 230).

Plantain Cashew Custard Tart

Makes one 11-inch tart

Plantains are a popular food in tropical regions. They are best cooked when they are overripe and their sugars have turned extra sweet. The flavor is the perfect complement to the creamy, nutty cashew in this tart. Without the caramel glaze, it can be served as a savory side dish to a main course.

Crust

1 batch Cashew Tart Crust (page 253)

Filling

2 large very ripe plantains

2 large eggs

¼ cup granulated sugar

¼ cup firmly packed light brown sugar

2 tablespoons all-purpose flour

¾ cup heavy cream

1 teaspoon vanilla extract

¼ cup ground roasted unsalted cashews

Topping

2 tablespoons chopped roasted unsalted cashews

2 tablespoons whole roasted unsalted cashews

⅓ cup Caramel Topping (page 91)

1. Butter and flour an 11-inch tart pan. Make the crust dough through step 5.

2. Preheat the oven to 450°F. Leaving their skins on, prick the plantains on all sides with a fork. Roast on a baking sheet for 35–40 minutes, or until soft (test with a knife). Cool on a rack and peel.

3. Purée three-fourths of the roasted plantains in a blender; you should have 1½–2 cups. Slice the remaining plantains on the diagonal with a knife and set aside.

4. Reduce the oven temperature to 375°F. Roll out the crust dough to form a circle about ¼ inch thick and 13½ inches in diameter. Drape the dough over the pan, allowing the excess to hang over the rim. Press the dough into the bottom edges, and cut off the excess with a knife. Prick the bottom with a fork. Top the crust with parchment paper and fill with pie weights. Blind-bake for 15 minutes, or until the crust is partially baked. Remove the paper and weights; cool on a rack.

5. Combine the eggs and both sugars in a large mixing bowl. Beat with an electric mixer on medium speed until light and fluffy. Add the flour, cream, and vanilla and mix until smooth. Add the ground cashews and puréed plantains to the cream mixture. Pour the filling into the tart shell and bake for 35–40 minutes, or until the custard is set. Cool on a rack for 30 minutes.

6. To serve, top with plantain slices, chopped and whole cashews, and caramel topping. Serve warm.

Chocolate Fig Ricotta Tart

Makes one 6 x 12-inch tart

This filling is based on the fillings in my favorite traditional Italian desserts—cannoli and cream puffs. The chocolate walnut shell and fresh figs add a contemporary California twist.

Ricotta Filling

3¼ cups ricotta cheese

2 large eggs

1 teaspoon vanilla extract

1 cup sifted confectioners' sugar

1 cup semisweet chocolate chips

¼ cup chopped dried apricots

2 tablespoons chopped candied orange

Crust

1 batch Chocolate Walnut Tart Crust (page 253)

10 fresh Mission figs, stemmed and halved

1. Preheat the oven to 375°F. Butter and flour a 6 x 12-inch tart pan.

2. To make the filling, beat the ricotta, eggs, and vanilla in a large mixing bowl with an electric mixer on medium speed. Gradually add the confectioners' sugar. Stir in the chocolate chips, apricots, and candied orange.

3. Roll out the crust dough to form a rectangle about 14 inches long, 8 inches wide, and ⅛ inch thick. Drape the dough over the pan, allowing the excess to hang over the rim. Press the dough into the bottom edges, and cut off the excess with a knife. Prick the bottom with a fork. Top the crust with parchment paper and fill with pie weights. Blind-bake for 15–20 minutes, or until the crust is partially baked. Remove the paper and weights cool on a rack.

4. Spoon the ricotta filling into the cooled crust until it comes almost up to the top of the rim. Press the fig halves into the

filling. Bake for an additional 25–30 minutes, or until the edge appears dry. Let cool for 20 minutes in the pan, and then remove from the pan and transfer to a rack to cool completely.

Variation

DRIED FIG TART: Replace the fresh figs with 10 coarsely chopped dried figs. Combine the figs and candied fruit in a bowl and soak in ¼ cup rum mixed with ¼ cup hot water for 20 minutes. Drain the liquid and add the fruit to the cheese mixture.

Crust

Large batch Basic Tart Crust
  (page 252)

Blueberry Topping

2 tablespoons water

2 tablespoons granulated sugar

1 tablespoon cornstarch

1 teaspoon grated lemon zest

3 cups fresh blueberries

Filling

2½ cups Pastry Cream
  (page 256)

2¾ cups Chocolate Pastry Cream
  (page 256)

Blueberry Custard Tart

Makes one 11-inch tart

Blueberries are fragile, precious, and delicately flavored. Their special flavor is heightened when combined with a custard or cream cheese filling. In this tart, the berries are cooked only just enough to sweeten and meld the flavors. But if your berries are really fresh, I recommend avoiding the cooking altogether. Just place the berries atop the pastry cream and sprinkle with confectioners' sugar.

1. Preheat the oven to 375°F. Butter and flour an 11-inch tart pan.

2. Roll out the crust dough to form a circle about ⅛ inch thick and 14 inches in diameter. Drape the dough over the pan, allowing the excess to hang over the rim. Press the dough into the bottom edges, and cut off the excess with a knife. Prick the bottom with a fork. Top the crust with parchment paper and fill with pie weights. Blind-bake for 15–20 minutes, or until the crust is partially baked. Remove the paper and weights; cool on a rack.

3. To make the topping, combine the water, sugar, cornstarch, and lemon zest in a medium saucepan. Bring to a boil over medium heat, stirring until the sugar is dissolved and the mixture has thickened.

4. Reduce the heat to a simmer and add the blueberries. Toss gently and cook for 2 minutes, or until the berries soften slightly. Remove from heat when the first few berries begin to pop and let cool for 30 minutes.

5. Once the shell and blueberry topping have cooled, spread the chocolate pastry cream in a circle in the center of the pan, leaving about 3 inches all around. Fill the space around the chocolate cream with a ring of the plain pastry cream. The cream should come almost up to the top of the shell. Gently spoon on the blueberry topping.

Variations

MINI CHOCOLATE BLUEBERRY ALMOND CREAM CHEESE TARTS: Prepare the crust in eighteen 2-inch tart pans. Omit the pastry creams and add ¼ teaspoon almond extract to the Cream Cheese Filling (page 255). Spoon the filling into a pastry bag fitted with a large round tip and fill the crusts. Chill for 2–3 hours, or until set. Top with fresh blueberries and whole almonds.

BLUEBERRY GINGER TART WITH GINGERSNAP CRUST AND CREAM CHEESE FILLING: Prepare a small batch of Gingersnap Crust (page 248) in a 9-inch tart pan and bake as directed above. Omit the pastry creams and add ½ teaspoon ground ginger to the Cream Cheese Filling (page 255). Chill in shell for 2–3 hours, or until set. Top with Blueberry Topping (above).

Crust

Medium batch (six disks) Chocolate Butter Crust (page 242)

Crème Brûlée Filling

3 large eggs
3 large egg yolks
½ cup granulated sugar
⅛ teaspoon salt
2 teaspoons vanilla extract
2 cups heavy cream

Topping

⅓ cup turbinado sugar, finely ground
¼ cup melted dark chocolate (at least 60% cacao)

Crème Brûlée Tarts with Chocolate Dots

Makes six 4½-inch tarts

The vanilla-and-toasted-sugar flavor of crème brûlée is one of the best taste sensations ever. When the custard is baked into a chocolate piecrust, however, it tastes even better. These tarts are baked in shallow dishes. But if you plan to bake them in tart pans and take them out of the pans before serving, make the bottom and side crusts extra thick so that they will hold the delicate filling. Otherwise, it's best to serve them in their dishes.

1. Preheat the oven to 350°F. Butter and flour six 4½-inch ramekins or tart pans.

2. Press the crusts a little at a time into the tart pans, making a ¼-inch-thick bottom and ½-inch-thick sides. Top with parchment paper and pie weights and bake for 20–25 minutes, or until tender. Cool in pans on a rack.

3. To make the filling, combine the eggs, yolks, sugar, and salt in a medium mixing bowl. Beat with an electric mixer on medium speed until pale; set aside.

4. In a saucepan, heat the cream over medium heat for about 4–5 minutes, or until hot but not boiling. Gradually add the warm cream to the egg mixture, stirring constantly. Return to the saucepan and whisk over medium heat for 4–5 minutes, or until thick. Pour the custard mixture through a fine-mesh sieve, then pour into the tart shells. Cover with plastic wrap, making sure the plastic touches the surface of the custard, and refrigerate for 4 hours.

5. Set the oven rack 2–3 inches from the broiler. When ready to serve, preheat the broiler. Sprinkle the top of each tart with 1½–2 teaspoons turbinado sugar. Broil the tarts about 1 minute, or until the sugar caramelizes. Watch closely so that the tarts don't burn (or, for more control, use a kitchen torch to caramelize). Let the tarts cool for 10 minutes.

6. Pour the melted chocolate into a pastry bag fitted with a

large round tip. Pipe dots of chocolate on the top of each tart. Serve warm.

Variations

WHITE OR DARK CHOCOLATE CRÈME BRÛLÉE TARTS: Add 3 ounces white or dark chocolate pieces to the cream and stir until melted.

SOUR CHERRY CRÈME BRÛLÉE TARTS: Sprinkle 4–5 chopped fresh sour cherries onto each shell before adding the custard.

Rice Pudding Tarts
Makes twelve 3-inch tarts

Rice pudding topped with whipped cream and maraschino cherries is a must-have dessert in a retro cafeteria. This more flavorful rendition, set in a chocolate pastry crust, incorporates fragrant basmati rice spiced with bay and orange.

Crust
Large batch (twelve disks)
Chocolate Sweet Tart Crust
(page 254)

Filling
4 cups plus 2 tablespoons whole
milk
⅛ teaspoon salt
2 bay leaves
½ cup basmati rice
¼ cup golden raisins
1½ tablespoons cornstarch
2 tablespoons granulated sugar
1 teaspoon vanilla extract
1 teaspoon grated orange zest

Topping
1½ cups Whipped Cream
(page 261)
2 tablespoons Dutch-process
cocoa powder
12 maraschino cherries

1. Preheat the oven to 350°F. Butter and flour twelve 3-inch tart pans.

2. Press the crusts a little at a time into the tart pans. Top with parchment paper and pie weights and bake for 25–30 minutes. Cool in pans on a rack.

3. To make the filling, bring 4 cups milk, salt, and bay leaves to a boil in a medium saucepan. Add the rice and raisins and return to a boil. Reduce the heat to simmer and cook for 15–20 minutes, or until the rice is tender and the milk has thickened slightly.

4. Mix the cornstarch, sugar, and remaining 2 tablespoons milk into a paste. Add to the rice mixture and stir for 1–2 minutes, or until very thick. Remove from heat and add the vanilla and orange zest. Remove the bay leaves. Let cool to room temperature.

5. Fill the shells with cooled pudding. When ready to serve, top with whipped cream and sprinkle with cocoa powder. Top with a maraschino cherry. Serve at room temperature or chilled.

Variation

CHOCOLATE RICE PUDDING TARTS: Omit the orange zest and raisins. Add 6 ounces melted dark (at least 60% cacao) chocolate to the rice mixture along with the paste. Top the tarts with 3 tablespoons lightly toasted pine nuts and dark chocolate curls.

Lemon Filling

⅔ cup freshly squeezed Meyer
   lemon juice
10 large egg yolks, at room
   temperature
¾ cup granulated sugar
⅓ cup cold unsalted butter, cut
   into cubes
Grated zest of 1 lemon

Crust

*Large batch (eight disks) Almond
Sweet Tart Crust (page 254)*

Topping

*3 cups Meringue Topping
(page 260)*

Meyer Lemon Meringue Tarts

Makes eight 3½-inch tarts

Lemon meringue is amazing enough by itself, but lemon meringue made with the sweeter and less acidic Meyer lemon deserves an extra-special treatment. Here are two options. One is made with a sweet almond crust and the other has a meringue crust and a meringue topping. Make them both and have your guests pick their favorite.

1. To make the filling, whisk the lemon juice, egg yolks, and sugar in a double boiler set over simmering water for about 5 minutes, or until thick. Add the butter and lemon zest, stirring until the butter is melted and the mixture is smooth. Transfer to a bowl and cover with plastic wrap, making sure the plastic touches the surface of the filling. Chill for 1–2 hours.

2. Butter and flour eight 3½-inch tart pans. Press the dough into the pans with your fingers, starting at the bottom and moving up the sides, creating a border flush with the top rim. Line the shells with parchment paper and fill with pie weights. Refrigerate for 1 hour.

3. Preheat the oven to 350°F. Blind-bake the shells for 8–10 minutes, or until partially baked. Remove the parchment and pie weights and bake for additional 8–10 minutes, or until golden. Cool shells in pans on a rack.

4. Divide the filling evenly among the shells.

5. Spoon the meringue topping into a pastry bag fitted with a large star-shaped tip. Pipe the meringue onto the center of each tart.

6. To toast the meringue with a kitchen torch, remove the cooled pies from the pans. Then hold a kitchen torch around 4 inches from the meringue and rotate pies one at a time to toast. To toast in the oven, leave the pies in the pans. Place the oven rack about 4 inches from the heat source and preheat the broiler. Place the tarts on a baking sheet and broil for 2–3 minutes, watching carefully, until the meringue browns. Cool on a rack. Then remove from pans.

Variations

UPSIDE-DOWN LEMON MERINGUE TARTS: Make a batch of Meringue Crust (page 250) and spoon it into a pastry bag fitted with a large round tip. Line two baking sheets with parchment paper. Preheat the oven to 200°F. Pipe the meringue onto the parchment in 3½-inch circles, so that the sides form a "bowl" around a well in the center. Bake for 60 minutes, or until firm and dry. Turn off the oven, leaving the door slightly ajar, and let sit for 2 more hours or overnight. Make the filling as directed in step 1 above, then pick up the recipe at step 4. Top with lemon wedges.

LAVENDER LEMON MERINGUE TARTS: Omit the almonds from the crust. Add ½ teaspoon dried lavender to the crust. Top the tarts with fresh lavender.

BLACKBERRY LEMON MERINGUE TARTS WITH GINGERBREAD CRUST: Prepare the Gingerbread Crust (page 224). Fill with lemon filling. Top with meringue and fresh blackberries.

ICE CREAM PIES

From the casual to the fancy, ice cream pies are without a doubt the "coolest" and easiest to make. Classic crumb crusts made with graham crackers or chocolate wafer cookies are featured in this chapter, but you will also find crusts made with waffle cones, pretzels, and amaretti. Use homemade or store-bought ice cream, and with just a few steps and simple toppings these pies will quickly transform an ordinary scoop into an extraordinary pie.

Amaretti Crust

2¼ cups crushed amaretti

¼ cup unsalted butter, melted

¼ cup chopped pistachios

Spumoni Filling

1 pint pistachio ice cream

1 pint chocolate ice cream

1 pint cherry ice cream

Topping

½ cup fresh sweet cherries, stemmed and pitted

¼ cup shaved dark chocolate (at least 60% cacao)

¼ cup chopped pistachios

Spumoni Ice Cream Pie with Amaretti Crust

Makes one 10-inch single-crust pie

Spumoni isn't a flavor of ice cream; rather, it is an Italian dessert comprising a three-layer presentation of cherry, chocolate, and pistachio ice creams. (Neapolitan ice cream, the American version, is made with vanilla, chocolate, and strawberry ice creams.) In this pie, the stripes are revealed when it is sliced. Amaretti (Italian almond macaroons) are used to make this crust. The cookies are crunchy outside and chewy inside, and they offer an interesting flavor variation on the traditional graham cracker crust.

1. To make the crust, toss 2 cups of the cookie crumbs and the butter in a bowl until well coated. Stir in the pistachios. Using your hands, press the crumbs into the bottom and up the sides of a 10-inch pie pan. Refrigerate for 30 minutes.

2. Preheat the oven to 325°F. Bake the crust for 7–8 minutes. Cool on a rack.

3. Soften the ice creams to a spreadable consistency. Spread the pistachio ice cream into the crust, covering the entire bottom. Spread the chocolate ice cream over the pistachio to form the middle layer, then spread the cherry ice cream on top. Cover with plastic wrap and freeze for 3 hours.

4. When ready to serve, top with the remaining amaretti crumbs, cherries, shaved chocolate, and chopped pistachios.

NEAPOLITAN ICE CREAM PIE: Omit the pistachios from the crust. Fill the pie with vanilla, chocolate, and strawberry ice creams. Top with fresh strawberries and shaved chocolate.

Salted Caramel Ice Cream Pie

Makes one 10-inch single-crust pie

Vanilla ice cream, mixed with a streak of caramel and set in a pretzel crust, offers a surprisingly sweet, smooth, buttery, and somewhat salty taste. Prepare the ice cream from scratch or purchase store-bought ice cream and mix in the caramel.

Filling

Vanilla or Caramel Ice Cream (page 256), or 1.5 quarts store-bought vanilla, dulce de leche, or caramel ice cream

Caramel Topping

1 9.5-ounce bag caramels
⅓ cup whole milk

Crust

Large Pretzel Crust (page 235), baked and cooled

Garnish

2 tablespoons crushed pretzels
¼ cup whole pretzels

1. Soften the ice cream until it reaches a spreadable consistency.

2. Combine the caramels and milk in a small saucepan and heat over medium-low heat, stirring occasionally, until melted and smooth. Cool for 5 minutes. If using vanilla ice cream, use a spatula to swirl three-fourths of the caramel mixture into the ice cream.

3. Spread the ice cream into the crust, then spread the caramel (or the remaining caramel, if using vanilla ice cream) on top. Cover with plastic wrap and freeze for 3 hours. When ready to serve, top with crushed and whole pretzels.

Green Tea and Chocolate Ice Cream Pie with Gluten-Free Coconut Crust

Make one 10-inch single-crust pie

This homemade ice cream pie is flavored with powdered green tea, or matcha. The coconut crust has a macaroon flavor and texture, and also makes a tasty gluten-free alternative to traditional piecrusts. Both the chocolate and green tea ice creams are homemade in this recipe, so plan to use your ice cream maker twice, or use two ice cream makers. If you want to simplify things, use your favorite brand of store-bought chocolate ice cream and buy green tea ice cream in a Japanese market. If you go with store-bought ice creams, you'll need 1 quart of green tea and 1 pint of chocolate.

Green Tea Ice Cream

1¾ cups heavy cream

1¾ cups half-and-half

¾ cup granulated sugar

5 tablespoons matcha

Pinch salt

Coconut Crust

2½ cups fresh or packaged
  unsweetened shredded coconut

2 tablespoons granulated sugar

⅓ cup unsalted butter, melted

Filling

2 cups Chocolate Ice Cream
  (page 257)

Topping

2 tablespoons dark chocolate (at
  least 60% cacao) shavings

1. To make the green tea ice cream, combine the cream, half-and-half, sugar, matcha, and salt in a large saucepan and whisk them together until combined. Set over high heat and bring to a boil, then reduce the heat to medium and cook, stirring, until it starts to foam. Remove it from the heat, cool, then transfer to a bowl and refrigerate for 1 hour.

2. Freeze in the ice cream maker, according to manufacturer's instructions, until almost firm but still soft and malleable.

3. Preheat the oven to 300°F. Butter and flour a 10-inch pie pan.

4. To make the crust, mix the coconut and sugar in a medium bowl. Add the melted butter a little at a time until well blended.

5. Press the crust into the pan. Bake for 10–15 minutes, or until lightly toasted. Cool on a rack.

6. Spread the green tea ice cream onto the crust, smoothing the top with an offset spatula. Cover with plastic wrap and freeze for 1 hour.

7. Soften the chocolate ice cream to spreading consistency. Using a spoon, dig out a spiral from the green tea ice cream and reserve the removed ice cream for another use. Spoon the chocolate ice cream into the spiral cavity. Cover with plastic wrap and freeze for 3 hours.

8. Sprinkle with chocolate shavings when ready to serve.

Oatmeal Cookies-and-Cream Ice Cream Pie

Makes one 9-inch single-crust pie

Most of us think of chocolate wafer cookies when we think of cookies-and-cream ice cream. For something a little different, though, the sweet chewiness of oatmeal cookies and vanilla ice cream in this pie will do the trick.

1. To make the ice cream, combine the half-and-half and sugar in a medium bowl. Beat with an electric mixer on medium speed until the sugar dissolves. Stir in the cream, cinnamon, and vanilla.

2. Pour into an ice cream maker and freeze according to

Oatmeal Cookies-and-Cream Ice Cream

1½ cups half-and-half

¾ cup granulated sugar

3 cups heavy cream

½ teaspoon ground cinnamon

2 teaspoons vanilla extract

2 cups coarsely ground oatmeal cookies

½ cup raisins

Crust

Small batch (1 disk) Oatmeal Crust (page 250)

Topping

2 cups Whipped Cream (page 261)

manufacturer's instructions, until the ice cream is almost firm but still soft and malleable.

3. Preheat the oven to 375°F. Butter and flour a 9-inch pie pan. Roll out the crust on a floured work surface into a circle about ⅛ inch thick and 12 inches in diameter. Drape the dough over the pie pan, allowing the excess to hang over the rim. Press the dough into the bottom edges, and trim the excess to a ¼-inch overhang. Fold the overhang over the rim and decoratively crimp the edge. Prick the bottom with a fork. Top the crust with parchment paper and fill with pie weights. Blind-bake for 15–20 minutes, or until the crust is golden. Remove from the oven and cool on a rack.

4. Remove the ice cream from the freezer. Add 1½ cups of the oatmeal cookies and the raisins and churn for 5 minutes. Spread into the piecrust. Cover with plastic wrap and freeze for 2–3 hours, until set.

5. Top the pie with whipped cream and remaining oatmeal cookies to serve.

Variation

COOKIES-AND-CREAM ICE CREAM PIE: Replace the crust with a small batch of Chocolate Wafer Crust (page 243). Replace the oatmeal cookies with chocolate wafer cookies.

Banana Date Nut Ice Cream Pie

Makes one 9-inch single-crust pie

The flavors in this pie are inspired by my visits to Indio, California, in the desert east of Los Angeles. Many of the world's dates are grown there, and if you are a date lover, as I am, the vanilla-date milk shakes alone are worth the drive. There are many types of dates you can use for this recipe. I used Medjool, which are the softest and chewiest. If you don't have an ice cream maker, combine the ingredients in a bowl and cover with plastic wrap. Stir every hour for 3 hours, then pour into the pie shell. Freeze overnight.

DATE VARIETIES

ABADA (A.K.A. BLACK DATE): Almost black in color, with a sweet taste and creamy texture

AMARI: Reddish-brown color, similar to the prized Medjool but available year-round

BARHI: Yellow in color, with a rounded oval shape and a vanilla flavor

DEGLET NOOR: Chewy and slightly dry

HALAWI: The most popular date—if a store only has one type, it is probably this; very sweet and well priced

KHADRAWI: Moist and soft

MEDJOOL: Called the King of Dates; medium-brown, large, juicy, and chewy

ZAHIDI: Round and light brown, with a firm skin and soft sweet center; less sweet than other dates; best used for baking

Banana Date Nut Ice Cream

1½ cups heavy cream

½ cup whole milk

⅔ cup granulated sugar

¼ teaspoon salt

1 teaspoon vanilla extract

¾ cup thinly sliced ripe bananas

1 teaspoon freshly squeezed lemon
   juice

¼ cup chopped pitted Medjool
   dates

¼ cup chopped walnuts

¼ cup desiccated coconut

Crust

Small batch Coconut Graham
   Cracker Cookie Crust (page
   249), baked and cooled

Topping

8 whole Medjool dates, pitted

½ cup banana slices

1 teaspoon freshly squeezed lemon
   juice

3 tablespoons walnut halves

2 tablespoons desiccated coconut

To make this pie using store-bought ice cream, first soften about 1 quart of high-quality vanilla ice cream by stirring it with a rotary beater in a large bowl. Fold in the bananas, lemon juice, dates, walnuts, and coconut, then spread into the frozen pie shell and cover with plastic.

1. To make the ice cream, beat the cream, milk, sugar, salt, and vanilla in a large mixing bowl until thick but not fully whipped. Toss the bananas with the lemon juice. Fold bananas, dates, walnuts, and coconut into the cream mixture. Refrigerate for 30 minutes.

2. Transfer to an ice cream maker and freeze according to manufacturer's instructions, until the ice cream is almost firm but still soft and malleable.

3. Spread the ice cream into the crust with a spatula, mounding it in the center. Cover with plastic wrap and freeze for at least 3 hours, or overnight.

4. When ready to serve, remove the pie from the freezer and top with whole pitted dates, banana slices tossed with lemon juice, and walnut halves. Sprinkle with desiccated coconut. Let soften for 5 minutes before serving, or refreeze until ready to serve.

Variation

FIG MINT ICE CREAM PIE: Prepare a small batch of Gingersnap Crust (page 248). Omit the bananas, walnuts, and coconut from the filling and topping. Substitute dried figs for the dates. Add 2 teaspoons chopped fresh mint to the ice cream, or use 1 quart store-bought mint-flavored ice cream.

4 large egg yolks

1⅓ cups confectioners' sugar

1½ teaspoons cornstarch

1 teaspoon vanilla extract

2 cups full-fat vanilla soy milk

1 cup plain soy yogurt

3 cups peeled and cubed fresh peaches (about 4 large)

Small batch Graham Cracker Cookie Crust (page 248), baked and cooled

Peach and Soy Ice Cream Pie

Makes one 9-inch single-crust pie

Dairy-free homemade peach soy ice cream is a lighter, protein-rich alternative to traditional ice cream.

1. To make the ice cream, combine the egg yolks, sugar, and cornstarch in a large mixing bowl. Beat with an electric mixer on medium speed until smooth. Add the vanilla.

2. Heat the soy milk in a saucepan over medium heat and add the egg mixture. Gently stir until the mixture thickens, about 7–10 minutes. Let the mixture cool to room temperature. Transfer to a bowl, cover with plastic wrap, and chill in the refrigerator for 1–2 hours.

3. Fold the yogurt and two-thirds of the peaches into the mixture. Transfer to an ice cream maker and freeze according to the manufacturer's instructions until almost firm but still soft and malleable.

4. Fill the cooled crust with ice cream, spreading to smooth. Cover with plastic wrap and freeze for 3 hours. When ready to serve, top with the remaining peaches.

Variation

CHOCOLATE CHIP ICE CREAM PIE: Replace the graham cracker crust with a small batch of Chocolate Wafer Crust (page 243). To make chocolate chip ice cream, replace the vanilla soy milk with plain soy milk and omit the peaches. Melt ½ cup semisweet chocolate chips with the soy milk in step 2. When the ice cream is partially set, but before it is added to the crust, stir in 1 cup chocolate chips.

Chapter 3

Special-Occasion Pies

BIRTHDAY PIES

Birthdays aren't just for cakes anymore; in fact, birthday pies are gaining ground. What better time than a special someone's birthday to show off your pie-making talents? This section includes pies for all ages—because we all have birthdays. The "can't stop at just one" Pie Pops and the Happy Pop-in-the-Oven Tarts are for the young or young at heart. The single-crust Cheesecake Pie is a dreamy, girlish pie. Or bake pies in jars for unique gifts.

If you're looking for an additional challenge, the Happy Birthday Nectarine Pie is the ultimate decorator's delight. It does a fine job of replacing cake as the party centerpiece and holds plenty of candles for the birthday boy or girl to blow out.

Pie Pops

Makes 24–30 1¾–2-inch pie pops

Everything tastes great on a stick—especially pie. These tiny sweet-savory party bites can be made out of some of the most flavorful crusts in this book. When assembling, place the top of the stick above the center point to keep the pie secure. Thread a fresh fruit on the stick to advertise the filling inside. Make one kind of dough or mix several different flavors. Serve these pops on their own, or with the Honey Syrup (page 183) as a dip.

1½ cups cherry, kumquat, or other fruit-flavored jam

Large batch (2 disks) Cornmeal Crust made with blue cornmeal (page 244), Cheddar Crust (page 130), or Nut Butter Crust made with almonds (page 243)

2 eggs, beaten

30 wooden coffee stirrers, lollipop sticks, or popsicle sticks

1. Preheat the oven to 350°F. Line two baking sheets with parchment paper.

2. Roll out each of the two pastry disks to a 10–12-inch square that is about ⅛ inch thick on a floured work surface. From one disk, cut out between twenty-four and thirty 1¾–2-inch squares and/or circles with cookie cutters. Cut an equal number of squares and/or circles from the second disk. Brush the edges with some of the beaten eggs.

3. Lay a wooden stick on each of half the cut-out shapes, pressing it into the dough so that the top falls slightly above the center. Spoon a teaspoon of jam into the center of each shape. Place the remaining shapes on top and press the edges to seal. With a sharp knife or bamboo skewer, draw patterns into the crusts, poking holes and making slits for venting. Place the pops on the baking sheets. Brush the remaining egg mixture over the tops. Cover sticks loosely with parchment to prevent burning. Bake for 12–15 minutes, or until golden. Cool on a rack in the pans.

Happy Pop-in-the-Oven Tarts
Makes 8 hand pies

Happy as can be, these pop-in-the-oven characters will bring cheer to birthday celebrations for the young at heart and fans of the classic toaster pastry. Using two crusts allows for flavor and color contrast. You'll need a full batch of both doughs to make eight tarts.

1. Line two baking sheets with parchment paper.

2. Divide each pastry disk in half. Roll out each half into a circle about ¼ inch thick and 14 inches in diameter. Using cookie cutters, a pastry wheel, or a knife, cut out a bottom crust and a top crust for each face—sixteen rectangles and/or circles in all. Place the bottom crusts—eight of the sixteen shapes—on the baking sheets.

3. Spread 2½–3 tablespoons of jam into the center of each

Extra-large batch (one disk)
   Basic Butter Crust (page 242)
Extra-large batch (one disk)
   Chocolate Butter Crust
   (page 242)
1½ cups strawberry jam
2 large eggs, beaten

bottom crust, leaving a ½-inch border (if a top piece is smaller than the bottom piece, spread the jam so it's ½ inch in from the edge of the top piece).

4. Cut vents in the top pieces. These could be holes for noses, eyelashes, freckles, eyes, or other facial features. Brush some of the beaten eggs on the backs of the top pieces and set them over the jam, pressing the edges of the top and bottom crusts together to seal.

5. Cut out the eyes, mouths, and other decorative details from leftover scraps of dough. Brush beaten eggs on the backs of these pieces and attach to the top pieces. Bake for 15–20 minutes, or until golden. Cool on a rack.

TO MAKE THE HAPPY RECTANGLE FACE: Cut out one 4-inch rectangle and one 3-inch rectangle. Pierce vents to make freckles. Cut out two 1-inch circles and two 2½-inch circles to make the eyes, and cut out a ½-inch semicircle for the mouth.

TO MAKE THE SQUARE GIRL: Cut out two 3-inch squares. Pierce vents to make the nose and eyelashes. Cut out two ½-inch circles and two ¼-inch circles to make the eyes and a ¾-inch semicircle for the mouth. Roll the dough into a log that's 5 inches long and ¼ inch thick and tie it into a bow.

TO MAKE THE ROUND GIRL: Cut out two 3 ½-inch circles. Pierce vents to make the nose and eyelashes. Cut out two ¾-inch circles and two ½-inch circles to make the eyes and a 1-inch semicircle for the mouth. Roll the dough into a log that's 4 inches long and ¼ inch thick and tie it into a bow.

TO MAKE THE MUSTACHE MAN: Cut out a 3½-inch rectangle and a 3-inch rectangle. Pierce vents in the smaller rectangle to make freckles. Cut out two 1½-inch circles and two ½-inch circles to make the eyes. Cut out two ½-inch semicircles for the eyebrow and a 2½-inch mustache.

Brownie Cream Cheese Pie

Makes one 9-inch single-crust pie

If you are a lover of gooey chocolate brownies, you will love the flavor and texture of this classic filling. Serve while the filling is still a bit warm.

1. Preheat the oven to 450°F. Butter and flour a 9-inch pie pan.

Small batch (one disk) Chocolate Cream Cheese Crust (page 245)

1 cup plus 3 tablespoons granulated sugar

½ cup (1 stick) unsalted butter, at room temperature

2 large eggs

2 tablespoons whole milk

⅓ cup all-purpose flour

1 teaspoon vanilla extract

3 ounces unsweetened chocolate, melted

¼ cup semisweet chocolate chips

¼ cup chopped walnuts

4 ounces cream cheese, at room temperature

2. Roll out the pastry disk on a floured work surface into a circle about ⅛ inch thick and 13 inches in diameter. Drape the dough over the pie pan, allowing the excess to hang over the rim. Press the dough into the bottom edges, and trim the excess to a ¼-inch overhang. Fold the overhang over the rim and decoratively crimp the edge. Prick the bottom with a fork. Top the crust with parchment paper and fill with pie weights. Blind-bake for 10 minutes. Remove from oven and cool on a rack. Reduce the heat to 375°F.

3. Combine 1 cup sugar, the butter, and the eggs in a large mixing bowl. Beat with an electric mixer on medium speed until fluffy. Beat in the milk, flour, vanilla, and chocolate until blended. Fold in half the chocolate chips and walnuts. Pour the mixture into the crust.

4. Combine the cream cheese with the remaining sugar in a medium mixing bowl. Beat with an electric mixer on medium speed until blended. One heaping teaspoon at a time, drop the cream cheese mixture over the filling, dispersing it evenly around the pie.

5. Bake for 10 minutes, then top with the remaining chocolate chips and walnuts, distributing them evenly over the pie and pressing them in with the back of a spoon. Bake for an additional 20–25 minutes, or until the center is puffy and a knife inserted in the center comes out clean. Cool slightly on a rack and serve warm.

Variations

MINI BROWNIE SUNDAE PIES: Prepare in six 3-inch pans. Omit the cream cheese. Top with Vanilla Ice Cream (page 256), Hot Fudge (page 259), walnuts, and maraschino cherries.

MARSHMALLOW BROWNIE PIE: Add 1½ cups miniature marshmallows to the brownie batter. Before serving, top with Marshmallow Meringue (page 259).

RASPBERRY BROWNIE PIE: Replace the cream cheese with ½ cup raspberry jam, dropping 1 tablespoon at a time over the batter. Top with fresh raspberries.

Filling

12 medium firm but ripe nectarines
  (about 4 pounds), pitted and
  sliced into wedges
2 teaspoons freshly squeezed lemon
  juice
1 cup granulated sugar
3 tablespoons cornstarch
2 tablespoons unsalted butter

Crust

Extra-large batch (three disks, one
  slightly larger than the other
  two) Basic Butter Crust
  (page 242)
2 large eggs, beaten with 3
  tablespoons heavy cream

Raspberry Sauce

½ cup water
½ cup granulated sugar
1 tablespoon freshly squeezed
  lemon juice
2 tablespoons cornstarch
2 cups fresh raspberries (about ½
  pound), puréed

Happy Birthday Nectarine Pie with Raspberry Sauce

Makes one 14-inch double-crust pie

For those who prefer pie to cake on their special day, this extra-large pie—made for serving to a large crowd—is a special birthday indulgence. It uses decorating techniques borrowed from cake baking and features a top embossed with a rubber stamp. The flowers, leaves, and birthday greeting are attached as an appliqué. To retain the detail, chill the pie in the freezer before baking. The accompanying raspberry sauce adds a formal touch and perfectly complements the flavor of the nectarines.

1. To make the filling, combine the nectarines and lemon juice in a large heavy saucepan. Stir in the sugar and bring to a boil over medium heat. Reduce the heat to a simmer and cook, carefully stirring occasionally, for 5 minutes to release some of the juices.

2. In a small bowl, combine the cornstarch and ¼ cup of the released juice and stir until dissolved. If you did not produce ¼ cup juice, add ¼ cup warm water to the cornstarch and stir to dissolve. Discard any remaining juices over ¼ cup. Add butter to the juice-and-cornstarch mixture, then stir into the nectarines. Continue to cook, stirring constantly, over medium heat for 5 minutes, or until the syrup has thickened. Remove from heat and let cool.

3. Roll out the large pastry disk on a floured work surface into a circle about ⅛ inch thick and 18 inches in diameter. Drape over the pie pan, allowing excess to hang over the rim. Brush the edge of the crust with some of the egg mixture. Prick the crust with a fork. Spoon the filling into the crust.

4. Roll out a second disk into a circle about ⅛ inch thick and 13 inches in diameter. Using a large rubber stamp, emboss a pattern into the surface. Lay the top crust over the filling. Trim the crusts flush around the rim of the pan. Press the edge of the top crust into the bottom crust and crimp decoratively.

5. Roll out the final disk into a rectangle about 12 inches long, 8 inches wide, and ⅛ inch thick. Using a cookie cutter, cut out about 48 1½ x 1-inch leaves. Using a knife or bamboo skewer, draw veins in the leaves. Cut out 5 flowers, ranging in size from 1 inch to 3½ inches in diameter. Using letter-shaped cookie cutters, or working freehand with a knife, cut out the phrase "Happy Birthday." Brush the back of the cutouts with some more of the egg mixture and press into the top crust. Prick vents in the top with a fork. Cover with plastic wrap and freeze for 1 hour.

6. Preheat the oven to 450°F. Remove the pie from the freezer and brush the top with the remaining egg mixture. Bake for 15 minutes. Reduce the temperature to 375°F and bake for an additional 30–40 minutes, or until the crust is golden and the juices are shiny and bubbly. Cool for 30–40 minutes on a rack until warm.

7. To make the raspberry sauce, combine the water, sugar, and lemon juice in a medium saucepan and stir over medium heat to dissolve. Add the cornstarch and mix to thicken. Stir in the raspberries and cook over low heat for 3–5 minutes, until the mixture forms a thick sauce. Serve on the plate, alongside the slices of pie.

Pie in a Jar

Makes eight ½-cup pies

If you're the experimenting type, you'll enjoy making these playful, crafty kitchen treats. The technique used here works with most fruit pie recipes when the filling and crust are baked together. Add a ribbon and a pretty cloth covering and you have an instant gift. This recipe makes eight pies that are the same size as the cute small half-cup jar shown in the foreground of the photo. For larger pies, the technique is the same, but the baking time will be a little longer.

If you want to make your pies in larger jars, you'll also need more filling for each jar. Shown in the photo are (clockwise from bottom): a single-crust pecan pie (½–⅔ cup filling), a double-crust Concord

Large batch (2 disks, one slightly larger than the other) Basic Butter Crust (page 242)

Large batch (2 disks, one slightly larger than the other) Basic Butter Crust (page 242)

4½–5 cups pie filling (choose from pecan [page 214], blueberry [page 202], raisin [page 65], cherry [page 46], and/or Concord grape [page 191])

2 tablespoons cold unsalted butter, cut into 8 cubes

2 large eggs, beaten with 2 tablespoons whole milk (for double-crust pies only)

grape pie (¾ cup filling), a double-crust cherry pie (1¾ cups filling), a lattice-top blueberry pie (1¼ cups filling), and a double-crust raisin pie (¾ cup filling).

1. Butter eight 4-ounce mason jars.

2. Roll out the larger disk of dough on a floured work surface into a 12 x 12-inch square that is about ⅛ inch thick. Using the ring top of a jar as a template, cut out sixteen circles about ½ inch larger than the ring. Press eight circles into the jars, fitting them part of the way up the sides. Reserve the remaining circles for the top crusts, if desired.

3. Roll out the second disk into a rectangle about 12 inches long, 8 inches wide, and ⅛ inch thick. Using a pastry wheel or knife, cut the dough into four 3 x 8-inch strips. Fit one strip into each jar, pressing onto the bottom crusts to seal and covering the sides with a little overlap on the top of the jar.

4. Spoon about ½–⅔ cup filling into each jar, pressing the mixture down to eliminate air pockets. Top each jar with a cube of butter.

5. If desired, make the top crust of your choice (see page 242) and place it on top of the filling. Brush with the egg mixture.

6. Prepare a water bath (see page 34). Set the water bath in the oven and preheat to 375°F. Place the jars in the preheated water bath and bake for 20–25 minutes, or until crusts are golden and juices are bubbling.

TO MAKE THE LATTICE-TOP PIE: Cut the second batch of eight dough circles into ¼-inch strips. Lay half of the strips over the filling, leaving space in between. Lay the other half crosswise over the first layer, or weave the strips over and under each other in a basketweave pattern. Press the ends of the strips into the rim of the jar. Fold over the overhang and press together with a fork. Brush lattice and rim with egg wash.

TO MAKE THE SINGLE-CRUST PIE: Fold the excess dough over the rim and crimp decoratively.

TIPS FOR BAKING PIES IN JARS

1. First, decide on the type of jar to use. I recommend mason jars, which are used for canning. For extra safety, bring the pies up to temperature in the oven slowly and bake them in a water bath to evenly dissipate the heat. This does affect the crust a bit—it won't brown as much as it would if the pies were baked on a baking sheet (which also helps dissipate the heat). Avoid tall jars the first time you make these. Work your way up to them once you have made them a few times and understand the process.

2. Depending on the shape of the jar and the kind of filling you use, you can take the pies out of the jars after they are baked or serve them in the jars. Jars with angled sides are the easiest to use. If you use square or irregularly shaped jars, you may want to press the dough into the jar rather than roll it out in strips. Just make sure that the crust is of even thickness.

3. Decide if you want to offer the pie with the jar's original lid on, or whether you want to cover the pie with cloth. This will determine your pie's topping. If you use a lid, you must keep the crusts under the top rim. After the pies are baked, you can place the metal lids back on and seal them. If you use a cloth top, you can build the crust up over the rim of the jar, drape the cloth over the pie, and then wrap a ribbon around the cloth on the jar to seal. If you plan on freezing the unbaked or baked pies, you will need to put the lid on. Never bake the pie with the lid on.

4. Decide on the topping for your pie. Crumb toppings and single-crust pies are easier to make than double-crust and lattice-top pies.

5. Pies can be frozen before they are baked or after. To bake frozen pies, increase the baking time by 10 to 15 minutes.

Crust

Medium batch Graham Cracker Cookie Crust (page 248), prepared through step 1

Lemon Mascarpone Cream Filling

3 tablespoons granulated sugar

¼ cup freshly squeezed lemon juice

1¼ cups heavy cream

1 cup mascarpone cheese

¼ teaspoon grated lemon zest

Topping

3 tablespoons graham cracker crumbs

2 tablespoons Cinnamon Sugar (page 258)

TO MAKE THE DOUBLE-CRUST PIE: Cut vents in the top crusts with cookie cutters or a knife. Place the top crusts over the filling. Press the edges firmly together to seal, then crimp decoratively. Brush egg wash evenly over the top crusts.

TO MAKE A PIE WITH CRUMBLE TOPPING (PAGE 258): Prepare as a single-crust pie. Leave about ¾ inch between the top of the filling and the top of the jar. Distribute the crumb topping evenly over the filling.

Mascarpone Cream Petits Fours Pies

Makes twelve 1¾-inch single-crust pies

These delicate, tiny petits fours pies are filled with a great creamy Italian cheese—mascarpone. If you can't find it, use cream cheese instead. Use paper liners set in mini muffin pans, which help hold the crust together. Serve the pies inside the liners or gently peel away to serve. Make an assortment of flavors and decorate with fondant flowers (page 111).

1. Preheat the oven to 325°F. Line a 12-compartment mini muffin pan with paper liners.

2. Press about 2 tablespoons crust into the bottom and sides of each liner.

3. Bake for 5–6 minutes. Cool in pan on a rack.

4. To make the filling, beat the sugar, lemon juice, cream, mascarpone, and lemon zest in a large mixing bowl with an electric mixer on medium speed until stiff. Spoon the filling into a pastry bag fitted with a large round tip and pipe some into each crust. Use a small offset metal spatula to smooth the tops flush with the tops of the crust.

5. Sprinkle some of the tops with the graham cracker crumbs and others with cinnamon sugar. Leave some plain. Set in a baking dish taller than the tops of the pies, cover with plastic wrap (being careful not to touch the tops), and chill for 1 hour.

6. Remove the pies from the muffin tin and decorate as desired before serving.

Variations

CHERRY MASCARPONE CREAM PETITS FOURS PIES: Replace the lemon juice with 2 tablespoons cherry jam.

ORANGE MASCARPONE CREAM PETITS FOURS PIES: Replace the lemon juice and zest with orange juice and zest. Add 2 drops of orange food coloring.

VANILLA MASCARPONE CREAM PETITS FOURS PIES: Replace the lemon juice with 2 teaspoons vanilla extract.

FONDANT FLOWERS

Makes enough for 12 flowers
½ cup Fondant (page 258)
Pink, orange, purple, and green food coloring
Confectioners' sugar for rolling
3 tablespoons confectioners' sugar mixed
*   with 1 teaspoon water*
Small round candies for garnish

TO MAKE THE PINK CHERRY BLOSSOMS: Color the fondant with pink food coloring. Roll out the fondant to ¹⁄₁₆ inch on a work surface covered with confectioners' sugar and cut out ¾-inch flowers with a flower-shaped cookie cutter or freehand with a knife. Curl up the edges of the petals and attach a small round candy to the center with the confectioners' sugar mixture. Dry on a curved surface (such as the inside of an egg carton) and let harden for 2–3 hours.

TO MAKE THE DAISIES: Color half the fondant with orange food coloring and half with purple food coloring. Roll out the fondant to ¹⁄₁₆ inch on a work surface covered with confectioners' sugar. Cut out ¾-inch orange flowers with a flower-shaped cookie cutter or freehand with a knife. Cut out a slightly smaller purple circle to place in back of the daisy. Cut out a very small purple circle to place in the center. Attach the circles with the confectioners' sugar mixture.

TO MAKE THE WHITE LOTUS FLOWER: Color one-third of the fondant with purple food coloring and one-third with pink food coloring. Leave one-third of the fondant white. Roll out the fondant to ¹⁄₁₆ inch on a work surface covered with confectioners' sugar. Cut out ¾-inch white flowers in the cherry blossom shape. Cut out ¾-inch purple flowers in the daisy shape. Cut out a slightly larger pink circle. Attach the daisy to the circle with the confectioners' sugar mixture and curve inward. Attach the white cherry blossom in the center with the confectioners' sugar mixture. Dry on a curved surface (such as the inside of an egg carton) and let harden for 2–3 hours.

TO MAKE THE ROSES: Color two-thirds of the fondant with orange food coloring and one-third with green food coloring. Form a ¼-inch ball of the orange fondant into a cone shape—you will use this core to support the rose petals. Roll the remaining orange fondant into tiny balls, one for each petal of the rose. Flatten the balls into petal shapes, about ¹⁄₈ inch thick. The petals should be slightly thicker at one end. Starting at the wide end of the cone, wrap a petal around the cone, with the thicker end on the bottom, and press it in. Use your fingers to curl the ends of the petal outward. Overlap a second petal onto the first petal. Repeat with 3–4 additional petals. Then roll out the green fondant to ¹⁄₁₆ inch. Use a leaf-shaped cookie cutter or a knife to cut out leaf shapes around 1¼ inches long, then use a toothpick to draw veins on the leaves. Dry leaves on a curved surface (such as the inside of an egg carton) and let harden for 2–3 hours.

Cheesecake Pie with Marzipan Butterflies

Makes one 9-inch single-crust pie

If you like cheesecake but can never get enough of that graham cracker crust, this pie is for you. And pie lovers take note: even though it's often classified as a cake, we all know that, technically, cheesecake is in fact a custard pie. Traditionally served with fresh strawberries or blueberries, cheesecake can be topped with just about anything— that's one of its virtues. Here, the tasty and decorative addition of marzipan butterflies makes this feminine pie appropriate for birthdays, Mother's Day, Quinceañeras, or bridal and baby showers.

Marzipan Butterflies

⅓ cup Marzipan (page 259)
Pink and green food coloring
Confectioners' sugar for rolling

Cheesecake Filling

12 ounces cream cheese, at room
   temperature
¼ cup plus 3 tablespoons granulated sugar
2 large eggs
¼ cup heavy cream
1 teaspoon vanilla extract
½ teaspoon grated lemon zest
Pinch salt

Crust

Small batch Graham Cracker
   Cookie Crust (page 248), baked
   and cooled

Topping

2 cups Whipped Cream
   (page 261)

1. To make the marzipan butterflies, divide the marzipan into two batches, one slightly larger than the other. Color the large batch pink and the small batch green. Roll out to ⅛ inch on a work surface covered with confectioners' sugar. Using butterfly-shaped cookie cutters, or working freehand with a knife, cut out 1- and 2-inch butterflies. Fold each butterfly inward on its center seam and let dry on a curved surface (such as the inside of an egg carton) overnight.

2. Prepare a water bath (see page 34). Set the water bath in the oven and preheat to 350°F.

3. Combine the cream cheese and sugar in a large mixing bowl. Beat with an electric mixer on medium speed until fluffy. Add the eggs, one at a time, beating well after each addition. Beat in the heavy cream, vanilla, lemon zest, and salt until smooth. Pour the batter into the crust.

4. Set the pan into the water bath and bake for 35–40 minutes, or until firm and a knife inserted in the center comes out clean. Remove water bath and pie from the oven and cool in pan on a rack for 1 hour, then cover and chill until ready to serve.

5. Spoon the whipped cream into a pastry bag fitted with a large star-shaped tip. Pipe rosettes of cream around the border of the pie. Top with marzipan butterflies.

WEDDING PIES

Pies are hot—actually they are cool, too. They are the latest wedding-dessert trend, and couples looking to do something a bit different are replacing multitiered wedding cakes with spreads of dozens of full-size pies. Miniature pies are also a good wedding choice—they are one of my favorite ways to serve a large crowd. If you pick an easy-to-make crust (such as a single-crust tart or a double-crust pie with a pretty border), they are easy to make in large quantities. If you can't give up serving a traditional wedding cake, mini pies make excellent take-home-and-enjoy-later wedding favors.

Wedding Pies

Makes twelve 3½-inch double-crust pies and one 12-inch double-crust pie

If you're getting married and want to skip the traditional wedding cake (I can't believe I just said that), make some pies instead. But don't skip the crafty fun of decorating. Embellish at least one large pie—such as this cherry pie, topped with braided hearts and flowers—as the table's centerpiece. Include an edible wedding topper, too, such as this marzipan bride and groom.

1. Preheat the oven to 425°F. Butter and flour twelve 3½-inch pie pans. Roll out one of the larger disks of dough on a floured work surface into a 16 x 16-inch square that is about ⅛ inch thick. Cut the square into twelve 4-inch circles. Fit the circles into the pans by pressing the dough against the bottom and up the sides, allowing the crusts to drape slightly over the rims. Brush some of the egg mixture on the top edge of the crusts. Prick holes in the bottoms and fill with filling. Top each pie with a butter cube.

2. Roll out a second larger disk of dough on a floured work surface into a 14 x 14-inch square that is about ⅛ inch thick. Cut the square into twelve 3½-inch circles. Using a rubber stamp, emboss patterns in each circle. Prick each circle with the tines of a fork to vent. Press the edges of these circles onto the top edge of the bottom crusts to seal. Trim excess

---

Sidebar:

2 extra-large batches (three disks each, one slightly smaller than the other two) Basic Butter Crust (page 242)

17–20 cups pie filling, 8 cups for the large pie and 9–12 cups (¾–1 cup each) for the mini pies (see sidebar, page 117)

3 large eggs, beaten with 6 table-spoons whole milk

4 tablespoons cold unsalted butter, each cut into 4 cubes

¼ cup granulated sugar

- Set up a dessert table with several different pies made from his and her families' treasured recipes. Top them with paper flags that identify the fillings and let guests choose their favorite.

- Create a blended pie recipe—if she likes blueberry pie and he likes peach pie, make blueberry peach pies.

- Go the symbolic color route and choose a red filling to symbolize love—strawberry for a spring wedding, cherry for a summer wedding, cranberry for a fall wedding, or pomegranate for a winter wedding. Or choose fillings that match the wedding colors.

- If you still aren't sure what kind of pie to make, see my list of suggestions (page 117). Although flavor is an important consideration, so is the time it will take to make the pies. When making one hundred or more individual pies, it will take substantially less time to make single-crust pies than double-crust pies. Avoid toasting meringue (it takes a watchful eye) and choose simple cream toppings. The fruits you choose for fillings also matter. Blueberries, which only need to be washed, are quicker than peaches, which can be baked with the skins on—and they're both quicker than apples, which are time-consuming to peel.

crust flush with the rims of the pans. Brush the top crusts with more of the egg mixture.

3. Roll out one of the smaller disks on a floured work surface into a 12 x 12-inch square that is about ⅛ inch thick. Using a pastry wheel or a knife, cut the square into twenty-four strips, each 12 inches long and ½ inch wide. Braid two strips together and press them around the circumference of each pie. Brush the braids with some of the egg mixture and then sprinkle with sugar.

4. Bake for 15 minutes. Reduce the heat to 350°F and bake for an additional 20–25 minutes, or until the crust is golden brown and the juices are bubbling. Cool on a rack.

5. To make the large pie, preheat the oven to 425°F. Butter and flour a 12-inch pie pan. Roll out one of the larger disks of dough on a floured work surface into a circle about ⅛ inch thick and 14 inches in diameter. Drape the dough over the pie pan, allowing the excess to hang over the rim. Press the dough into the bottom edges, and trim the excess to a ¼-inch overhang. Brush egg mixture on the top edge of the crust. Prick holes in the bottom and fill with filling. Top with the remaining butter cubes.

6. Roll out the remaining larger disk on a floured work surface into a circle about ⅛ inch thick and 13 inches in diameter. Punch vents in the top of the pie with the tines of a fork. Place the top crust over the filling, pressing the edge into the bottom crust. Crimp decoratively. Brush top with egg mixture.

7. Divide the remaining smaller disk in half. Roll out one piece on a floured work surface to about 7 inches square. Using cookie cutters, cut out three sets of 1¼-inch flowers and ¾-inch leaves. Break the remaining piece of dough in half and roll out both pieces into two logs, each about 18 inches long. Braid the two logs together and place them on the center of the pie, creating a heart shape. Pinch the edges together in the middle to complete the heart. Place the

FILLING SUGGESTIONS FOR WEDDING PIES

Here are some suggestions for wedding-pie fillings, listed in order from easiest to most time-consuming:

Single-Crust Pies	Recipe page number	Double-Crust Pies	Recipe page number	Double-Crust Pies	Recipe page number
Pecan	214	Blueberry	220	Pomegranate	63
Pumpkin	212	Blackberry	53	Concord grape	191
Coconut custard	80	Raspberry	53	Cherry	46
Key lime	196	Peach	49	Apple	138
Chocolate pastry cream	256	Apricot	59	Mango	52
Banana	70	Strawberry	45	Mincemeat	234
		Pineapple	164	Blackberry apple	121
		Rhubarb	56	Raspberry apple	123
		Plum	60	Apple cranberry	221

MARZIPAN BRIDE AND GROOM WEDDING TOPPER

Instead of using the colors called for in this recipe, you could use food coloring that matches the hair and skin colors of the bride and groom.

    ½ cup Marzipan (page 259)

    Black, white, red, and brown food coloring

Divide the marzipan into two batches, one slightly larger than the other. Roll the smaller batch into two 1-inch balls to create the heads. Roll the remaining marzipan into a log about 1¼ inches in diameter and 5 inches long. Cut the log in half to make two bodies. Taper one end of each log by pressing down on one side as you roll. If desired, shape the logs according to the height of the bride and groom. Attach the head to the body by pressing the two pieces together, or use toothpicks—but make sure whoever will be eating the topper knows they are there. Let the marzipan sit overnight to dry. Once dry, paint the wedding dress and man's shirt with white food coloring. Paint hair on the heads. Let dry. Paint the tuxedo and the tie on the shirt and the flowers on the wedding dress.

BRIDE PIES

Bride pies, or wedding pies, were common at affluent wedding ceremonies up until the middle of the seventeenth century, well before cake took off as the mainstay of a proper wedding. Bride pies were usually filled with sweetbreads, lamb, or dried fruit. A glass ring was baked inside the pie, and the girl who found the ring in her slice was supposedly the next to be married. If you want to make a bride pie, try using the lamb filling in the Shepherd's Pie (page 149) or the filling from the Mincemeat Pie (page 234)—they're closest to the traditional fillings.

flowers on the top and on the sides around the heart. Brush with egg mixture.

8. Bake for 15 minutes. Reduce the heat to 350°F and bake for an additional 30–40 minutes, or until the crust is golden brown and the juices are bubbling. Cool on a rack.

*Extra-large batch (one disk)
Sweet Tart Crust (page 253)
3–4 cups Pastry Cream (page
256), Cream Cheese Filling
(page 255), Chocolate Ganache
(page 258), or Lemon Curd
(page 255)
4 cups assorted fresh fruit (see
below for suggestions)
¼ cup edible flowers*

TOPPINGS FOR MINI TARTS

FRESH FRUITS

Blackberries

Blueberries

Champagne grapes

Currants

Golden and red raspberries

Gooseberries

Kumquats

Sliced figs

Sliced grapes

Sliced kiwifruit

Small strawberries

EDIBLE FRESH FLOWERS

Chamomile

Dandelions

Lavender

Marigolds

Pansies

Roses

Fruit Tarts with Sweet Tart Shells

Makes twelve 3-inch tarts or twenty-four 2½-inch tarts

The appeal of these tarts is in the variety of flavors you can achieve by mixing and matching just a few basic elements. Choose mini tart pans in assorted sizes and shapes, then prepare the sweet tart shells and top them with fresh fruits arranged in graphic patterns. When serving a large crowd, prepare both the plain and chocolate crusts as well as several different fillings. Guests will love picking and choosing their favorites to enjoy.

1. Preheat the oven to 425°F. Butter and flour twelve 3-inch tart pans or twenty-four 2½-inch tart pans.

2. Roll out the dough on a floured work surface into a circle about ⅛ inch thick and 15 inches in diameter. Place the tart pans upside down on the dough and score it by pressing the entire rim of each pan lightly into the dough. Using a knife, cut the dough into circles slightly bigger than the diameter of the pans. You can also use cookie cutters that are larger than the tart pans; use cutters with fluted edges to make decorative edges.

3. Drape the dough over the pie pans, allowing the excess to hang over the rim. Press the dough into the bottom edges and up the sides, so the dough rises slightly above the rims of the pans. Decoratively crimp the edges. Line the shells with parchment paper and fill with pie weights. Blind-bake the shells for 7–8 minutes, then remove the parchment and weights. Prick the bottoms of the shells with a fork and bake for an additional 7–10 minutes, or until the edges are golden brown. Cool on a rack for 30 minutes, then gently remove from tart pans.

4. Fill the shells with pastry cream, cream cheese filling, chocolate ganache, or lemon curd. Top with fresh fruits and flowers.

PIES FOR BABY CELEBRATIONS

Celebrate the arrival of a new baby—or a baby shower, christening, or baby event—with a "cutie pie." The Southern-style Marshmallow Cookie Pies and the Sesame Peanut Butter and Jam Pie are both nostalgic, feel-good pies that echo the carefree days of childhood. If you want to experiment with decorative toppings, try the Blackbird Pies, topped with cute baby blackbirds or robins made of fondant. Inspired by the nursery rhyme, they are sure to make guests smile.

Marshmallow Cookie Pies

Makes twenty-four 3-inch sandwich pies

Marshmallow cookie pies—also known as MoonPies—originated as a snack pie in the American South. They have recently become popular as a retro-style dessert. The classic recipe we all know and love features a sugar cookie made with brown sugar instead of white. In my double-decker version, the cookie is made with a shortbread piecrust dough. One jar of marshmallow crème will be enough for a thin layer of filling, but I recommend using two jars so that the filling is extra thick.

> *Large batch (three disks) Short-bread Cookie Crust (page 252)*
>
> *2 jars (7½ ounces each) marsh-mallow crème*
>
> *16 ounces semisweet chocolate chips*
>
> *⅓ cup vegetable oil*

1. Preheat the oven to 350°F. Line three baking sheets with parchment paper.

2. Roll out the chilled pastry disks on a floured work surface into three 15 x 15-inch squares that are slightly more than ⅛ inch thick. Using cookie cutters, cut out seventy-two 3-inch circles from the dough and place them on the baking sheets. Refrigerate for 20 minutes.

3. Bake the disks for 10–12 minutes, or until lightly browned. Cool on the pans for 5 minutes, then transfer to a rack to cool completely.

4. To assemble, spoon the marshmallow crème into a pastry bag fitted with a large round tip. Mound about 1½ tablespoons onto the center of a disk. Top with another disk and gently press to spread the marshmallow to the edges.

Add another marshmallow mound on top of the second disk, and top with another round, gently pressing again to spread the filling to the edge. Place the filled pies on a wire rack set over a baking sheet lined with wax paper as you finish them. Repeat with the rest of the disks and marshmallow crème.

5. Combine the chocolate chips and vegetable oil in the top of a double boiler set over simmering water and stir until melted and smooth. Pour the melted chocolate over each pie so that it covers the tops and runs down the sides. Return the chocolate on the baking sheet to the double boiler. Let the cookies dry for 2 hours, or transfer to wax paper and chill to dry more quickly. If you would like to coat the bottoms, reheat the melted chocolate, turn the pies over, and repeat the coating.

Variation

PEANUT BUTTER MARSHMALLOW COOKIE PIES: Spread ½ teaspoon peanut butter on each disk before topping with the marshmallow crème.

Blackbird Pies

Makes four 4-inch deep-dish double-crust pies

The nursery rhyme "Sing a Song of Sixpence," along with the vintage pie birds available in antique stores and on auction Web sites, inspired these pies, which I like to say are suffering from "terminal cuteness." The blackbird pies are filled with blackberry apple filling and the red robin variations are filled with raspberry apple filling. The center of the crust is designed to look torn, to give the impression that the birds are breaking out of the pies. In order to achieve this effect, the little cuties are popped in the freezer a bit before they are baked, to harden the dough, and the triangular pieces of dough surrounding each bird are held in place with a ball of aluminum foil in the center. If you would like to simplify this, though, just cut a hole in the center of the pie and do away with the "torn dough" effect.

1. Butter and flour four 4-inch pie pans.

6 medium apples (about 1¼ pounds), peeled, cored, and sliced (see page 43 for varieties)

¼ cup apple juice or water

1 cup granulated sugar

2 tablespoons cornstarch

3 cups fresh blackberries

Medium batch (two disks, one slightly larger than the other) Basic Butter Crust (page 242)

2 large eggs, beaten

2 tablespoons cold unsalted butter, cut into cubes

Fondant Pie Birds (see page 123)

FOUR AND TWENTY BLACKBIRDS

It is believed that the origin of this nursery rhyme is the sixteenth-century European practice of placing live birds in pies for the amusement of noblemen. When the pies were cut, the birds flew out. The European blackbird is similar to the American red robin, which is usually the first bird to sing in the morning.

Sing a song of sixpence,
A pocketful of rye.
Four and twenty blackbirds
Baked in a pie.
When the pie was opened,
The birds began to sing.
Wasn't that a dainty dish
To set before the king?

FONDANT PIE BIRDS

This recipe makes enough for four birds; to make the robins, substitute red or brown food coloring for the black used here.

⅓ cup Fondant (page 258)
Black and yellow food coloring
3 tablespoons confectioners' sugar mixed with 1 teaspoon water

Color three-fourths of the fondant with black food coloring. Pull off a ½-inch ball of the remaining fondant and leave it white. Color the remaining fondant yellow. Roll out the black fondant into a rectangle that is about 10 inches tall, 8 inches wide, and ⅛ inch thick on a surface covered with confectioners' sugar. Cut out four 2¼ x 1¼-inch blackbirds freehand with a knife. Roll out the yellow fondant to a thickness of ⅛ inch and cut out a 1-inch crescent shape for the breast and a ⅓-inch beak. Roll a ¼-inch dot of the white for the eye and a ⅟₁₆-inch dot of black for the pupil. Attach the breast, beak, and eye to the bird's body with the confectioners' sugar mixture. Dry for 1–2 hours.

2. To make the filling, combine the apples, apple juice, sugar, and cornstarch in a large saucepan. Stir to coat. Cook 6–8 minutes over medium heat, until the mixture boils and thickens. Remove from heat and let cool. Stir in the blackberries.

3. Roll out the larger disk of dough on a floured work surface into a 16 x 16-inch square that is about ⅛ inch thick. Cut four 8-inch circles from the dough. Fit the crusts into the pans by pressing the dough against the bottom and up the sides, allowing the excess to drape slightly over the rims of the pans. Brush some of the beaten eggs on the top edges of the crusts. Prick holes in the bottoms and add the filling. Top with butter cubes.

4. Roll out the second disk of dough on a floured work surface into a 9 x 9-inch square that is about ⅛ inch thick. Cut out four 4½-inch circles from the dough. Using a knife, cut ¾-inch slits in the center of each circle. The slits should form triangular "tabs" that radiate in from the center. Transfer the circles to the pies, pressing the top and bottom crusts together. Trim the excess flush with the rims of the pans. Crimp to form a decorative edge on each pie.

5. Roll small pieces of aluminum foil into balls about 1 inch in diameter. Bend the slits in the top crusts up and place the ball in the center. Rest the triangles against the ball. Freeze the pies for 30 minutes.

6. Preheat the oven to 425°F. Brush the tops with remaining beaten eggs. Bake for 15 minutes. Reduce the heat to 350°F and bake for an additional 20–25 minutes, or until the crusts are golden brown and the juices are bubbling. Cool on a rack. Place fondant pie birds in the opening.

Variation

ROBIN RASPBERRY APPLE PIES: Replace the blackberries with raspberries and the fondant blackbirds with fondant robins.

Cherry Chocolate Chocolate Chip Cookie Pie

Makes one 12-inch single-crust pie

1½ cups semisweet chocolate chips

2½ cups all-purpose flour

1 teaspoon baking powder

½ teaspoon baking soda

½ teaspoon salt

1½ cups (3 sticks) unsalted butter,
     at room temperature

¾ cup granulated sugar

¾ cup firmly packed light brown
     sugar

2 teaspoons vanilla extract

4 large eggs

¾ cup chopped walnuts

½ cup dried cherries

Medium batch (one disk) Choco-
     late Butter Crust (page 242)

2 cups Vanilla Ice Cream
     (optional; page 256)

Do you like homemade gourmet chocolate chocolate chip cookies with lots of goodies mixed in? This filling is just that—cookie dough made with dried cherries and walnuts. Since I define pies as "anything having a pastry shell," I can turn the cookie dough into pie filling by baking it in a shortbread-type crust, which offers a crunchy texture to contrast with the chewy filling. If you like a cookie-and-ice-cream combination, top the pie with mounds of vanilla ice cream in the center.

1. Preheat the oven to 325°F. Generously butter and flour a 12-inch pie pan. Melt ½ cup of chocolate chips and set aside to cool.

2. To make the filling, combine the flour, baking powder, baking soda, and salt in a medium mixing bowl; set aside.

3. Combine the butter, sugars, and vanilla in a large mixing bowl. Beat with an electric mixer on medium speed until fluffy. Beat in the eggs one at a time, beating well after each addition. Add the reserved melted chocolate, ¾ cup of the remaining chocolate chips, ½ cup of the walnuts, and ¼ cup of the dried cherries. Add the flour mixture, stirring until incorporated.

4. Roll out the crust on a floured work surface into a circle about ⅛ inch thick and 15 inches in diameter. Drape over the pie pan, allowing excess to hang over the rim. Press the dough into the bottom edges, and trim the excess to a ¼-inch overhang. Fold the overhang over the rim and decoratively crimp the edge. Prick the bottom with a fork.

5. Add the filling and bake for 45–50 minutes, or until firm. Transfer to a rack to cool for 20 minutes.

6. Top with the remaining dried cherries, walnuts, chocolate chips, and the ice cream, if desired.

Peanut Butter Filling

1 cup cold heavy cream

4 ounces cream cheese, at room
   temperature

¾ cup creamy peanut butter

½ cup confectioners' sugar

2 tablespoons whole milk

1 tablespoon vanilla extract

⅔ cup raspberry jam

Crust

Small batch (one disk) Sesame
   Graham Cracker Cookie Crust
   (page 248), baked and cooled

Topping

½ cup peanut butter chips

¼ cup whole sesame-coated
   peanuts

1 cup fresh raspberries

2 teaspoons sesame seeds

Sesame Peanut Butter and Jam Pie

Makes one 9-inch single-crust pie

Sesame seeds jazz up this childhood favorite icebox pie.

1. To make the filling, whip the cream in a medium mixing bowl, using an electric mixer on medium speed, until it holds soft peaks; set aside.

2. Combine the cream cheese, peanut butter, sugar, milk, and vanilla in a large mixing bowl. Beat with an electric mixer on medium speed until smooth. Fold in the whipped cream.

3. Spread ⅔ cup jam on the inside of the crust. Spread the filling over the jam. Top with peanut butter chips and peanuts. Cover with plastic wrap and freeze for 1 hour. Transfer to the refrigerator 30 minutes before you are ready to serve. Top with fresh raspberries and sesame seeds just before serving.

Variations

PEANUT BUTTER AND JAM PIE: Omit the sesame seeds from the crust and topping, and top with whole unsalted peanuts instead of sesame-coated peanuts.

CHOCOLATE PEANUT BUTTER PIE: Prepare the pie in a small batch of Chocolate Wafer Crust (page 243). Replace the toppings with chocolate chips, whole unsalted peanuts, and peanut butter chips.

PEANUT BUTTER MARSHMALLOW PIE: Replace the jam with 1 cup marshmallow crème. Replace the toppings with dollops of marshmallow crème and miniature marshmallows.

PEANUT BUTTER BANANA PIE: Replace the jam with 1½ cups sliced bananas.

Party Pies

BRUNCH PIES

The best part of planning what to make for brunch is that you get to take a little bit of inspiration from both breakfast and lunch. I suggest serving a mix of sweet and savory, such as the Deep-Dish Pear Cheddar Pie, or for an all-savory pie menu make the Quiches with Herb Wheat Germ Crusts. If you want something sweet and savory at the same time, try the Butternut Squash Custard Pie. All you need is a salad and you have a complete, and completely impressive, meal.

Quiches with Herb Wheat Germ Crusts

Makes twenty-four 2½-inch single-crust pies

I highly recommend this herb wheat germ crust for its earthy flavor, which goes well with a variety of fillings. Customize each quiche by adding vegetables, spices, herbs, and cheeses that complement or contrast with the flavor of the crust. Your guests will all have their favorites and won't be able to stop at just one.

1. Preheat the oven to 350°F. Butter and flour two 12-cup muffin tins.

2. Roll out both disks of dough on a lightly floured surface into two circles, each about ⅛ inch thick and 13 inches in diameter. Using a cookie cutter or the top of a glass as a guide, or working freehand with a knife, cut twenty-four

1 batch (two disks) Herb Wheat Germ Crust (page 249)
5 large eggs
¾ cup heavy cream
½ cup yogurt or sour cream
6 ounces Monterey Jack cheese, grated
3 cups mix-ins (see page 128)

QUICHE MIX-INS

VEGETABLES

Asparagus

Bell peppers

Leeks

Mushrooms

Olives

Onions

Spinach

Sun-dried tomatoes

Tomatoes

Zucchini

MEATS

Bacon

Ham

Sausage

CHEESES

Blue cheese

Cheddar

Feta

Gouda

Mozzarella

Parmesan

Pepper Jack

Ricotta

Swiss

3½-inch circles from the dough. Fit the circles in the muffin cups; they should reach about halfway up the sides. Roll the top edges of the circles down to form thick sides. Line the crusts with parchment paper and fill with pie weights. Blind-bake for 7–10 minutes, or until light golden in color. Set the muffin tins on racks to cool until ready to fill.

3. To make the filling, combine the eggs, heavy cream, yogurt, and cheese in a medium bowl and whisk until blended. Divide the egg mixture among the crusts, leaving about ⅓ inch of room at the top for additional ingredients.

4. Spoon ⅛ cup mix-in ingredients onto each quiche. Stir the mix-ins into the egg mixture, repeating ingredients—or not—as you like. Top with additional mix-in ingredients.

5. Bake the quiches for an additional 17–22 minutes, or until the filling has puffed and set and the tops are golden brown. Cool on a rack for 15 minutes. With a small spatula, remove the quiches from the muffin cups. Serve warm.

Deep-Dish Pear Cheddar Pie

Makes one 11-inch double-crust pie

I tend to have more success making rustic, deep-dish pies—such as this slightly salty Cheddar crust with a sweet pear filling—from firm fruits, such as pears and apples, which hold a nice shape once they're sliced. I usually make this pie with Anjou or Bartlett pears, because they are the most common, but if you can find some of the other varieties (see page 131) feel free to experiment. Here, the Cheddar is in the crust, but for extra cheesy flavor, top the pie with thin slices of cheese about five minutes before it is finished baking. This might soon become your favorite breakfast pie!

1. To make the crust, combine the flour, salt, and sugar in a large bowl. Using a pastry blender or your fingertips, quickly work the butter into the dry ingredients until it resembles coarse meal. Toss the cheese into the mixture.

Cheddar Crust

3 cups all-purpose flour

1 teaspoon salt

1 tablespoon confectioners' sugar

½ cup (1 stick) cold unsalted butter, cut into cubes

1 cup cold grated Cheddar cheese

½ cup cold water

1 large egg white, beaten

Pear Filling

9–10 large firm Anjou or Bartlett pears, cored, peeled, and thinly sliced

1 cup water, mixed with 2 tablespoons freshly squeezed lemon juice

1 cup pear nectar or apple juice

¼ cup firmly packed light brown sugar

3 tablespoons cornstarch

½ teaspoon ground nutmeg

½ teaspoon ground ginger

1½ teaspoons ground cinnamon

1 teaspoon vanilla extract

2. Sprinkle the water over the mixture and mix with a fork or your fingertips until the dough holds together. If necessary, add more cold water, 1 tablespoon at a time. Divide the dough in half, flatten each half into a disk, wrap in plastic wrap, and chill for 1 hour.

3. Preheat the oven to 450°F. Butter and flour an 11-inch deep-dish pie pan.

4. Toss the pears in the water-lemon mixture and let sit until ready to use. Bring the fruit juice to a boil in a heavy-bottomed saucepan over high heat. Add the sugar, cornstarch, nutmeg, ginger, and cinnamon and stir until dissolved. Remove from the heat and add the vanilla. Let cool.

5. Roll out one pastry disk on a floured work surface into a circle about ⅛ inch thick and 14 inches in diameter. Drape over the pie pan, allowing the excess to hang over the rim.

6. Drain the pears from the liquid and transfer to a large mixing bowl. Add the cooled juice mixture to the pears, tossing gently to coat. Set aside 1 cup of sliced pears and pour the rest into the crust, pressing the pears down to eliminate air pockets. Arrange the remaining pear slices on top of the filling, starting from the outside of the crust and radiating inward toward the center.

7. Roll out the second disk on a floured work surface into a circle about ⅛ inch thick and 13 inches in diameter. Cut four large vents into the crust with a knife or cookie cutter. Brush the edge of the bottom crust with some of the egg white and place the top crust over the filling. Press the edges of the crusts firmly together to seal. Press grooved lines into the crust with the back of a knife. Brush the remaining egg white over the top of the crust.

8. Bake for 10 minutes, then reduce the heat to 350°F and bake for an additional 45–50 minutes, or until the pears are tender and the juices are bubbly. Cover the crust with an edge shield if it becomes too brown.

PEAR VARIETIES

ANJOU: The most common type of pear, available year-round; bright green skins, sometimes with a reddish blush; skins retain original color when ripened

BARTLETT: Turn from bright green to golden yellow when ripe; sweet, distinctive pear flavor and somewhat creamy texture that softens quickly with baking

BOSC: Brownish-green skins; crunchy texture and sweet-spicy flavor; sweet early in the ripening process

CONCORDE: Golden-green skins with golden yellow spots; long necks and a hint of vanilla flavor; hold their shape and flavor at high heat

FORELLE: Green skins with reddish freckling; small, crisp, firm, and tangy

Variation

BLUE CHEESE PEAR FIG PIE: In the crust, replace the Cheddar with ⅓ cup crumbled blue cheese. Replace the nutmeg and ginger in the filling with 1 teaspoon ground cardamom. Add 3 tablespoons of honey and 10 chopped dried figs to the juice in step 4.

Butternut Squash Custard Pie with Tres Leches Sauce

Makes one 9-inch single-crust pie

There is something about orange vegetables—such as pumpkins, carrots, and butternut squash—that makes me feel good. I must somehow instinctively know that they are packed with beta-carotene, and by "going orange" I am making a healthy choice.

Butternut squash is one of my favorite winter squashes. It has a hard rind, so roast it with the rind on, then scoop out the squash and purée. This is a not-so-sweet pie, so it can cross over from brunch to lunch—as a side dish—or to dinner, as a dessert. If you would like to sweeten it, sprinkle some sugar on top before you cover it with the tres leches sauce. Remember to check on the pie after about 25 minutes of baking and cover the edges if needed.

1. Preheat the oven to 350°F. Butter and flour a 9-inch pie pan. Line a baking sheet with parchment paper.

2. Roll out the pastry disk on a floured work surface into a circle about ⅛ inch thick and 12 inches in diameter. Drape the dough over the pie pan, allowing the excess to hang over the rim. Press

Crust

Small batch (one disk) Cornmeal Crust (page 244)

Filling

¼ cup granulated sugar

½ cup firmly packed light brown sugar

1½ tablespoons cornstarch

2 teaspoons ground cinnamon

½ teaspoon ground ginger

Pinch ground nutmeg

1 butternut squash, about 1½ pounds, roasted, seeded, and puréed (about 3 cups)

½ cup (1 stick) unsalted butter, at room temperature

2 large eggs

¼ cup apple juice

1 tablespoon vanilla extract

Tres Leches Sauce

⅛ teaspoon baking soda

1 can (12 ounces) evaporated milk

6 tablespoons granulated sugar

⅓ cup sweetened condensed milk

½ cup heavy cream

½ teaspoon ground cinnamon

the dough into the bottom edges, and trim the excess to a ¼-inch overhang. Fold the overhang over the rim and decoratively crimp the edge. Prick the bottom with a fork. Top the crust with parchment paper and fill with pie weights.

3. Reroll the leftover scraps of dough and cut out shapes (such as leaves, flowers, hearts, or stars) with a cookie cutter. Place the shapes on the baking sheet. Blind-bake the shell together with cutouts for 7–10 minutes. Cool on a rack.

4. To make the filling, combine the sugars, cornstarch, cinnamon, ginger, and nutmeg in a small bowl; set aside.

5. Combine the squash, butter, eggs, apple juice, and vanilla in a large mixing bowl. Beat with an electric mixer on medium speed until smooth. Add the sugar mixture and mix until blended. Spread into the crust.

6. Bake for 45–55 minutes, or until a knife inserted in the center comes out clean. Cool on a rack. Top with the reserved cutouts.

7. To make the sauce, dissolve the baking soda in 2 teaspoons water in a small bowl; set aside.

8. Heat the evaporated milk and sugar in a medium saucepan over high heat until it comes to a boil. Reduce the heat to medium and stir in the baking soda mixture. Continue to cook, stirring, until the mixture boils again. Reduce the heat to low and simmer for about 30 minutes, or until the liquid is reduced to ½ cup and turns a light caramel color. Stir in the sweetened condensed milk, cream, and cinnamon and cook for an additional 3–5 minutes, or until thick. Spoon the sauce on serving plates or directly on the slices to serve.

Spinach, Fig, and Feta Turnovers

Makes 9 turnovers

Sweet and salty flavor contrasts are all the rage these days, and these turnovers exemplify that contrast by juxtaposing the sweetness of

Pastry

1 batch Puff Pastry (page 251),
   or 1 (14-ounce) box frozen puff
   pastry, thawed
1 large egg white, beaten with 3
   tablespoons whole milk

Spinach, Fig, and Feta Filling

2½–3 pounds fresh spinach leaves,
   washed, trimmed, steamed, and
   drained (about 2 cups)
8 fresh Mission figs, stemmed and
   cut into ¼-inch pieces
1½ cups crumbled feta cheese
2 tablespoons chopped fresh mint
3 tablespoons confectioners' sugar
1 teaspoon freshly squeezed lemon
   juice
2 large eggs, beaten

Topping

2 tablespoons sesame seeds

figs with the saltiness of feta cheese. This recipe is inspired by spana-
kopita, a popular Greek pastry traditionally made with phyllo dough.
For these turnovers, though, I prefer to use puff pastry.

1. To make the filling, mix the spinach, figs, cheese, mint,
   sugar, and lemon juice in large bowl. Stir in the eggs and set
   aside.

Blue Corn Crust

1 ½ cups all-purpose flour

½ cup blue corn flour

2 ½ teaspoons baking powder

¼ teaspoon salt

¼ teaspoon freshly ground black pepper

⅔ cup shortening, chilled

⅔ cup whole milk

4 slices bacon, cooked and crumbled (about ¼ cup)

2 large eggs, beaten with 2 tablespoons whole milk

Filling

2 tablespoons unsalted butter

8 large eggs

¼ cup whole milk

3 scallions, chopped

Salt and freshly ground black pepper to taste

½ cup grated Cheddar cheese

½ pound bacon, cooked and crumbled

2. Line two baking sheets with parchment paper. Roll out the puff pastry dough on a floured work surface into a 15-inch square that is about ⅛ inch thick. Using a pastry cutter, cut the dough into nine 5-inch squares.

3. Spoon about ⅓ cup of filling into center of each square. Brush some of the egg white mixture on the edges and fold each square in half to make a triangle. Press down and pinch the edges together with your fingertips to seal tightly.

4. Place the turnovers on baking sheets. Brush the tops with the remaining egg white mixture and sprinkle with sesame seeds. Chill for 20 minutes.

5. Preheat the oven to 400°F. Bake the turnovers for 15 minutes, then reduce the heat to 350°F and bake for an additional 10–15 minutes, or until golden brown. Cool for 10–15 minutes on a rack. Serve warm.

Variations

GOAT CHEESE AND SUN-DRIED TOMATO TURNOVERS: Replace the feta with goat cheese, the figs with ¼ cup chopped sun-dried tomatoes, and the mint with fresh basil.

APRICOT AND BLUE CHEESE TURNOVERS: Replace the feta with blue cheese and the figs with 6 chopped fresh apricots. Omit the mint.

Bacon and Egg Pocket Pies

Makes eight hand pies

For an on-the-go breakfast, package a classic combo of bacon and eggs—or your own favorite scramble—in these fluffy pastry pockets, made from a blue corn crust. Don't overcook the eggs or bacon—in fact, undercook them slightly, because they will continue to cook in the oven.

1. To make the crust, combine the flours, baking powder, salt, and pepper in a large mixing bowl. Cut in the shortening with a pastry blender or your fingertips until the mixture resembles coarse meal. Gradually add the milk (you may

not use it all), blending until the dough sticks together and forms a ball. Flatten into a disk, wrap in plastic wrap, and chill for 30 minutes.

2. To make the filling, melt the butter in a large skillet over medium heat. Add the eggs, milk, scallions, salt, and pepper, and scramble until almost cooked but not completely set. Sprinkle with cheese and bacon. Cover with a lid and allow the cheese to melt.

3. Preheat the oven to 400°F. Line a baking sheet with parchment paper. Knead the crumbled bacon into the pastry, then roll out the dough on a floured surface to form a rectangle 18 inches long, 9 inches wide, and ⅛ inch thick. Cut the rectangle into eight 4½-inch squares. Brush the egg wash around the edges of each square, then spoon one-eighth of the filling into the center of each. Fold the dough in half, forming triangles. Crimp the edges to seal. Prick holes on the top with a fork. Place on the baking sheet.

4. Bake the pies for 15–20 minutes, or until golden brown. Serve warm.

LUNCHEON PIES

These lunchtime pies are light, casual, and easy to transport, whether to a picnic in a fancy hamper or to school or work in a utilitarian lunch box. You can also make them for a fresh and special lunch at home.

Potato Knishes

Makes 8 knishes

This recipe produces a traditional New York–style knish, with sour cream added to give the potato filling some tang. Add just about anything you like to the filling—try a cup of cubed corned beef, chopped hard-boiled eggs, minced sautéed chicken livers, ground sausage, or herbs and grated cheese. For a sweetened version, add ¼ cup confectioners' sugar and fresh or dried chopped fruits and nuts to the filling.

1. To make the filling, mash the potatoes until smooth. Add eggs, sour cream or yogurt, flour, salt, and pepper; mix well. Add the mix-ins, if desired. Cover with plastic wrap and chill for 1 hour.

2. To make the dough, combine the flour, baking powder, salt, and pepper in a medium bowl. Make a well in the center and set aside.

3. Beat the egg, oil, vinegar, and water in a small bowl. Pour into the well in the dough and mix with a spatula to combine. Transfer to a floured work surface and knead gently into a ball. Return to the dough to the bowl, cover with plastic wrap, and let sit at room temperature for 1 hour.

4. Preheat the oven to 350°F. Line a baking sheet with parchment paper. Roll out half the dough on a floured work surface into a rough rectangle about 13 inches wide, 6 inches long, and ⅛ inch thick. Spoon half the filling onto the dough in a long log shape, leaving about 2 inches from the bottom and top long edges of the rectangle. Brush some of the egg mixture on the remaining exposed dough. Roll the dough around the filling,

Potato Filling

4 large Yukon Gold potatoes (about 2 pounds), peeled, diced, and boiled until tender

2 large eggs

⅓ cup sour cream or plain yogurt

¼ cup all-purpose flour

¼ teaspoon salt

¼ teaspoon freshly ground black pepper

1 cup mix-ins (see opposite page), if desired

Dough

1 ¾ cups all-purpose flour

1 teaspoon baking powder

½ teaspoon salt

¼ teaspoon freshly ground white pepper

1 large egg

½ cup vegetable oil

1 teaspoon cider vinegar

½ cup lukewarm water

2 large eggs, beaten with 2 tablespoons whole milk

Garnish

¼ cup prepared mustard

first rolling the short sides around the filling and then rolling the long sides away from you. Press the egg edge into the log to seal. Repeat with the remaining dough and filling.

5. Using a sharp knife, cut each log into four segments. Pinch and twist the dough at the open ends to seal, then press one end onto the work surface to flatten into a compressed cylinder. Press the top end flat with the palm of your hand. Then press the center down to close. Build up a decorative rim around the top edges. Set the knishes on the baking sheet as you finish them. Brush the entire outsides of the pastry with the remaining egg mixture. Bake for 30–35 minutes, or until golden brown. Cool for 10 minutes on a rack and serve hot, with mustard.

KNISH MIX-INS

Blue cheese, walnuts, and apricots
Caramelized onions
Cheddar and thyme
Dried apricots and cranberries
Hard-boiled eggs and bacon
Leeks and tarragon
Peas, ham, and Swiss cheese
Pecans and raisins
Roasted red peppers and pears
Sausage, tomato, and rosemary
Sautéed chicken livers
Spinach and mushrooms

Cornish Pasties

Makes eight hand pies

At a time in the British Isles when women's work was in the kitchen and men's work was down in the mines (I am usually pro-equality, but in this case I would much rather be in the kitchen than in a mine), women made pasties for their husbands' lunches. These handheld pies included both lunch and dessert in one pie. The English hot-water crust, made from shortening or lard, was strong and sturdy so it

Crust

1 cup shortening or lard

1 ½ cups boiling water

1 teaspoon salt

4 ½–5 cups all-purpose flour

3 large eggs, beaten with 3 tablespoons whole milk

Apple Walnut Filling

3 tablespoons unsalted butter

6 medium apples (about 2 pounds), peeled, cored, and thinly sliced (see page 43 for varieties)

Juice of ½ lemon

3 tablespoons apple juice or water

½ cup firmly packed light brown sugar

½ teaspoon ground cinnamon

Pinch ground nutmeg

1 tablespoon cornstarch

⅓ cup chopped walnuts

Sausage Filling

¾ pound apple sausage or mild Italian sausage (about 3–4 links), removed from casings

½ cup diced onion

1 cup diced cooked potatoes

½ cup diced cooked carrots

¼ teaspoon salt

¼ teaspoon freshly ground black pepper

Topping

Cinnamon Sugar (page 258)

wouldn't break if the lunch boxes were dropped down the mine shaft. Some were made with a handle, so that the miner could conveniently hold the pie, and most were embossed with initials, so each miner could identify his own.

My version of pasties has a savory sausage filling for the main course and a sweet apple filling for dessert. Assemble the pies on the baking sheet; it will make your life much easier. Prepare the fillings so they are almost fully cooked, because they'll finish cooking during the baking process. There are several steps to this recipe, so if you want to take a shortcut (gasp!) use canned apple pie filling.

1. To make the crust, spoon the shortening or lard into a large mixing bowl. Pour the boiling water over it and stir until melted. Add the salt. Gradually mix in the flour until it forms a stiff dough (you may not use all the flour). Flatten the dough into two disks, one about 25% larger than the other, wrap in plastic wrap, and chill for 1 hour.

2. To make the apple walnut filling, melt the butter in a large skillet over medium heat. Add the apples and sauté 5–7 minutes, or until browned. Stir in the lemon and apple juices, reduce the heat to low, and simmer until juices are absorbed. Transfer the apples to a medium bowl and stir in the brown sugar, cinnamon, nutmeg, cornstarch, and walnuts. Set aside.

3. To make the sausage filling, combine the sausage and the onion in a sauté pan and cook, breaking apart the sausage with a wooden spoon, until the sausage is almost completely cooked. Transfer to a medium bowl. Add the potatoes, carrots, salt, and pepper.

4. Preheat the oven to 350°F. Line a baking sheet with parchment paper.

5. Roll out the smaller pastry disk on a floured work surface into a rectangle 11 inches long, 12 inches wide, and ⅛ inch thick. Using a pastry wheel or a knife, cut the dough into eight 3 x 5 ½-inch rectangles. Transfer the rectangles to the baking sheet. Brush some egg wash over the entire surface of the pastries.

6. Place a scant ½ cup of sausage filling and a scant ½ cup of apple filling on each pastry, positioning each mound about ¼ inch from the edges and leaving ¾ inch between the two mounds.

7. Remove a 3-inch ball of dough from the larger pastry disk and set aside. Roll out the larger disk on a floured work surface into a rectangle 11 inches long, 12 inches wide, and ⅛ inch thick. Using a pastry wheel or a knife, cut the dough into eight 3 x 5½-inch rectangles. Using a cookie cutter, cut out 2-inch circles from one side of each rectangle, leaving about ½ inch from the edges. Cut 1½-inch cross-shaped slits in the other side of each rectangle, leaving about 1 inch between the slits and the hole and ¾ inch on each side, as shown in the photo. Add the dough scraps to the reserved ball.

8. Roll out the ball on a floured work surface into a 6 x 6-inch square that is ⅛ inch thick. Cut the square into two 3 x 6-inch rectangles. Use both of these rectangles to cut 5–6¼-inch lattice strips for each pie. Weave the lattice strips over the apple walnut filling. Brush the backs of the cut rectangles with egg wash and place the side with the hole over the lattice strips. Line up the rectangles with the bottom crusts and press the edges, as well as the space in between the two mounds of filling, together. Score a pattern around all the edges and in the middle with a knife. Brush the entire top with egg wash. Sprinkle the lattice strips with cinnamon sugar. Open the cross-shaped slits a little to vent.

9. Bake for 20–25 minutes, or until golden. Serve warm or at room temperature.

Panda Bento Box
Makes one 3½-inch double-crust pie and one 2-inch double-crust pie
Ready for this? Opening up a bento box is about as much fun as lunch can be—especially when it contains two pies. The panda pie, made with chicken pot pie filling, is a savory pie, and the chocolate raspberry pie is for a sweet dessert. A full batch of dough will make several luncheon pies at one time. Make a week's worth of pies (create different

BENTO BOX LUNCHES

There is an old Japanese saying, "Eat with your eyes," which means that food tempts us with its beauty as well as with its flavor and aroma. Today, parents express their love for their children by packing them adorable bento box lunches. Character bentos (called *kyaraben*), such as this panda, are all the rage—and healthful, too.

Medium batch (one disk) Basic
    Butter Crust (page 242)
Small batch (one disk) Chocolate
    Butter Crust (page 242)
1 cup Chicken Pot Pie Filling
    (page 220), or your favorite
    vegetable or meat stew, drained
1 ½-inch ball Marzipan (page
    259)
3 drops black food coloring
1 ½ tablespoons raspberry jam
½ cup assorted fresh fruit, such
    as cherries, blueberries, grapes,
    blackberries, kumquats, kiwi-
    fruit, and pineapple
1 large egg, beaten
Confectioners' sugar for dusting
1 tablespoon confectioners' sugar
    mixed with ¼ teaspoon water

characters and desserts) and freeze them after assembling. You can also make these pies with extra scraps of dough and filling from other pies. If you're short on time, you can use store-bought pie dough and ready-made meat stew. Pack your pies in a traditional multilayer bento box, as shown in the photo, or in a plastic storage container. The box I used is about 5 inches x 4 inches x 3 inches high.

1. Preheat the oven to 400°F. Butter and flour one 3½-inch pie pan for the panda pie and one 2-inch pan for the chocolate raspberry pie.

2. To make the panda pie, roll out the basic butter crust on a floured work surface into a rectangle about 12 inches long, 6½ inches wide, and ⅛ inch thick. For the bottom crust, cut out a 6½-inch circle. Drape the dough over the larger pie pan, allowing the excess to hang over the rim. Press the dough into the bottom edges. Prick the bottom with a fork and brush the top edges with some of the beaten egg. Spoon in the chicken pot pie filling.

3. Cut out a 3½-inch circle from the remaining dough and place it over the filling. Press the edges of both crusts firmly together to seal. Cut slits in the center of the pie for venting and crimp the edges decoratively.

4. Using a cookie cutter, or working freehand with a knife, cut out a circular panda face about 2¼ inches in diameter from the remaining crust. Brush some more of the egg over the entire top of the crust and attach the face. Prick holes in the crust with a straw where the eyes will be; these will help vent the pie. Brush more egg over the face and bake for 10 minutes, then reduce the heat to 350°F and bake for an additional 15–20 minutes, or until the filling is bubbling. Set on a rack to cool.

5. Color a 1-inch ball of marzipan black and leave the rest white. Roll out the black marzipan on a work surface covered with confectioners' sugar and cut out the panda's ears, nose, mouth, and eyes. Roll the white marzipan into

two ¼-inch balls to make the pupils of the eyes. Attach to the black eyes with the confectioners' sugar mixture.

6. To make the chocolate raspberry pie, roll out the chocolate dough into a rectangle that is 7 inches long, 4½ inches wide, and ⅛ inch thick. For the bottom crust cut out a 4½-inch circle; for the top crust, cut out a 2½-inch circle. Drape the dough over the smaller pie pan, allowing the excess to hang over the rim. Press the dough into the bottom edges. Prick the bottom with a fork and brush the top edges with some of the beaten egg. Spoon in the raspberry jam. Place the smaller circle over the top of the pie, roll up the edge of the bottom crust to cover the edge of the top crust, and press with your fingers to seal. Cut slits in the center of the pie for venting and crimp the edges decoratively.

7. Roll out the scraps of the basic butter crust into a 2-inch square that is ⅛ inch thick. Using a leaf-shaped cookie cutter, cut out two leaves. Using a bamboo skewer, a toothpick, or a knife, draw veins in the leaves. Attach to the top of the raspberry pie with beaten egg. Bake at 350°F for 12–15 minutes. Cool on a rack. Remove pie from pan.

8. To make the fruit salad, place 3 fresh pineapple rings, each about 3½ inches in diameter, in a silicone cupcake or muffin tin liner. Using a knife, cut a slice of kiwifruit into an octagon. Cut a kumquat in half. Stack the kiwifruit on top of the pineapple, then place the kumquat on top of the kiwifruit. Cut the remaining kumquat half into 4 slices and place them on top of the pineapple.

9. To fill the bento, place the panda pie on the box's top "shelf." Fill the shelf with cherries and other fruits. Thread blueberries onto a bamboo skewer and grapes onto a second skewer. Place the chocolate raspberry pie and fruit salad on the bottom shelf of the box. Fill the spaces with remaining berries.

Medium batch (one disk) Basic
    Butter Crust (page 242)

4 large eggs

¾ cup fresh or packaged unsweet-
    ened shredded coconut

1 ¼ cups grated Cheddar cheese

1 can (13½ ounces) full-fat
    coconut milk

¼ cup granulated sugar

1 tablespoon cornstarch

¼ teaspoon salt

Cheddar Coconut Pies

Makes ten 2½-inch single-crust pies

Think of these as a sweet and salty treat with Southeast Asian flair. Served with a salad or soup, they make a delicious lunchtime meal.

1. Preheat the oven to 350°F. Butter and flour ten 2½-inch pie pans or ten cups in a muffin tin.

2. Roll out the crust on a floured surface into a circle that is ⅛ inch thick and 15 inches in diameter. Cut out ten 5-inch circles from the dough. Drape the circles over the pans, pressing into the bottoms and sides and trimming the edges flush with the tops of the pans. Prick the bottom of the crusts with a fork. Line with parchment paper and fill with pie weights. Blind-bake for 7–10 minutes, or until light golden. Cool completely on a rack.

3. To make the filling, combine the eggs, coconut, and cheese in a large mixing bowl and whisk until blended. Set aside.

4. Combine the coconut milk, sugar, cornstarch, and salt in a medium saucepan over medium heat. Cook, stirring, for 5–7 minutes, or until blended and thickened. Stir into the egg mixture. Add the filling to the partially baked crusts. Bake for an additional 17–22 minutes, or until the filling has puffed and set and tops are golden brown. Cool on a rack for 15 minutes. Serve warm.

DINNER PARTY PIES

Pie can be a comforting, savory dinner entrée—I'm especially fond of serving the Macaroni Pie and the Tamale Pie as a casual main course. Pies like the Zucchini Pie can also work well as a pastry-encased side dish. Of course, pie is the perfect way to top off a meal. If you're looking to make a showstopping dessert for an elegant dinner party, try the Deconstructed Cherry Pies or the Blueberry Ravioli. Sit down with pie and a glass of wine, or beer, or a cappuccino and enjoy the fruits of your labor.

Macaroni Pie

Makes one 12-inch single-crust pie

Pasta is available in many shapes and sizes, and here I highlight a few of them on the top of this cheesy baked-macaroni pie. The olive oil–semolina crust adds a classic Italian flavor. Freezing olive oil takes a while, so make the crust several hours before you plan on eating the pie.

1. Preheat oven to 425°F. Coat a 12-inch pie pan with olive oil.

2. Mix the ricotta, eggs, mozzarella, basil, and 1½ cups tomato sauce in a large bowl. Set aside.

3. Roll out the crust into a circle about ⅛ inch thick and 15 inches in diameter. Gently drape the crust over the pie pan. Press the dough into the bottom edges and up the sides of the pan, so the top edge is flush with the top of the pan. Prick the bottom of the crust with a fork.

4. Cook 8 ounces of the pasta in boiling water for 7–10 minutes, or until al dente. Drain and reserve about 2 ounces of assorted pasta shapes for the top. Add the remainder of the cooked pasta to the cheese mixture. Spoon the filling into the crust. Decorate the top with the reserved pasta and cover tightly with aluminum foil. Bake for 15 minutes, then reduce the temperature to 375°F and bake for an additional 35–45 minutes. Remove the foil and bake for an additional 10–15 minutes to lightly brown the top. Cool on a rack for 5–10 minutes.

5. Heat the remaining tomato sauce and serve on top or to the side of each slice.

---

1 ¾ cups ricotta cheese

2 large eggs

1 ½ cups grated mozzarella cheese

¼ cup chopped fresh basil leaves

4 cups tomato sauce

1 batch Olive Oil Crust (page 251), chilled for 30 minutes

10 ounces assorted dried pasta

Chili Filling

1 teaspoon kosher salt

½ teaspoon freshly ground black
    pepper

¼ teaspoon cayenne pepper

1 pound ground beef

1 tablespoon olive oil

3 garlic cloves, minced

1 large yellow onion, diced

2 jalapeño peppers, minced (seeds
    and ribs removed)

1 celery stalk, chopped

1 can (14 ounces) diced tomatoes

1 can (6 ounces) tomato paste

1 tablespoon chili powder

1 teaspoon ground cumin

1 teaspoon dried cilantro

2 tablespoons cider vinegar

¼ cup unsulfured molasses

Juice of 2 limes

2 cups fresh corn kernels

1 can (14 ounces) kidney beans,
    drained

Creamy Cornmeal Crust

5 cups chicken broth

2 ¼ cups cornmeal

¾ cup whole milk

1 ½ cups sour cream

1 large egg, beaten

4 scallions, chopped

⅛ teaspoon freshly ground black
    pepper

1 ½ cups grated Cheddar cheese

Tamale Pie

Makes one 9-inch single-crust pie

Think of this as the Southwestern version of a shepherd's pie. A creamy cornmeal crust is filled with a spicy sweet chili. Increase the heat by adding as many jalapeño peppers as you like.

1. Sprinkle ½ teaspoon kosher salt, ¼ teaspoon black pepper, and cayenne pepper in a large skillet. Heat the pan, add the ground beef, and cook, breaking apart the beef, until almost done. Drain the grease and transfer to a medium bowl. Wipe the skillet with a paper towel to remove excess grease.

2. Add the olive oil, garlic, onion, jalapeños, and celery to the skillet. Cook over medium heat until the garlic is lightly browned, about 2 minutes.

3. Add the tomatoes, tomato paste, chili powder, cumin, cilantro, vinegar, molasses, and remaining salt and pepper. Reduce the heat to low and cook, stirring occasionally, for 5 minutes. Add the ground beef and cook for an additional 5 minutes. Add the lime juice, corn, and kidney beans and remove from the heat.

4. Preheat the oven to 400°F. Butter a 9 x 9-inch baking dish.

5. To make the crust, heat the chicken broth in a large saucepan. Whisk in the cornmeal, a little at a time, until smooth. Remove from heat and add the milk, ¾ cup sour cream, egg, half the scallions, and pepper.

6. Spread a layer of cornmeal mixture (use a little more than half) over the bottom of the baking dish. It should come part of the way up the sides. Add the meat mixture. Top with remaining cornmeal mixture. Sprinkle cheese over top. Bake for 30–35 minutes, or until bubbly and light golden on top. Cool on a rack for 5 minutes. Spoon onto plates with a dollop of the remaining sour cream and sprinkle with the remaining scallions.

Shepherd's Pie with Sweet Potato Crust

Makes one 2-quart single-crust pie

2 pounds ground lamb

2 garlic cloves, minced

3 tablespoons unsalted butter

1 medium white onion, diced

1 celery stalk, chopped

2 medium carrots, peeled and chopped

¼ pound fresh mushrooms, sliced

3 slices bacon, cut into pieces, cooked, and drained

½ teaspoon freshly ground black pepper

1 teaspoon chopped fresh rosemary

1 bottle (12 ounces) amber beer

1 package (10 ounces) frozen peas, loosely broken apart

2 large sweet potatoes (about 8 ounces each), peeled, cooked, and mashed

½ cup grated white Cheddar cheese

I've always made shepherd's pie with ground beef, and then it hit me—shepherds tend sheep, not cattle! I looked it up, and I had indeed been misinformed. A real shepherd's pie is made with ground or cubed lamb. What I was making was technically a cottage pie, which features ground beef. To confuse matters even more, I had been adding a layer of bread crumbs to the pie, which technically made it a Cumberland pie. The one constant in all these: mashed potatoes form the top crust. I prefer sweet potatoes to regular potatoes, but you can use either.

1. Cook the ground lamb and garlic in a large skillet over medium heat. Drain the grease and transfer to a medium bowl. Wipe the skillet with a paper towel to remove excess grease.

2. Preheat the oven to 400°F. Add 1½ tablespoons butter and the onion to the skillet and cook over medium heat until the onion is clear and soft, about 10 minutes. Add the celery, carrot, mushrooms, bacon, pepper, and ½ teaspoon rosemary. Cook for 1–2 minutes, then add the beer and cook, stirring occasionally, until vegetables are almost tender. Add the peas at the very end and cook for 1–2 minutes, until peas are separated. Spoon the lamb mixture into a shallow 2-quart baking dish. Add the vegetables on top.

3. Combine the mashed sweet potatoes, the remaining butter and rosemary, and the cheese in a large bowl. Spoon the potato mixture into a pastry bag fitted with a large star-shaped tip. Pipe the potatoes over the lamb, cover tightly with foil, and bake for 15 minutes. Remove the cover and cook for an additional 10–15 minutes, or until potatoes are lightly browned.

Deconstructed Cherry Pies

Makes 8 plated pies

Deconstructing pies, or breaking them down into their separate components and rearranging them, provides many opportunities to plate creatively. It also allows you to change the ratio of ingredients and cook each to its optimal degree of doneness. Here, homey cherry pie is jazzed up and turned into a plated landscape, one that features minimal crust and tons of cherries and whipped cream. The cherries are cooked very quickly, so they retain their juices and texture.

Medium batch (four disks)
Almond Sweet Tart Crust (page 254)

½ cup granulated sugar

¼ cup water

1 teaspoon cornstarch

3 pounds fresh Bing or other sweet cherries, stemmed and pitted (about 6 cups)

4 cups Whipped Cream (page 261)

¼ cup ground almonds

1. Preheat the oven to 375°F. Butter and flour four 3½-inch tart pans. Roll out each disk of dough on a floured work surface to form four circles, each about ¼ inch thick and 5 inches in diameter. Fit the crusts into the pans, pressing into the bottom edges. Line the crusts with parchment paper and fill with pie weights. Blind-bake for 20 minutes. Remove the parchment paper and weights and bake for an additional 7–12 minutes, or until golden. Cool for 20 minutes in the pans on a rack, and then remove from the pans and transfer to a rack to cool completely.

2. Combine the sugar, water, and cornstarch in a large saucepan. Cook over medium heat, stirring, until the sugar has dissolved and the mixture is thickened. Stir in the cherries and cook for an additional 3–5 minutes, or until the liquid coats the cherries and the juices are bubbly but the cherries are still firm. Set aside to cool slightly.

3. To assemble the desserts, cut each tart shell in half. Spoon the whipped cream into a pastry bag fitted with a large star-shaped tip. Pipe a ¼-cup mound on one side of a serving plate. Lean one half of a tart shell against the whipped cream at an angle, using the whipped cream for support. Spoon about ¾ cup cherry filling onto the plate next to the shell. Pipe a second ¼-cup mound of whipped cream on the other side of the plate. Sprinkle with 1½ teaspoons ground almonds. Repeat with the remaining whipped cream, shells, and filling.

Large batch (two disks) Egg Crust
   (page 246)
2 large eggs, beaten with ¼ cup
   whole milk
3 cups Blueberry Filling
   (page 202)

Blueberry Ravioli

Makes sixteen 2¼-inch ravioli, or about 4 hearty servings

For your next dinner party dessert, prepare a plate full of sweet ravioli. These are filled with blueberry filling, but have fun with the form and play around with different fillings to come up with something equally yummy! The venting holes on top can be cut with cookie cutters in a variety of shapes.

1. Preheat the oven to 425°F. Line two baking sheets with parchment paper.

2. Roll out one disk of dough on a floured work surface into a 9 x 9-inch square that is ⅛ inch thick. Cut the square into four 2¼-inch squares. Transfer the squares to the baking sheets. Brush egg mixture on the edges of the squares. Spoon a heaping tablespoon of filling onto each square.

3. Roll out the second disk of dough on a floured work surface to the same size and cut into four 2¼-inch squares. Punch venting holes in the squares with a straw or cookie cutter. Place the squares over the filling and press the edges together with your fingers or a fork. Brush the tops with remaining egg mixture.

4. Bake for 7–8 minutes, then reduce the temperature to 350°F and bake for an additional 10–15 minutes, or until the crust is golden brown and the juices are bubbling. Cool on the baking sheets on a rack for 10 minutes.

5. Heat the remaining blueberry filling in a saucepan until just warm. Arrange three or four ravioli on each plate and spoon the sauce on top or on the side.

Meringue

1 teaspoon white vinegar

1 teaspoon vanilla extract

2 teaspoons cornstarch

Pinch salt

4 large egg whites

¼ cup superfine sugar

⅓ cup ground hazelnuts

Filling

1 cup hazelnut spread (Nutella)

1 cup toasted whole hazelnuts

Hazelnut Meringue Pie

Makes one 10-inch single-crust pie

This pie is inspired by Pavlova, the creamy meringue dessert from Australia. The size of the pie and the baking time keep the crust chewy in the center, and although this chewiness is what makes the pie so good, it is also what makes it messy. If you bake the pie in a pan, it can be difficult to cut and remove the slices. So I simply form the meringue into a pie shape on a piece of parchment and bake it without the pan.

1. Preheat the oven to 250°F. Line a baking sheet with parchment paper.

2. Combine the vinegar, vanilla, cornstarch, and salt in a small bowl, stirring until the cornstarch has dissolved.

3. In a separate bowl, beat the egg whites with an electric mixer at high speed until soft peaks form. Then beat in the sugar, 1 teaspoon at a time, until it is completely dissolved, the whites are no longer gritty, and stiff peaks form.

4. Gently fold the vinegar mixture into the egg white mixture. Add the ground hazelnuts.

5. Use a spatula to spread the meringue on the parchment, shaping it into a 10-inch circle with a raised border. Bake the meringue about 1 hour and 10 minutes, or until the outside is crisp, dry, and cream-colored. Cracks may form in the top; this is normal. Turn off the oven and let the meringue cool in the oven with the door slightly ajar, which will prevent droplets of moisture from forming on the meringue.

6. Once the meringue is cooled, spoon half the hazelnut spread into the well. Smooth the top with an offset spatula. Spoon the other half into a pastry bag fitted with a star-shaped tip. Pipe stars over the hazelnut spread. Top with whole hazelnuts.

Variation

BERRY PAVLOVA PIE: Replace the hazelnut cream with your favorite berry jam and the whole hazelnuts with fresh berries.

SUMMER PARTY PIES

Come summer, grilled fruit, fresh melons, and s'mores are familiar out-of-this-world favorites, especially when they make their appearance in pies. For a savory appetizer at your next barbecue or picnic, try the Chicken Empanadas. They are a good movable feast, allowing you to circulate among your guests and "work the crowd."

Crust

Medium batch Chocolate Wafer Crust (page 243), prepared in twelve 3½-inch square tart pans

Barbecued Fruit

4 cups cubed and sliced assorted fresh fruit, such as mangoes, plums, melons, kiwifruit, and peaches
3 tablespoons unsalted butter, melted
2 tablespoons firmly packed light brown sugar
Juice of 2 medium oranges
2 tablespoons olive oil

Barbecued-Fruit Ice Cream

Makes 8 cups
6 large egg yolks
2 cups whole milk
1 cup granulated sugar
¼ teaspoon salt
¼ cup desiccated coconut
2 cups heavy cream
1 teaspoon vanilla extract

Barbecued-Fruit Ice Cream Tarts

Makes twelve 3½-inch tarts

Looking for a not-so-mainstream ice cream tart to serve at a summertime barbecue? These, made with grilled fruit, are as delicious as they are pretty. When grilling the fruit, cut it into pieces of approximately equal size for best results and even cooking. Thread fruits that are similar in size and texture or density onto the same skewers.

1. Preheat the oven to 350°F. Bake the crust for 6–8 minutes, or until it darkens. Cool in the pans for 10 minutes, then transfer crusts to a rack to cool completely.

2. To make the grilled fruit, thread the fruit onto metal skewers. Combine the butter, sugar, and orange juice in a small mixing bowl. Brush the fruit lightly with the sauce.

3. Set the grill up for direct grilling and preheat to high. Brush olive oil on the grill. Grill the fruit, turning several times, for 4–8 minutes, or until softened. Remove from heat and set aside.

4. To make the ice cream, combine the eggs and milk in a double boiler set over simmering water, whisking until combined. Add the sugar, salt, and coconut and cook, stirring occasionally, until the mixture thickens and coats the back of a metal spoon. Remove from heat and let cool.

5. Stir in the heavy cream and vanilla. Transfer to an ice cream maker and freeze according to manufacturer's instructions until almost firm but still soft and malleable. Mix in 2 cups of the grilled fruit. Return to the ice cream maker and freeze until firm.

6. To assemble the tarts, spoon a large scoop of ice cream into the shells and top with remaining fruit. Serve immediately, or cover and refreeze until ready to serve.

Empanada Pastry Dough

3 ¼ cups all-purpose flour

½ teaspoon salt

1 cup (2 sticks) plus 2 tablespoons cold unsalted butter, cut into cubes

1 large egg

2 tablespoons red wine vinegar

1 cup cold water

2 egg whites, beaten

¼ cup cold whole milk

Chicken Filling

Makes 4 ½ cups

3 cups shredded cooked chicken

2 Roma (plum) tomatoes, cubed

3 scallions, chopped

2 tablespoons chopped red bell pepper

1 teaspoon chopped jalapeño pepper (seeds and ribs removed)

1 tablespoon ground cumin

½ teaspoon chopped fresh dill

⅓ teaspoon celery salt

½ teaspoon freshly ground black pepper

Chicken Empanadas with Yogurt Kiwi Dipping Sauce

Makes 6 hand pies

Wrapped in a buttery pastry crust, these savory chicken empanadas, served with sweet yet tangy dipping sauce, are perfect as a party snack. Empanadas can be made in all shapes and sizes. To create this oblong shape, I used oval cutters in two sizes—the bigger size for the tops and the smaller size for the bottoms.

1. To make the pastry, combine the flour and salt in a large bowl. Using a pastry blender or your fingertips, cut in the butter until the mixture resembles coarse meal. Blend in the whole egg and vinegar. Gradually add the water, using only as much as needed to form the dough.

2. On a floured surface, knead the dough gently a few times until smooth. Flatten into two disks, wrap in plastic wrap, and chill for 30 minutes.

3. Preheat the oven to 400°F. Line a baking sheet with parchment paper.

4. To make the filling, combine all ingredients in a large bowl and mix well.

5. Roll out both disks of dough on a floured surface into a circle about ⅛ inch thick and 18 inches in diameter. Using cookie cutters, or working freehand with a knife, cut out six ovals from each disk. Half the ovals from each disk should be slightly larger than the others. Brush egg whites around the edges of the smaller ovals.

6. Divide the chicken filling among the smaller ovals. Place the larger ovals over the filling and press the edges of the crusts together to seal. Transfer to the baking sheet and brush milk over the tops. Bake for 25–30 minutes, or until

Yogurt Kiwi Dipping Sauce

1 ½ cups plain Greek-style or
   whole-milk yogurt

1 cup sour cream

1 tablespoon olive oil

1 tablespoon red wine vinegar

1 tablespoon freshly squeezed
   lemon juice

2 garlic cloves, minced

¼ teaspoon salt

¼ teaspoon freshly ground white
   pepper

4 kiwifruit (or 2 cucumbers),
   peeled and diced

1 teaspoon chopped fresh dill

golden. Cool for 10 minutes and serve warm with the sauce on the side.

YOGURT KIWI DIPPING SAUCE

1. Blend the yogurt and sour cream with a whisk in a medium bowl; set aside.

2. Blend the olive oil, vinegar, lemon juice, garlic, salt, and pepper in a small bowl. Add to the yogurt mixture and mix well. Fold in the kiwifruit and dill. Chill for 1 hour before serving.

Walnut Crust

1 ½ cups all-purpose flour

½ cup confectioners' sugar

½ cup chopped walnuts

¼ teaspoon salt

1 cup (2 sticks) cold unsalted butter, cut into cubes

1 teaspoon freshly squeezed lemon juice

5 tablespoons cold water

Filling

1 ½ cups Lemon Curd (page 255)

3 ½ cups melon balls (such as cantaloupe, honeydew, golden honeydew, and watermelon)

Four-Melon Tart

Makes one 9-inch tart

At the height of summer, honeydew, golden honeydew, cantaloupe, and watermelon abound. And since these melons lose their flavor if cooked, they should be served in a tart only when fresh. This tart is simple to make, allowing you plenty of time to arrange the melon balls in an attractive pattern that showcases their colors. Bake the crust—which tastes like a big walnut cookie—in a square or rectangular pan, and use a melon baller and a small ice cream scoop to scoop the colorful fruits in different sizes.

1. Butter and flour a 9-inch square tart pan with a removable bottom.

2. To make the crust, combine the flour, sugar, walnuts, and salt in a medium bowl. With a pastry blender or your fingertips, cut in the butter until the mixture resembles coarse meal. Gradually add the lemon juice, then water to dampen, and stir until the dough begins to stick together. Form it into a ball with your hands.

3. Roll out the dough on a floured work surface into an 11 x 11-inch square that is ¼ inch thick. Press it into the bottom and sides of the tart pan, making a ½-inch edge. Cover and chill for 30 minutes.

4. Preheat the oven to 350°F. Line the crust with parchment paper and fill with pie weights. Blind-bake for 10 minutes, or until the crust begins to brown. Remove the parchment and weights

and bake for an additional 10–15 minutes, or until fully browned. Cool in the pan on a rack for 1 hour.

5. Spread the lemon curd on the bottom of the crust. Top with melon balls.

Chilly Milk Chocolate S'more Pie

Makes one 9-inch single-crust pie

If you think a real summertime treat is to dig into a melty, creamy s'more, just wait until you try it frozen! Keep in mind that marshmallows are sold in many different flavors and colors, so your pie can contain a hint of strawberry, orange, lemon, or lime (among many other flavors) if you want some variety.

14 ounces miniature marshmallows

4 ounces milk chocolate

1 ½ cups heavy cream

1 tablespoon granulated sugar

1 teaspoon vanilla extract

Small batch Graham Cracker Cookie Crust (page 248), baked and cooled

1 cup Hot Fudge (page 259)

¼ cup graham cracker crumbs

1. Combine half the marshmallows, the chocolate, and ½ cup heavy cream in the top of a double boiler set over simmering water and stir until the marshmallows and chocolate are melted. Remove from heat and let cool.

2. Combine the remaining 1 cup cream, sugar, and vanilla in a medium mixing bowl. Beat with an electric mixer on medium speed until thick. Fold into the marshmallow mixture along with half the remaining marshmallows. Spread the mixture into the crust and smooth the top with a spatula. Cover and freeze for 2 hours.

3. Spread ¾ cup of the hot fudge over the pie; cover and freeze for an additional 2 hours.

4. Remove from freezer and top with reserved fudge, the remaining marshmallows, and graham cracker crumbs. Let sit for 5–10 minutes to soften before serving.

Variation

PEPPERMINT MARSHMALLOW PIE: Make the pie in a small batch of Coconut Graham Cracker Cookie Crust (page 249). Replace the vanilla with ½ teaspoon peppermint extract. Top with 2 tablespoons crushed peppermint candies and ¼ cup sweetened flaked coconut.

COCKTAIL-PARTY PIES

In my opinion, traditional cocktail party foods—snacky mini bites that can be eaten as guests drink and mingle—are really just pies in various states of dress or undress! In previous sections, I've introduced several recipes that would be appropriate for cocktail parties—including Pie Pops (page 99), Chicken Empanadas (page 156), and Quiches with Herb Wheat Germ Crusts (page 127). But what makes the pies in this section especially suited for cocktail parties is that the recipes themselves include alcohol: each indulgently spirited pie is flavored with a little kick to pique your guests' taste buds.

Rum Raisin Pudding with Piecrust Chips

Makes six 4-inch double-crust pies and 36 piecrust chips

I'm a big fan of dessert parties—much more so than traditional cocktail parties, because I spend so much time mixing drinks that it's hard to enjoy my guests. But when I host a dessert party I booze up the recipes, and I prepare them in advance so I can enjoy the party, too. This recipe is a takeoff on chips and dip—serve the pudding in a piecrust "bowl" with additional piecrust "chips" for dipping. Fun party fare all around.

1. To make the pudding, soak 1 cup raisins in the rum for 30 minutes to soften.

2. Combine the eggs, sugar, and cinnamon in a large mixing bowl. Beat with an electric mixer on medium speed until blended. Add the cornstarch and whisk until smooth. Add the hot milk and stir until smooth.

3. Pour the mixture into a saucepan and cook over medium heat, stirring constantly, for 2–3 minutes, or until mixture thickens. Return mixture to the bowl. Beat in the butter until melted. Stir in the soaked raisins and their liquid. Let cool slightly, then cover with plastic wrap, making sure that the plastic touches the surface. Chill for 2 hours.

4. Preheat the oven to 450°F. Butter and flour six 4-inch pie pans and line a baking sheet with parchment paper. Roll out

Rum Raisin Pudding

1 cup plus 2 tablespoons golden raisins

⅓ cup golden rum

8 large eggs

½ cup granulated sugar

½ teaspoon ground cinnamon

3 tablespoons cornstarch

3 cups hot whole milk

¼ cup unsalted butter, at room temperature

Crust

Large batch (two disks, one slightly larger than the other) Basic Butter Crust (page 242)

¼ cup unsalted butter, at room temperature

2 tablespoons Cinnamon Sugar (page 258)

the larger disk of dough into a rectangle that is 12 inches long, 18 inches wide, and ¼ inch thick. Cut out six 6-inch circles. Drape the circles over the pie pans, allowing excess to hang over the rim. Trim the excess and press flush with the top of the pie pan. Line with parchment paper and fill with pie weights. Blind-bake for 10 minutes, then reduce the heat to 350°F and bake for an additional 10–15 minutes, or until golden. Cool on a rack, but leave the oven on.

5. To make the chips, roll out the second disk of dough into a rectangle that is 5 inches long, 18 inches wide, and ⅛ inch thick. Brush with half the softened butter, then sprinkle with half the cinnamon sugar. Using a cookie cutter, cut dough into 2–2½-inch triangles or circles. Place the shapes on the baking sheet. Bake for 10–12 minutes, then turn the shapes over, brush with the remaining butter, and sprinkle with half the remaining cinnamon sugar. Bake for an additional 3–5 minutes, or until just browned. Cool on a rack.

6. Once cooled, remove the pie bowls from the pans. Spoon the pudding into the bowls and top with 2 tablespoons raisins and the remaining cinnamon sugar. Serve with piecrust chips on the side.

Piña Colada Cream Pies

Makes eight 3-inch single-crust pies

Pineapple custard fills these creamy, dreamy, over-the-top cocktail pies. Accent the custard with a fruit garnish, as you would for a piña colada cocktail.

1. To make the filling, heat the milk in a heavy saucepan until just below the boiling point. Remove the skin that forms on the surface of the milk. Transfer to a double boiler set over simmering water. Add the sugar, egg yolks, cornstarch, and salt. Cook, stirring, for about 10 minutes, until the mixture thickens and heavily coats the back of a wooden spoon. Remove from the heat and stir in the butter until melted.

Pineapple Custard Filling

1 ¼ cups whole milk

⅓ cup granulated sugar

2 large egg yolks

2 tablespoons cornstarch

Pinch salt

1 ½ tablespoons unsalted butter

3 tablespoons golden rum

1 ¼ cups canned crushed
    pineapple, drained, or crushed
    fresh pineapple

Crust

Medium batch (two disks) Coconut Lemon Crust (page 243)

Topping

2 ½–3 cups Coconut Lemon
    Whipped Cream (page 261)

½ cup toasted desiccated coconut
    (see page 25)

8 maraschino cherries

2 fresh pineapple rings, cut into
    wedges

Add the rum and pineapple. Transfer to a bowl and cover
with plastic wrap, making sure the plastic touches the surface
of the custard. Chill for 2 hours.

2. Butter and flour eight 3-inch pie pans. Preheat the oven to
   425°F.

3. Roll out each disk of dough into a 10 x 10-inch square that
   is about ⅛ inch thick. Cut each square into four 4½-inch
   circles. Drape the circles over the pie pans, allowing excess
   to hang over the rim. Trim the excess and press flush with
   the top of the pie pan. Line with parchment paper and fill
   with pie weights. Blind-bake for 15 minutes, then reduce the
   heat to 350°F and bake for an additional 10–15 minutes, or
   until golden. Cool on a rack.

4. Spoon the pineapple filling into the shells, making a taller
   mound in the center than around the edges.

5. Spoon the coconut lemon cream into a pastry bag fitted
   with a star-shaped tip. Pipe mounds of cream on top of
   the pies, covering the filling and the crust. Spread the
   toasted coconut on a plate and roll the pies in the coconut,
   holding them at an angle so that only the lower half of the
   cream topping touches the coconut. Top with cherries and
   pineapple wedges.

Brandied Butterscotch Pie

In the spirit of after-dinner drinks, this creamy pie has a luscious sweetness that appeals to the child in all of us as well as a brandy flavor that's
all grown up. Booze it up even more by reducing the milk and adding
more brandy to taste.

1. To make the filling, melt the butter in a large skillet and
   continue to cook until it turns brown. Add the sugar and stir
   with a wooden spoon until bubbly. Add the water and stir
   until smooth. Remove from heat and set aside.

Butterscotch Filling

6 tablespoons unsalted butter

1 cup firmly packed dark brown
    sugar

1 cup boiling water

2 tablespoons all-purpose flour

3 tablespoons cornstarch

¼ teaspoon salt

1 ⅔ cups whole milk

3 large egg yolks

3 tablespoons brandy

Crust

Small batch (one disk) Butter-
    scotch Graham Cracker Cookie
    Crust (page 249), baked and
    cooled

Topping

2 cups Brandied Whipped Cream
    (page 261)

⅓ cup Candied Pecans
    (page 257)

2. Combine the flour, cornstarch, and salt in a medium saucepan. Set over medium heat and gradually add the milk, stirring until smooth. Add the brown butter mixture and continue to stir until the mixture comes to a boil. Let boil for 1 minute, then remove from heat.

3. In a medium bowl, combine 3 tablespoons of the hot milk mixture with the egg yolks, and whisk until smooth. Add the egg mixture to the saucepan with the milk mixture. Return to a simmer and cook until the mixture comes to a low boil. Reduce the heat and simmer for 1 minute, or until smooth and thickened. Remove from heat and stir in the brandy. Pour into the crust and smooth out the top. Cover with plastic wrap, making sure the plastic touches the filling, and chill for 3 hours.

4. To serve, spoon the whipped cream into a pastry bag fitted with a star-shaped tip. Pipe mounds of cream on top of the filling, then top with candied pecans.

Variation

PLAIN BUTTERSCOTCH PIE: Replace the brandy in the filling with 1½ teaspoons vanilla extract. Top with Whipped Cream (page 261), miniature marshmallows, and butterscotch chips.

Chapter 5

Holiday Pies

NEW YEAR'S PIES

Celebrate New Year's Eve with the savory Baked Brie, which goes well with Champagne, or the stay-up-late Mocha Pie. Then for brunch the next day, start the year off right with the Pine Nut Tart—pine nuts are a symbol of new beginnings, good fortune, and prosperity in many cultures, ranging from the Native American to the European.

Baked Brie in Short Crust Pastry

Makes one 6-inch single-crust pie

New Year's Eve is the ideal time to entertain, and Champagne paired with a sweet and savory baked Brie is especially festive. To deepen the flavor of this traditional short crust, I added corn flour and ground pine nuts. Traditionally, short crust has no leavening agent, but I added a little baking powder so the crust will puff a little. Top the pastry with three colors of grapes and toasted pine nuts, and serve with water crackers. Be careful not to overcook the grapes: remove them from the sauté pan as soon as a few just begin to pop. I prepared this recipe using a 5½-inch wheel of Brie and a 6-inch cake pan, but you can use any size wheel of Brie. Just make sure the pan is ½–1 inch larger than the cheese, and adjust the thickness of the crust and baking time accordingly. I leave the rind on the Brie, but if you don't like the taste you can cut it off with a knife before wrapping it in the pastry.

Short Crust

1 ¼ cups all-purpose flour

¾ cup corn flour

1 teaspoon baking powder

¼ cup ground pine nuts

10 tablespoons (1 ¼ sticks) cold
    unsalted butter, cut into cubes

1 large egg

2 large eggs, separated

¼ cup granulated sugar

Filling

5 ½-inch wheel of Brie, with rind
    on

2 ½ cups red, green, and black
    seedless grapes

¼ cup pine nuts, toasted

½ cup apple juice or white grape
    juice

1. To make the crust, combine both flours and the baking powder in a food processor. Pulse in the pine nuts and butter several times until the mixture resembles coarse meal.

2. Combine the egg, egg yolks, and sugar in a medium mixing bowl. Whisk with an electric mixer on medium speed until smooth. Add to the flour mixture and pulse until the mixture gathers into a ball. If the dough is too crumbly, add a bit of the egg whites; if it is too sticky, add a bit more flour.

3. Divide the dough into two flattened disks, one slightly larger than the other. Cover in plastic wrap and chill for 30 minutes.

4. Preheat the oven to 350°F. Line a cake pan that is 6 inches in diameter and 2 inches deep with parchment paper, leaving a 1-inch overhang around the edges.

5. Roll out the larger disk of dough on a floured surface into a circle about ¼ inch thick and 10 inches in diameter. Fit the dough into the pan so that it covers the bottom and drapes over the sides. Set the Brie into the crust. Cut half the grapes in half. Spread the cut grapes and half the pine nuts over the Brie.

6. Roll out the smaller disk of dough into a circle about ¼ inch thick and 6 ½ inches in diameter. Cut a 2-inch vent in the center with a cookie cutter. Brush egg white around the edges of the dough and place it over the grapes, pressing the crusts together to seal. Press lines into the top of the crust, circling inward, and brush the top with more egg white. Bake for 35–40 minutes, or until light golden. Cool in the pan on a rack for 10 minutes.

7. Sauté the remaining grapes and juice over low heat in a medium sauté pan for 5–7 minutes, or until the grapes brown a little and start to pop. Drain the excess juice.

8. Using the parchment paper, lift the baked Brie out of the pan and peel the paper off. Set the Brie on a serving platter and mound the sautéed grapes and remaining pine nuts in the center. Serve warm.

Small batch (one disk) Mocha
   Cream Cheese Crust (page 246)
¾ cup (1½ sticks) unsalted butter
4 ounces dark chocolate (at least
   60% cacao)
1 tablespoon vanilla extract
2 teaspoons instant coffee granules, dissolved in 2 tablespoons
   water
3 large eggs
1¾ cups granulated sugar
6 tablespoons all-purpose flour
¼ teaspoon salt
2 cups Whipped Cream
   (page 261)
¼ cup chocolate-covered espresso
   beans

Mocha Pie

Makes one 9-inch single-crust pie

Celebrate the night with this stay-awake-late pie, which provides two jolts of caffeine—one in the crust and another in the filling.

1. Preheat the oven to 350°F. Butter and flour a 9-inch pie pan.

2. To make the crust, roll the one pastry disk on a floured work surface into a circle about ⅛ inch thick and 12 inches in diameter. Drape the dough over the pie pan, allowing the excess to hang over the rim. Press the dough into the bottom edges, and trim the excess to a ¼-inch overhang. Fold the overhang over the rim and decoratively crimp the edge. Prick the bottom with a fork. Top the crust with parchment paper and fill with pie weights. Blind-bake for 10 minutes. Remove from the oven and cool on a rack.

3. To make the filling, melt the butter and chocolate in the top of a double boiler set over simmering water. Add the vanilla and coffee mixture and stir until smooth. Set aside.

4. Combine the eggs and sugar in a large mixing bowl. Beat with an electric mixer on medium speed until foamy. Beat in the flour and salt. Stir in the chocolate mixture until smooth. Pour into the cooled shell. Bake for 35–40 minutes, or until a knife inserted in the center comes out mostly clean but a little bit sticky. Cool on a rack.

5. To serve, top with whipped cream and chocolate-covered espresso beans.

Variation

HAZELNUT MOCHA PIE: Prepare the pie in a small batch of Nut Butter Crust, using hazelnuts (page 243). Add ½ cup ground hazelnuts to the filling after the chocolate. Top with whole hazelnuts.

Crust

Large batch (one disk) Sweet Tart
Crust (page 253)

Pine Nut Paste

¼ cup granulated sugar

¼ cup clover honey

¼ cup water

½ cup ground pine nuts

2 tablespoons unsalted butter,
melted

½ cup whole pine nuts

Confectioners' sugar for dusting

Mascarpone Filling

8 ounces mascarpone cheese

1 large egg

¼ cup granulated sugar

Pine Nut Tart

Makes one 11-inch tart

If you like the taste of bear claws and other sweets made with almond paste, you'll like this tart, which is made with pine nut paste. It has the same vibe as almond paste, as well as a highly intensified yumminess and a markedly different flavor. The mascarpone filling complements the pine nuts with its flavor and its texture.

1. Butter and flour an 11-inch tart pan. Press the dough into the pan, working it up the sides to create an edge flush with the rim of the pan. Prick the bottom of the crust with a fork. Line with parchment paper and fill with pie weights. Refrigerate for 1 hour.

2. To make the pine nut paste, combine the sugar, honey, and water in a small saucepan and stir over medium heat until the sugar has dissolved. Remove from heat. Transfer the ground pine nuts, sugar mixture, and butter to the food processor and pulse until the mixture forms a smooth paste. Add more honey if necessary. Work the whole pine nuts into the paste by kneading it on a work surface covered with confectioners' sugar. Set aside.

3. To make the filling, combine the mascarpone, eggs, and sugar in a medium mixing bowl. Beat with an electric mixer on medium speed until smooth. Cover with plastic wrap and chill until ready to use.

4. Preheat the oven to 375°F. Bake the crust for 10 minutes. Remove the parchment and pie weights. Spread the mascarpone mixture into the crust and top with the pine nut paste. Bake for an additional 15–20 minutes, or until golden.

5. Cool on a rack for 30 minutes. Remove from the pan and transfer to a rack to cool completely.

VALENTINE'S DAY PIES

On February 14, chocolate is the flavor of the day. It is also the main ingredient in these "lots of love" pies. Here, you will find heartfelt handheld delectables, from Chocolate Chili Hearts to tiny Truffle Pies, to give out as valentines to your sweeties. And for the fruit pie lover, the Fruit Rose Pies are super pretty and tasty, too.

Chocolate Chili Hearts

Makes six 3-inch tarts

Is your heart on fire this Valentine's Day? In these rich chocolate tarts, chili powder can be combined with dark chocolate to suit your level of heat tolerance. For most people, ¼ teaspoon is where the hot starts, so that's what I use in this recipe. You can use more or less. I baked these in silicone rather than metal heart-shaped pans so the crumb crust was easy to remove. And yes, you can eat the garnish—it all depends on how daring you are.

1. Butter and flour six 3-inch heart-shaped tart pans. Press the crust crumbs into the pans, working it up the sides to create an edge flush with the rims of the pans. Cover with plastic wrap and chill for 30 minutes.

2. To make the filling, heat the heavy cream in a small saucepan until it just comes to a boil. Remove from heat, then whisk the cream and melted chocolate together until glossy. Add the eggs, cinnamon, chili powder, and salt.

3. Preheat the oven to 325°F. Pour the filling into crusts. Bake for 15 minutes, or until the filling has puffed up but is still slightly jiggling in the center. Cool on a rack.

4. Spoon the whipped cream into a pastry bag fitted with a round tip. Pipe some cream on top of each heart. Garnish with chili peppers.

Crust

Small batch Chocolate Chili Wafer Crust (page 243), prepared through step 1

Chocolate Chili Filling

¾ cup heavy cream
6 ounces dark chocolate (at least 60% cacao), chopped and melted
1 large egg
¼ teaspoon ground cinnamon
¼ teaspoon chili powder
⅛ teaspoon salt

Topping

2 cups Cinnamon Whipped Cream (page 261)
6 whole dried red chili peppers

Fruit Rose Pies

5 sheets (14 x 18 inches each) country-style phyllo dough, thawed if frozen

¼ cup unsalted butter, melted

2 cups apple juice

¼ cup freshly squeezed lemon juice

1 unpeeled Granny Smith apple, cored and cut into paper-thin slices

1 unpeeled Golden Delicious apple, cored and cut into paper-thin slices

1 unpeeled Gala apple, cored and cut into paper-thin slices

1 ½ cups apple butter

2 kiwifruit, peeled and cut horizontally into paper-thin slices

2 mangoes, peeled and sliced into long paper-thin wedges

3 firm unpeeled plums, sliced into long paper-thin wedges

Makes six 3½-inch single-crust pies

Phyllo can be molded into many different shapes; here it forms shallow bowls that hold "roses" made from paper-thin slices of fresh fruit. The creamy white apples, orange mangoes, red-purple plums, and the green kiwifruit "leaves" make quite a colorful arrangement. Leave the skins on the apples to highlight their different colors as well. The apples need to be cooked and softened to be malleable, but firm yet soft mangoes, plums, and kiwifruit are easy to shape without cooking.

1. Preheat the oven to 350°F. Butter six medium muffin cups. Using kitchen shears, cut each phyllo sheet into six 6-inch squares. Set one square of phyllo in each of the muffin cups, pressing against the bottom and sides. Brush with some of the melted butter. Repeat with the remaining sheets, brushing each layer with melted butter and positioning each successive sheet so it is slightly offset from the sheet underneath it. Bake for 8–10 minutes, or until golden. Cool on a rack.

2. Combine the apple juice, 2 tablespoons of the lemon juice, and the sliced apples in a skillet over low heat. Cook for 5–7 minutes, turning occasionally, until the apples have softened. Remove from the heat and let cool.

3. Carefully remove the phyllo crusts from the pan and place on serving plates. Divide the apple butter among the phyllo cups.

4. Using a leaf-shaped cookie cutter, or working freehand with a knife, cut the kiwifruit rounds into leaf shapes.

5. Form the apples into rosettes by curling a small slice into a circle, then wrapping additional slices around it; use three or four slices for each rosette. Place in the center of each crust. Form the plums and then the mangoes into rosettes using the same technique. Place around the apple rosettes. Fill each crust with alternating fruit rosettes.

Crust

*Medium batch (one disk) Basic
   Tart Crust (page 252)*

Chocolate Lavender Filling

1½ cups heavy cream

*1 tablespoon fresh lavender flowers
   or ½ teaspoon dried lavender
   flowers*

*12 ounces dark chocolate (at
   least 60% cacao), chopped and
   melted*

2 tablespoons light corn syrup

½ teaspoon grated orange zest

Topping

*2 teaspoons Dutch-process cocoa
   powder*

2 teaspoons confectioners' sugar

¼ cup fresh lavender flowers

Dark Chocolate Lavender Tart

Makes one 9-inch tart

If you like the aroma and color of lavender, you should taste it, too. It is one of the more modern dessert flavors, especially when combined with chocolate, as it is in this dark chocolate ganache filling. The hint of lavender is just enough to evoke springtime.

1. Butter and flour a 9-inch tart pan with a removable bottom. Roll out the dough on a floured surface into a circle about ¼ inch thick and 11 inches in diameter. Transfer the crust to the pan, pressing it firmly into the bottom and up the sides. The dough should rise slightly above the rim. Prick the bottom with a fork. Line with parchment paper, cover with plastic wrap, and freeze for 30 minutes, or until firm.

2. Preheat the oven to 350°F. Line the shell with parchment paper and fill with pie weights. Blind-bake the crust for 25–30 minutes. Remove the paper and pie weights and cool in pan on a rack.

3. To make the filling, heat the cream in a small saucepan over low heat until bubbles appear. Do not allow the cream to boil. Remove from the heat and add the lavender. Let sit, allowing the flavor to infuse, for 20 minutes. Strain the cream through a fine-mesh sieve and discard the lavender.

4. Mix the dark chocolate, corn syrup, and orange zest in a medium bowl until smooth. Stir in the lavender cream.

5. Pour the filling into the tart shell, cover with plastic wrap, and chill for 2 hours. When ready to serve, dust with cocoa powder and confectioners' sugar. Sprinkle with lavender flowers.

Variation

MILK CHOCOLATE MINT TART: Replace the lavender in the filling with 10 chopped fresh mint leaves and use milk chocolate instead of dark chocolate. Garnish with fresh mint.

Large batch (two disks) Chocolate
Cream Cheese Crust (page 245)
Small batch (one disk) Cream
Cheese Crust (page 245)
1 ⅓ cups Chocolate Ganache
(page 258)
3 tablespoons sweetened flaked
coconut
2 tablespoons chocolate-covered
almonds
3 tablespoons chopped almonds
1 large egg, beaten
½ cup Vanilla Icing (page 260)

Truffle Pies

Makes about 6 double-crust and 12 single-crust pies, each 1½–2 inches

These tiny pies are a real treat to give to loved ones on Valentine's Day. Filled with chocolate ganache, almonds, and coconut, they can also be prepared with other truffle-like fillings, such as fruit jam and buttercream (page 260). Wrap them individually in tins or cellophane bags, or, for that extra-special someone, offer them in a large heart-shaped box or on a heart-shaped plate.

1. Preheat the oven to 350°F. Butter and flour an assortment of eighteen round and square mini muffin tins and small square tart pans. Line a small baking sheet with parchment paper.

2. Roll out the one of the chocolate disks into a circle about ⅛ inch thick and 14 inches in diameter. Measure the bottoms and sides of the pans. Using cookie cutters or a knife, cut the crust into shapes that will form bottom crusts ½ inch larger than the measured dimensions of the pans. Drape the shapes over the pans, allowing the excess to hang over the rims. Press into the bottom edges of the pans with your fingers.

3. To make the single-crust pies, fold the edges inward and crimp decoratively. Cut slash marks in the edges with a knife, if desired. Spoon in some of the ganache. Sprinkle a bit of coconut on some of the pies, some chopped almonds on others, and leave some plain.

4. To make the double-crust pies, spoon the remaining ganache into the remaining shells. Roll out the second disk of chocolate dough into a circle that is about ⅛ inch thick and 14 inches in diameter. Cut out top crusts that are ¼ inch larger than the top dimensions of the pans. Brush some of the beaten egg on the edges of the bottom crusts, then set the top crusts over the fillings, pressing the edges together to seal and crimping to form a decorative edge.

5. Roll out the plain disk into a circle about ⅛ inch thick and 14 inches in diameter. Cut out hearts and flowers from each circle in assorted sizes, from ½ inch to 1¾ inches. Brush

some of the beaten egg on the backs of some of the shapes and attach them to the tops of the double-crust pies.

6. Place the remaining hearts and flowers on the baking sheet and bake for 5–7 minutes, or until golden and dry. Cool on a rack.

7. Bake smaller pies for 12 minutes and larger pies for 15 minutes. Cool on a rack.

8. Remove pies from pans. Sprinkle the remaining shredded coconut and chopped almonds over the single-crust pies. Spoon the icing into a pastry bag fitted with a small round tip. Using the icing as a glue, attach chocolate-covered almonds, hearts, and flowers to the tops of the double-crust pies. Then decorate with small icing dots, x's, and o's.

Chocolate Almond Tart

Makes one 9-inch tart

This chocolate almond tart has the rich gooeyness of a pecan pie. It's luscious enough for special occasions but simple enough to make when you're short on time. It also tastes wonderful if you substitute pecans or walnuts for the almonds.

1. Preheat the oven to 350°F. Butter and flour a 9-inch tart pan.

2. Roll out the disk of dough on a floured work surface into a circle about ⅛ inch thick and 12 inches in diameter. Drape the dough over the pan, allowing the excess to hang over the rim. Press the dough into the bottom edges and up the sides, forming a thick edge that is flush with the top of the pan. Prick the bottom with a fork. Top the crust with parchment paper and fill with pie weights. Blind-bake for 7–10 minutes to set. Remove the paper and the weights and sprinkle the chopped almonds over the crust.

3. Combine the eggs, honey, and sugar in a medium mixing bowl. Beat with an electric mixer on medium speed until

---

Small batch (one disk) Chocolate Almond Butter Crust (page 242)

1 cup chopped almonds

3 large eggs

1 cup clover honey

½ cup granulated sugar

½ teaspoon salt

¼ cup unsalted butter, melted

2 ounces dark chocolate (at least 60% cacao), melted

2 teaspoons vanilla extract

¾ cup whole almonds

combined. Add the salt, butter, chocolate, and vanilla and blend well. Pour the filling into the crust. Arrange the whole almonds on top in a decorative pattern. Bake for an additional 20–25 minutes, or until crust is deep brown and the filling has puffed. Cool on a rack for 30 minutes and serve warm.

German Chocolate Pie

Makes one 8½-inch single-crust pie

No matter how you slice it, in a cake or a pie, sweet chocolate with pecans and coconut is one of the tastiest flavor combinations ever created. This pie has a brownie-like fudge filling, a crust flavored with pecans and coconut, and a gooey topping held together with coconut milk. If you don't have the square springform pan called for in the recipe, you can use an 8-inch round springform pan.

German Chocolate Pecan Crust

1 ¼ cups all-purpose flour

¼ cup sweetened flaked coconut

¼ cup ground pecans

2 tablespoons granulated sugar

¼ teaspoon salt

½ cup (1 stick) cold unsalted butter, cut into cubes

1 ounce German sweet chocolate, melted and cooled

3–4 tablespoons cold water

1. To make the crust, combine the flour, coconut, pecans, sugar, and salt in a medium mixing bowl. Cut in the butter with a pastry blender or your fingertips until the mixture resembles coarse meal. Stir in the chocolate until blended. Gradually add the cold water until the dough holds together. Form into a ball, flatten slightly, and wrap in plastic wrap. Chill for 30 minutes.

2. Preheat the oven to 350°F. Butter and flour an 8½ x 8½-inch shallow square springform pan. Roll out the disk of dough on a floured work surface into a 12-inch square that is about ⅛ inch thick. Drape the dough over the pan and press it into the bottom and up the sides. Cover with plastic wrap and chill in the refrigerator.

3. To make the filling, melt the butter and chocolate in a small saucepan over low heat. Remove from heat and let cool. Combine the egg, sugar, flour, and salt in a medium mixing bowl. Beat with an electric mixer on medium speed until blended. Beat in the chocolate mixture and vanilla. Fold in the pecans. Pour into the crust.

Fudge Filling

¾ cup (1 ½ sticks) unsalted butter

3 ounces German sweet chocolate

1 large egg

1 ½ cups granulated sugar

6 tablespoons all-purpose flour

¼ teaspoon salt

1 tablespoon vanilla extract

½ cup chopped pecans

Coconut Pecan Topping

¼ cup full-fat coconut milk

1 large egg yolk

1 ounce German sweet chocolate, chopped

1 teaspoon vanilla extract

¼ cup granulated sugar

¼ cup unsalted butter

¼ cup fresh or packaged unsweetened shredded coconut

¼ cup chopped pecans

4. Bake for 35–45 minutes, or until a knife inserted in the center comes out clean. Cool on a rack.

5. To make the topping, heat the coconut milk, egg yolk, chocolate, and vanilla in a large saucepan, stirring until blended. Add the sugar and butter and cook, stirring, for 10–12 minutes, or until thickened. Remove from heat. Stir in the coconut and pecans and mix well. Let cool, then spread on top of pie to serve.

EASTER PIES

There are so many egg- and bunny-shaped sweets filling Easter baskets that I decided to move past them and focus on other cultural traditions for the Easter pies in this section. For example, the delicate phyllo-based Pistachio Nests are a symbol of new beginnings and spring for some Armenians (I live in Glendale, California, home to one of the largest Armenian communities outside of Armenia; here, these delicate pastries are available every year come springtime). The Ricotta Pie reflects my Italian heritage and my family's own Easter tradition. For the many families who enjoy their Easter meal after church, the fruit-laden Chicken Hand Pies are a delicious savory choice for an afternoon brunch.

Ricotta Pie

Makes one 9-inch double-crust pie

It isn't Easter in an Italian household without a sweet ricotta pie. Every family has its heirloom recipe—this one is mine. The filling is very simple, with just a few raisins for sweetness and a bit of lemon and orange zest for zing, and the crust is particularly flaky. Leave the top plain or, using a stencil, sprinkle confectioners' sugar on the top in the shape of a cross. The pie can be served plain or dressed up with Raspberry Sauce (page 105). For a more cannoli-like filling, use the Ricotta Filling on page 83.

3½ cups ricotta cheese

½ cup confectioners' sugar sifted

2 large eggs, beaten

2 large egg yolks, beaten

½ teaspoon grated lemon zest

½ teaspoon grated orange zest

2 tablespoons golden raisins, plumped in 2 tablespoons boiling water

Large batch (two disks, one slightly larger than the other) Flaky Crust (page 247)

1 large egg, beaten

1. Preheat the oven to 400°F. Butter and flour a 9-inch pie pan.

2. To make the filling, combine the ricotta, sugar, eggs, and yolks in a large mixing bowl. Beat with an electric mixer on medium speed. Stir in the lemon and orange zests and raisins.

3. Roll out the larger disk of dough on a floured work surface into a circle about ⅛ inch thick and 12 inches in diameter. Drape over the pie pan, pressing into the bottom edges and allowing the excess to hang over the rim. Prick the bottom with a fork. Pour the filling into the crust, pressing the mixture down to eliminate air pockets.

4. Roll out the second disk of dough into a circle about ⅛ inch thick and 10 inches in diameter. Using a knife or a cookie cutter, cut a large vent into the center of the crust. Brush the edges of the bottom crust with beaten egg and place the top crust over the filling. Press the edges firmly together to seal. Brush the remaining beaten egg over the top crust.

5. Bake for 10 minutes, then reduce the temperature to 350°F and bake for an additional 40–50 minutes, or until brown. Cool on a rack. Serve at room temperature.

Crust

1 pound country-style phyllo
 dough (eight 18 x 14-inch
 sheets), thawed if frozen
½ cup (1 stick) unsalted butter,
 melted

Filling

1 cup chopped pistachio nuts

Honey Syrup

¼ cup honey
5 tablespoons water

Topping

¼ cup ground pistachio nuts

Pistachio Nests

Makes twelve 2½-inch single-crust pies

This recipe will make you a fan of the light and crispy texture of phyllo pastry. Pistachio nuts and honey syrup add sweetness to this classic flaky layered pie. Use either square or round pans to form the nests.

1. Preheat the oven to 350°F. Butter twelve 2½-inch muffin cups.

2. Divide the phyllo dough into two stacks of four sheets each. Using kitchen shears, cut the stacks in half lengthwise to make sixteen 9 x 14-inch sheets.

3. Cut each sheet into six 4½-inch squares. Lay one square in each muffin cup, pressing the dough against the bottom and sides of the pan. Brush with some of the butter and lay another sheet on top. Repeat with the remaining dough and butter to make twelve 8-layer nests. Sprinkle a heaping tablespoon of chopped pistachios in the center of each nest. Bake for 8–10 minutes, or until golden.

4. Combine the honey and water in a small saucepan and cook over medium heat, stirring, until the mixture is smooth. Remove from the heat and let cool a few minutes, until just warm, before using. Then spoon the honey syrup into the nests. Top with ground pistachios to serve.

Chicken Filling

Makes 4 cups

2 ½ cups chopped cooked chicken

2 tablespoons orange juice

¼ cup raisins

¼ cup chopped dried apricots

2 scallions, chopped

⅓ teaspoon celery salt

½ teaspoon freshly ground black pepper

½ cup heavy cream

3 tablespoons unsalted butter, melted

Crust

1 batch Yeast Empanada Dough (page 52)

2 large eggs, beaten

Chicken Hand Pies

Makes eight hand pies

These sweet-savory pocket pies combine dried fruits with meat and vegetables. Begin making the filling when the dough is almost finished rising. Partially cook the chicken until golden on the outside but still pink on the inside. It will finish cooking in the oven.

1. Combine the chicken, orange juice, raisins, apricots, scallions, celery salt, and pepper in a large bowl. Add the cream and butter; set aside.

2. Preheat the oven to 350°F. Line two baking sheets with parchment paper.

3. Knead the risen dough again for 30 seconds on a lightly floured surface. Divide the dough in half and roll out one batch at a time on a floured surface into a rectangle that is 12 inches long, 10 inches wide, and ⅛ inch thick. Cut each batch into four 5 x 5½-inch rectangles.

4. Brush some of the beaten egg around the edge of each rectangle. Spoon about ½ cup of filling down the center of each. Fold over the dough to create long rectangles (about 5 inches x 2¼ inches), overlapping the long sides by about ½ inch. Press the long sides together with your fingers and press the short sides together with a fork. Flip the rectangles over and place them on the baking sheets, seam side down. Brush with the remaining egg.

5. Bake for 20–25 minutes, or until golden. Cool for 7–10 minutes on a rack and serve warm.

PIES FOR JEWISH HOLIDAYS

There are many traditional foods associated with each Jewish holiday. Here, I've tried to reinterpret some of these traditions in pie form. For example, the tradition of enjoying sweet wine during Passover finds its way into my bite-size Concord Grape Pies. Instead of a *sufganiyah*, the traditional jelly doughnut of Hanukkah, try my fruit-filled Fried Fruit Pies. And the practice of dipping apples in honey, a tradition of Rosh Hashanah, is reflected in my Honey-Sweetened Apple Tart.

Fried Fruit Pies

Makes 24 hand pies

Fried foods are a traditional delicacy of Hanukkah, which celebrates the miracle of the oil. Fill these with your favorite combination of dried fruits, or try one of the combinations suggested on the following page.

1. To make the filling, combine the fruits and rinds in a saucepan and fill with water to just about cover the fruit. Bring to a boil, reduce heat, and let cook for 15–20 minutes, or until softened. Drain and transfer the rinds and fruits to a food processor. Pulse into a chunky paste. Mix in the sugar and cinnamon and set aside.

2. To make the dough, combine the flour, baking powder, and cinnamon in a large bowl. Add the shortening and eggs. Add the milk, a little at a time, until the dough comes together. Knead the dough on a floured work surface, adding a little more flour if sticky or a little milk if dry.

3. Divide the dough in half. Roll out each piece of dough into a rectangle that is 16 inches long, 12 inches wide, and ⅛ inch thick. Using cookie cutters or a knife, cut each rectangle into twelve circles and squares of about 4 inches each. Reroll any scraps, then cut out twelve 1½-inch stars.

4. To make the dipping sauce, combine the honey, water, and orange zest in a small saucepan and set over medium heat. Cook, stirring, until the mixture is smooth. Remove from

---

Filling

2 cups assorted dried fruits, chopped into small pieces if necessary

Rind of 1 lemon, roughly chopped

Rind of 1 orange, roughly chopped

¼ cup granulated sugar

1 teaspoon ground cinnamon

Crust

4 cups all-purpose flour

2 teaspoons baking powder

¼ teaspoon ground cinnamon

½ cup shortening, melted

2 large eggs

¾ cup whole milk

2 large eggs, beaten

Vegetable oil for frying

Honey Sauce

½ cup clover honey

¼ cup water

½ teaspoon grated orange zest

the heat and let cool a few minutes, until just warm, before serving.

5. Brush beaten eggs on the edges of the circles and squares. Spoon about 1 heaping teaspoon filling onto each pastry. Press the edges together with your fingers to seal. Brush more beaten eggs on top and press stars into the center.

6. Pour 2 inches of oil into a large deep pot and set over medium-high heat. Test the oil temperature with a piece of bread; if it browns, the oil is hot enough. Fry the pies, a few at a time, for about 2–2½ minutes on each side, or until golden brown. Drain on paper towels. Serve hot, with honey sauce for dipping.

DRIED-FRUIT FILLING COMBINATIONS FOR FRIED PIES

Apples, apricots, and cranberries
Apricots, cranberries, and golden raisins
Cherries and nectarines
Mission figs, dates, and currants
Peaches and candied ginger
Pineapples, mangoes, and papayas
Strawberries, blueberries, and pears

Honey-Sweetened Apple Tart

Makes one 9-inch lattice-top tart

One of the ways of celebrating Rosh Hashanah, the Jewish New Year, is to dip apples in honey as a symbol of hope for a sweet year ahead. Inspired by that tradition, these honey-sweetened tarts are so versatile that they can be eaten for brunch, an afternoon snack, or an after-dinner dessert throughout the holiday season.

1. Preheat the oven to 450°F. To make the filling, combine the apples and lemon juice in a large heavy saucepan. Stir in the cinnamon, nutmeg, cloves, and salt. Bring to a boil, lower

Filling

5 medium Braeburn or other good
   pie apples (see page 43), peeled,
   cored, and sliced
Juice of ½ lemon
1½ teaspoons ground cinnamon
Pinch nutmeg
Pinch ground cloves
Pinch salt
1 tablespoon cornstarch
3 tablespoons apple juice or water
⅓ cup gently warmed honey
3 tablespoons cold unsalted butter,
   cut into cubes

Crust

Medium batch (two disks, once
   slightly larger than the other)
   Sweet Tart Crust (page 253),
   chilled for only 30 minutes
1 large egg, beaten with 2
   tablespoons heavy cream

the heat to medium, and cook for 5–7 minutes, or until the
apples are tender.

2. Combine the cornstarch and apple juice in a small bowl and
   stir until dissolved. Add to the apple mixture and continue to
   stir over medium-low heat for 5 minutes, or until the syrup is
   translucent and thickened. Remove from heat and stir in the
   honey. Let cool.

3. Preheat the oven to 425°F. To make the bottom crust, roll out the larger disk on a floured work surface, forming a circle about ⅛ inch thick and 12 inches in diameter. Drape the dough over the pan, pressing it flush with the rim. Brush the edge with some of the egg mixture. Prick the bottom with a fork. Spoon the apple mixture into the crust. Top with butter cubes.

4. To make the top crust, roll out the smaller disk into a circle about ⅛ inch thick and 10 inches in diameter. Using a pastry wheel or a knife, cut the dough into 10 strips, each about 1 inch wide. Lay half the strips over the filling, leaving space in between. Lay the other half of the strips on top of them, on the diagonal. Press the ends of the strips into the edge of the bottom crust. Fold the overhang over the rim to conceal the edges of the lattice. Seal by pressing together the top and bottom crusts with a fork. Brush the exposed crust with the remaining egg wash.

5. Bake for 15 minutes. Reduce the temperature to 375°F and bake for an additional 30–40 minutes, or until crust is golden and the juices are shiny and bubbly. Cool completely on a rack before removing from the tart pan.

Concord Grape Pies

Makes eighteen 2-inch single-crust pies

The hearty New England Concord grape, used to make the sweet Passover wine Manischewitz, will also be very happy in these bite-size pies at your next seder. If you can't find Concord grapes, use any purple sweet grapes and add up to ¼ cup of additional sugar, if necessary, to intensify the sweetness of the fruit.

Sometimes, grapes are peeled before they go into a pie filling, but I like to leave the skins on. It saves so much work, and the extra fiber gives the pie a more earthy taste. The texture of the purée will still be pretty smooth.

1. Preheat the oven to 350°F. Butter and flour eighteen 2-inch muffin cups or 2-inch tart pans.

Grape Filling

1½ pounds Concord grapes,
  washed, cut in half, and seeded
  (about 3 ½ cups)
½ cup granulated sugar
2 tablespoons instant tapioca

Crust

Large batch (one disk) Basic
  Butter Crust (page 242)

Topping

2 cups Meringue Topping (page
  260)

2. To make the filling, combine the grapes and ¼ cup sugar in a saucepan and bring to a boil. Reduce the heat to medium and cook for 6–7 minutes, or until the juices are released.

3. Transfer the grape mixture to a food processor and purée until smooth. Return to the saucepan. Add the tapioca and remaining sugar and cook, stirring, for 5–6 minutes, or until the mixture has thickened. Remove from heat and let cool.

4. Roll out the dough on a floured surface into a circle about ⅛ inch thick and 18 inches in diameter. Measure the bottoms and sides of the pans. Using cookie cutters or a knife, cut the crust into shapes that will form crusts ¼ inch larger than the measured dimensions of the pans. Drape the shapes over the pans, pressing the dough into the bottom and up the sides with your fingers. Prick the bottoms of the crusts with a fork.

5. Spoon the cooled filling into the crusts and bake for 15–20 minutes, or until crusts are golden and juices are bubbling. Cool on a rack.

6. Spoon the meringue topping into a pastry bag fitted with a large round tip. To toast the meringue with a kitchen torch, remove the cooled pies from the pans. Pipe mounds of meringue on top. Then hold a kitchen torch around 4 inches from the meringue and rotate pies one at a time to toast. To toast in the oven, leave the pies in the pans. Place the oven rack about 4 inches from the heat source and preheat the broiler. Pipe mounds of meringue on top of the pies. Place the pans on a baking sheet and broil for 2–3 minutes, watching carefully, until the meringue browns. Cool on a rack. Then remove from pans.

FOURTH OF JULY PIES

Pie is the great American dessert—I wish there were enough pages in this book to include a pie from every state in the union. Instead, I've chosen a few pies that capture the ingredients, traditions, and flavors of each region. Make your Fourth of July picnic or barbecue unique this year by picking a few to try out.

American Slab Pie with Star Pie Pops

Makes one 8 x 12-inch slab pie plus twenty-four 2½-inch pie pops

I am a big fan of free-form pies, and this slab pie—really a big tart—is one of my favorites. I have also used this versatile technique (and my extensive cookie cutter collection) to make a Valentine's Day slab pie with a chocolate cream cheese crust, chocolate ganache, and heart-shaped pie pops, as well as a Christmas slab pie with a gingerbread crust, cranberry filling, and gingerbread-man pie pops. Here, cut out festive Fourth of July stars from the top crust so that you can see the filling's juices flow, and serve with these magic wand–inspired star-shaped pie pops. Cream cheese dough is easy to work with but isn't as tender as the Basic Butter Crust (page 242), which you can use if you prefer.

Large batch (four disks) Cream Cheese Crust (page 245)

2 large eggs, beaten with 3 tablespoons whole milk

2½ cups Raspberry Filling (page 53)

2½ cups Blueberry Filling (page 202)

24 popsicle sticks

1. Preheat the oven to 425°F. Line two baking sheets with parchment paper.

2. To make the bottom crust, roll out one disk of dough on a floured surface into a rectangle that is 15 inches long, 11 inches wide, and ⅛ inch thick. Trim the edges with a pastry wheel or knife to make them straight and clean. Cut 1½-inch slits all the way through the dough on a 45-degree angle in each corner. Transfer the dough to a baking sheet and brush egg mixture around the edges.

3. Spoon ½ cup blueberry filling lengthwise down the center of the pastry, stopping about 2 inches from the short ends. Spoon two rows of raspberry filling (about ½ cup each) on either side of the blueberry filling, leaving a border of about 2 inches on all sides.

4. To make the top crust of the slab, remove a 3-inch ball of dough from another pastry disk and set aside. Roll out this disk into a rectangle about 12 inches long, 8 inches wide, and ⅛ inch thick. Using a cookie cutter, cut out thirteen 1-inch stars in 3 rows, as shown in the photo. Cut 1-inch slits on 45-degree angles in each corner. Add the dough scraps to the 3-inch ball.

5. Carefully place the top crust over the filling. Fold over the ends, overlapping the 45-degree angles, and press together to seal. Using your finger, press diagonal indentations in the edges to form a decorative border.

6. Roll out the ball and scraps into a circle about ⅛ inch thick and 12 inches in diameter on a floured surface. Cut out thirteen 2¼-inch stars with a knife or cookie cutters. Cut out ¾-inch stars in the center of each. Brush the back of each star with egg mixture and place them over the 1-inch star cutouts on the top crust. Brush egg mixture over the entire top crust. Bake for 10 minutes, then reduce the temperature to 350°F and bake for an additional 20–25 minutes, or until the top is golden and juices are bubbling. Cool on the baking sheet on a rack.

7. To make the pie pops, roll out each of the two remaining disks on a floured surface into a circle about ⅛ inch thick and 15 inches in diameter. Cut out forty-eight 2½-inch stars. Brush the edges with egg mixture. Press a popsicle stick into each of twenty-four stars, slightly above the center. Spoon about 1 teaspoon of filling into the center of each, then cover with the remaining stars and press the edges to seal. Using a bamboo skewer, poke holes large enough for venting at the points of each star. Transfer the pops to the second baking sheet. Brush remaining egg mixture over the tops. Cover the sticks loosely with parchment. Bake for 12–15 minutes, or until golden. Slide the parchment onto a rack and cool the pops.

Crust

Small batch Basic Butter Crust
  (page 242)
1 egg white, lightly beaten

Buttermilk Pie Filling

3 large eggs
¾ cup granulated sugar
¼ cup all-purpose flour
2 cups buttermilk
5 tablespoons unsalted butter,
  melted
2 teaspoons vanilla extract
1 teaspoon grated orange zest
⅛ teaspoon salt
1½ tablespoons confectioners'
  sugar

Peach Sauce

¾ cup water
¼ cup granulated sugar
2½ tablespoons cornstarch
½ teaspoon ground ginger
3 large fresh peaches, peeled, sliced,
  and cubed (about 2 cups)

Buttermilk Pie with Peach Sauce

Makes one 9-inch single-crust pie

Buttermilk is right up there with pecan, sweet potato, and Key lime as favorite flavors in the canon of Southern hospitality pies. If you aren't familiar with buttermilk pie, you can think of its sugary top and creamy custard as resembling a large crème brûlée. Serve it on its own or with peach sauce on the side.

1. Preheat the oven to 425°F. Butter and flour a 9-inch pie pan.

2. Roll out the pastry disk on a floured surface into a circle about ⅛ inch thick and 12 inches in diameter. Drape the dough over the pie pan, allowing the excess to hang over the rim. Press the dough into the bottom edges, and trim the excess to a ¼-inch overhang. Fold the overhang over the rim and decoratively crimp the edge. Prick the bottom with a fork. Top the crust with parchment paper and fill with pie weights. Blind-bake for 15 minutes, or until the crust is partially baked. Remove the paper and weights and brush the crust with egg white.

3. To make the filling, combine the eggs and sugar in a large mixing bowl. Beat with an electric mixer on medium speed until light. Add the flour, buttermilk, butter, vanilla, orange zest, and salt, and beat until blended. Pour the filling into the crust.

4. Set the pan into the water bath and bake for 10 minutes, then reduce the temperature to 325°F and bake for an additional 35–40 minutes, or until the filling is puffy in the center. Do not worry if the filling cracks or shrinks a bit. Remove water bath and pie from oven and cool on a rack for 2 hours. When ready to serve, sprinkle the top with confectioners' sugar, then slice and put on serving plates.

5. To make the sauce, bring the water, sugar, cornstarch, and ginger to a boil in a medium saucepan. Add the peaches and boil for 2 minutes. Cool slightly, then spoon some of the sauce over or alongside each slice on the plate.

Variations

BLACKBERRY BUTTERMILK PIE: Omit the peach sauce. Cut 1 cup fresh blackberries in half and fold into the custard before pouring into the crust. Top with 1 cup whole fresh blackberries.

BOOZY BUTTERMILK PIE: Omit the peach sauce. Replace the vanilla with 2 tablespoons Grand Marnier (top with orange segments) or amaretto (top with slivered almonds).

Key Lime Pies

Makes six 4-inch single-crust pies

Key limes, from the Florida Keys, give these pies a tangy bite. The crust is made with a shortbread cookie dough, so it won't brown much—a characteristic of shortbread. Line the pans with parchment paper to make it easy to lift the baked pies from the pans.

Key Lime Filling

½ cup (1 stick) unsalted butter
⅔ cup granulated sugar
4 large eggs
1 cup Key lime juice, preferably freshly squeezed

Crust

Medium batch (one disk) Short-bread Cookie Crust (page 252)

Topping

2 Key limes, cut into wedges
2 mangoes, cut into wedges

1. To make the filling, melt the butter over low heat in a saucepan. Add the sugar, eggs, and lime juice and cook, stirring constantly, until thickened. Allow to cool, then transfer to a bowl, cover with plastic wrap touching the surface, and refrigerate for 3 hours. The filling will continue to thicken while cooling.

2. Preheat the oven to 350°F. Line six 4-inch square tart pans with parchment paper, leaving a 1-inch overhang on each side.

3. Roll out the dough on a floured surface into a rectangle about 18 inches long, 12 inches wide, and ⅛ inch thick. Cut the rectangle into six 6-inch squares.

4. Drape the squares over the pans, trimming the excess to make the edges flush with the top rims of the pans. Prick holes in the bottom of the crusts with a fork. Line with parchment paper and fill with pie weights. Bake for 10–15 minutes, or until firm. Cool on a rack.

5. Remove the crusts from the pans and place on serving plates. Divide the filling equally among the crusts. Top with mango slices and lime wedges.

Variations

PAPAYA KEY LIME PIES: Distribute 1 cup cubed fresh papaya among the shells, then top with the lime filling. Top with ½ cup cubed fresh papaya.

MANGO KEY LIME PIES: Peel and chop 2 mangoes. Purée in a blender, then add to the filling before chilling.

Shoofly Pie

Makes one 9-inch single-crust pie

A Pennsylvania Dutch tradition, shoofly pie is as American as it gets. Made with molasses and pantry staples, it is a good pie to whip up when you only have a few ingredients on hand and feel like baking something homey and sweet. All the crumbs can be put on top of the pie, or mix some in with the filling to add depth and texture.

1. Preheat the oven to 425°F. Butter and flour a 9-inch pie pan.

2. Roll out the dough on a floured surface into a circle about ⅛ inch thick and 12 inches in diameter. Drape the dough over the pie pan, allowing the excess to hang over the rim. Press the dough into the bottom edges, and trim the excess to a ¼-inch overhang. Fold the overhang over the rim and decoratively crimp the edge. Prick the bottom with a fork. Top the crust with parchment paper and fill with pie weights. Blind-bake for 10 minutes, or until the crust is partially baked. Remove the paper and weights and bake for an additional 5–7 minutes, or until golden. Remove from the oven and cool on a rack.

3. Reduce the temperature to 350°F. To make the topping, combine the flour, brown sugar, and cinnamon in a food processor and pulse a few times to blend. Add the butter and pulse few times until it forms crumbs.

4. To make the filling, place the baking soda in a large heatproof mixing bowl and pour boiling water over it. Add the egg, molasses, and vanilla, stirring to combine. Add ⅓ cup of the crumb mixture to the filling. Pour the filling into the crust.

5. Sprinkle the remaining crumbs evenly over the filling. Bake

Crust

Small batch (one disk) Spiced Crust (page 243)

Crumble Topping

¾ cup all-purpose flour

½ cup firmly packed dark brown sugar

½ teaspoon ground cinnamon

¼ teaspoon salt

3 tablespoons cold unsalted butter

Filling

1 teaspoon baking soda

¾ cup boiling water

1 large egg, beaten

1 cup unsulfured molasses

1 teaspoon vanilla extract

for 35–45 minutes, or until the filling puffs. Cool completely on a rack before serving.

Sour Cherry Pie
Makes one 9-inch double-crust pie

Which pie is more American, cherry or apple? I think it depends on where you are from. Northeasterners and Westerners would say apple, but I would guess that Midwesterners would say cherry. Some love the home-baked goodness of a sweet cherry pie (see page 46 for my version), but sour cherries have this fantastic zing that you don't get from sweet cherries. The secret ingredients in this pie—which is still plenty sweet—are almond extract and cider vinegar. The flavors are not obvious, but they'll keep you guessing. Fresh sour cherries have a short season; to enjoy this pie year-round, use 4 cups frozen sour cherries; partially thaw them before proceeding with the recipe.

4 cups fresh sour cherries, such as Montmorency or Morello, washed, stemmed, and pitted
1 cup granulated sugar
3 tablespoons instant tapioca
½ teaspoon almond extract
½ teaspoon vanilla extract
½ teaspoon cider vinegar
Large batch (two disks) Flaky Crust (page 247)
1 large egg, beaten
1 tablespoon cold unsalted butter, cut into cubes

1. Preheat the oven to 400°F. Butter and flour a 9-inch pie pan.

2. Combine the cherries, sugar, tapioca, almond and vanilla extracts, and vinegar in a large bowl.

3. Roll out one disk of dough on a floured surface into a circle about ⅛ inch thick and 13 inches in diameter. Drape over the pie pan, press the crust into the bottom edges, and allow the excess dough to hang over the rim. Brush the edge with beaten egg. Spoon the filling into the bottom crust, pressing the mixture down to eliminate the air pockets. Top with butter cubes.

4. Roll out the second disk of dough into a circle about ⅛ inch thick and 11 inches in diameter. Cut vents in the center with a knife or cookie cutter. Place the crust over the filling. Press the edges of the crusts firmly together to seal, then fold toward the center to make a thick edge. Brush the remaining egg over the entire top crust.

5. Bake for 10 minutes, then reduce the temperature to 350°F and bake for an additional 40 minutes, or until the filling is bubbling. Cover the entire crust with aluminum foil if the crust begins to brown too much. Cool on a rack until warm.

Crust

Small batch Chocolate Wafer
Crust (page 243), prepared in a
9-inch pie pan

Filling

12 ounces plus ½ cup semisweet
chocolate chips
2 cups heavy cream
½ cup chopped pecans
½ cup chopped walnuts
¾ cup crushed chocolate wafer
cookies
2 cups Marshmallow Meringue
(page 259)

Chocolate Icing

3 ounces semisweet chocolate
1 tablespoon unsalted butter
¼ cup hot water
1 cup confectioners' sugar

Crunchy Mississippi Mud Pie

Makes one 9-inch single-crust pie

There are as many recipes for Mississippi mud pie as there are bends
in the great river itself. There is one constant, though: the messier the
pie, the better it is. Some people dig through their cabinets and toss
in everything but the kitchen sink. Try it for your next Fourth of July
picnic.

1. Preheat the oven to 325°F. Bake the crust for 8–10 minutes,
   or until it darkens. Cool in the pan for 10 minutes, then
   transfer to a rack to cool completely.

2. To make the filling, place 12 ounces of the chocolate
   chips into a large heatproof bowl. Heat the heavy cream
   in a small saucepan until it just comes to a boil. Pour over
   the chocolate and whisk together until smooth. Add half
   the pecans, half the walnuts, and ¼ cup of the remaining
   chocolate chips to the mixture. Pour the filling into the
   crust, cover with plastic wrap, and chill for 4–6 hours, or
   until hardened. Then remove from the refrigerator and top
   with half the crushed cookies.

3. Using a spatula, pile the marshmallow meringue into a
   large mound on the top of the pie. Preheat the broiler.
   Line a baking sheet with foil. Place the pie on the baking
   sheet and broil for 1–2 minutes, or until the meringue is
   lightly browned. Keep a close watch, as it can burn quickly.
   (Alternatively, you can toast the meringue with a kitchen
   torch.)

4. To make the icing, combine the chocolate, butter, and hot
   water in the top of a double boiler set over simmering water,
   stirring until melted and smooth. Stir in the confectioners'
   sugar until the icing reaches a pourable consistency. Let it
   cool for 5 minutes, then pour the icing over the meringue,
   allowing it to drip over the pie. Top with remaining pecans,
   walnuts, chocolate chips, and crushed wafer cookies.

2 Meyer lemons (with peel), seeded
   and cut into paper-thin slices
2 cups granulated sugar
4 large eggs
4 tablespoons unsalted butter,
   melted
3 tablespoons all-purpose flour
Large batch (two disks) Flaky
   Crust (page 247)
1 large egg, beaten with 1
   tablespoon whole milk

Shaker Lemon Pie

Makes one 9-inch double-crust pie

Renowned for their thrift of resources, sense of community, and simplicity of lifestyle, the Shakers were also known for their baked goods. Lemons were precious, and even the rind would be used to avoid waste. I have updated this traditional recipe, which usually uses ordinary lemons, with Meyer lemons, which have a sweeter, less acidic taste.

Slice the lemons as thin as you can to prevent the rind from becoming too chewy—if you have a mandolin, that's the ideal implement to use. Also, if you can, allow the lemons to sit in the sugar overnight. Stir them occasionally—that is, when you aren't sleeping!

1. Mix the lemons and sugar in a large, nonreactive bowl. Cover with plastic wrap and let sit at room temperature for at least 12 hours, stirring occasionally.

2. Preheat the oven to 450°F. Butter and flour a 9-inch pie pan.

3. Whisk the eggs in a medium mixing bowl until frothy. Whisk in the butter and flour until smooth. Add the lemon mixture.

4. Roll out one disk of dough on a floured surface into a circle about ⅛ inch thick and 12 inches in diameter. Drape over the pie pan, pressing the dough into the bottom edges and allowing the excess to hang over the rim. Brush the edge of the crust with some of the egg mixture. Prick the bottom of the crust with a fork. Spoon in the lemon filling.

5. Roll out the second disk into a circle about ⅛ inch thick and 12 inches in diameter. Cut vents in the dough with the tip of a straw or small cookie cutters. Lay the circle on top of the filling, folding the bottom crust over and pressing the edges together firmly. Seal by pressing with the tines of a fork. Brush the top crust with the remaining egg mixture.

6. Bake for 15 minutes, then reduce the temperature to 375°F and bake for an additional 20–25 minutes, or until the top is golden. Cool on a rack.

Blueberry Filling

1½ pounds fresh blueberries
  (about 5 cups)
¾ cup granulated sugar
¼ cup cornstarch
1 ½ tablespoons freshly squeezed
  lemon juice
½ teaspoon grated lemon zest
½ teaspoon ground cinnamon
¼ teaspoon ground nutmeg
2 tablespoons cold unsalted butter,
  cut into cubes

Crust

Large batch (two disks, one
  slightly larger than the other)
  Flaky Crust (page 247)
1 large egg, beaten with 2 tablespoons whole milk
¼ cup heavy cream

Blueberry Pies

Makes four 4½-inch double-crust pies

These pies are casual and easy enough to make so that you don't have to wait for a special occasion to serve them—unless, of course, the occasion is the arrival of blueberry season, which happens to be in full force on the Fourth of July.

1. Preheat the oven to 425°F. Butter and flour four 4½-inch pie pans.

2. To make the filling, combine 2½ cups blueberries, sugar, cornstarch, and lemon juice in a saucepan set over medium heat. Cook, stirring frequently, for 6–8 minutes, or until the mixture boils and thickens. Remove from heat and add the lemon zest, cinnamon, and nutmeg. Cool, then stir in the remaining blueberries.

3. Roll out the larger disk of dough on a floured surface into a 13 x 13-inch square that is about ⅛ inch thick. Cut the square into four 6½-inch circles. Drape the circles over the pans, pressing the dough into the bottom edges and allowing the excess to hang over the rims. Brush the egg mixture on the edges of the crust. Prick holes in the bottoms, then fill with filling. Top with butter cubes.

4. Roll out the second disk of dough into a 10 x 10-inch square that is about ⅛ inch thick. Cut out four 4½-inch circles. Punch venting holes in the circles with a straw, then set the circles over the filling. Press the crusts together, then trim the excess flush with the rims of the pans. Brush the tops with the heavy cream.

5. Bake for 15 minutes, then reduce the temperature to 350°F and bake for an additional 20–25 minutes, or until the crust is golden and the juices are bubbling. Cool on a rack and serve warm.

½ cup cold water

1 packet (¼ ounce) unflavored
    gelatin

¾ cup granulated sugar

⅛ teaspoon salt

½ cup orange juice

1 ½ tablespoons freshly squeezed
    lemon juice

1 ½ tablespoons freshly squeezed
    lime juice

4 large egg yolks

¼ teaspoon grated orange zest

¼ teaspoon grated lemon zest

¼ teaspoon grated lime zest

1 ½ cups heavy cream

¾ cup confectioners' sugar

Small batch Lemon Graham
    Cracker Cookie Crust
    (page 249), baked for only
    6–8 minutes

2 tablespoons Lemon Icing
    (page 261)

2 tablespoons Orange Icing
    (page 261)

Three-Citrus Chiffon Pie

Makes one 9-inch single-crust pie

Los Angeles, California, is home to a variety of citrus fruits. For me, a neighborhood stroll entails a walk through a tricolored landscape of citrus trees. Their fruits inspired this fluffy, unbaked pie, the filling for which is light, dreamy, and creamy.

1. Stir the water and gelatin together in a small saucepan off the heat. Let sit for 7–10 minutes, or until the gelatin is dissolved. Add the sugar, salt, all three juices, and the egg yolks. Stir until blended. Cook over medium-low heat, stirring constantly, for 7–8 minutes, or until the mixture becomes smooth. Make sure the heat is low enough to prevent the mixture from boiling. Remove from the heat and transfer to a medium bowl. Let cool.

2. Combine the cream and confectioners' sugar in a medium mixing bowl. Beat with an electric mixer on medium speed until soft peaks form. Fold the cream completely into the gelatin mixture.

3. Spread the filling into the cooled crust, cover with plastic wrap, and chill for 4–5 hours, or until firm. Remove from the refrigerator 20–30 minutes before serving. Drizzle the icings over the top.

Pineapple Macadamia Brown Sugar Slab Pie

Makes one 10½ x 15-inch slab pie

In honor of our nation's fiftieth—and my favorite—state (sorry, California, you are number two), this slab pie is full of Hawaiian flavors. It is easy to make and great for feeding a large crowd—and is highly portable, perfect for a Fourth of July picnic.

2 fresh pineapples, peeled, cored, and cut into ¼-inch slices (about 18 slices)

2 tablespoons freshly squeezed lemon juice

⅓ cup chopped macadamia nuts, toasted

1 cup firmly packed light brown sugar

⅛ teaspoon salt

Large batch (two disks, one slightly larger than the other) Nut Butter Crust made with macadamia nuts (page 243)

1 large egg, beaten with 2 tablespoons heavy cream

⅓ cup Lemon Icing (page 261)

1. Preheat the oven to 425°F. Line a 10½ x 15-inch jelly-roll pan with parchment paper.

2. Gently toss the pineapple, lemon juice, ¼ cup macadamia nuts, brown sugar, and salt in a medium bowl. Set aside.

3. Roll out the larger disk of dough on a floured surface into a rectangle about 17 inches long, 12 inches wide, and ⅛ inch thick. Transfer to the jelly-roll pan, allowing the excess to overhang the sides. Brush the edges with some of the egg wash. Spread the pineapple mixture over the crust.

4. Roll out the second disk into a rectangle about 16 inches long, 11 inches wide, and ⅛ inch thick. Place the rectangle over the filling. Roll the edge of the bottom crust over the top crust and press the edges together to seal. Using a fork, prick the top crust all over to vent. Brush the top with the remaining egg wash.

5. Bake for 15 minutes, then reduce the temperature to 375°F and bake for an additional 25–30 minutes, or until golden. Cool on a rack.

6. Drizzle the icing over the top. Sprinkle with the remaining nuts. Let the icing dry before serving.

HALLOWEEN PIES

Readers of my other books know that I enjoy the sweet flavors of Halloween—caramel apples, pumpkins, and chocolate candy—more than I like the dressing-up part of the holiday. So instead of laboring over a costume each year, I put my time into coming up with new recipes and "dressing up" my favorite flavors.

Baked Caramel Apples

Makes four 3½-inch dumplings

Old-fashioned apple dumplings get a flavor makeover when caramel is added to the mix. The trick to this recipe is to time the baking so that the apple is soft on the inside (but not so soft that it collapses) and the crust is golden brown on the outside. This recipe uses large apples, so if you use smaller apples be sure to adjust the baking time accordingly. Leaving the skin on helps to keep the crust firm, but you can peel the fruit if you prefer. Vent the apples with slashes before wrapping with dough to ensure even baking.

1. Core the apples. Cut ¼ inch off the bottoms so they stand upright. Peel about 1 inch of skin from the top of each and cut ½-inch slits 1 inch apart all around the widest parts of the apple; set aside.

2. Combine the apple juice, lemon juice, sugar, honey, butter, and cinnamon in a small bowl; set aside.

3. Preheat the oven to 450°F. Generously butter a 9 x 9-inch baking pan. Line a baking sheet with parchment paper.

4. Roll out the smaller disk of dough into a 14 x 14-inch square that is ⅛ inch thick. For each apple, cut out two 3-inch circles, one 2-inch circle, and two 1-inch leaves with cookie cutters or a knife. Roll some of the remaining dough into 1-inch stems for the tops of the apples. Place the leaves and stems on the baking sheet. Bake for 7–10 minutes, or until golden.

5. Roll out the larger disk into a rectangle about 16 inches long, 10 inches wide, and ⅛ inch thick. Using a pastry wheel or a knife, cut the dough into twenty ¾ x 10-inch strips.

4 large (about 7 ounces each) unpeeled baking apples, such as Braeburn, Empire, Honeycrisp, Jonathan, or Rome

½ cup apple juice

2 teaspoons freshly squeezed lemon juice

6 tablespoons firmly packed light brown sugar

3 tablespoons clover honey

1 ½ tablespoons unsalted butter, at room temperature

¼ teaspoon ground cinnamon

Large batch (two disks, one slightly larger than the other) Basic Butter Crust (page 242)

3 large eggs, beaten with 3 tablespoons whole milk

½ cup warm Caramel Topping (page 91)

6. Wrap the 3-inch circles around the bottom of the apples, then begin wrapping the strips around each, brushing them with egg wash and overlapping the layers about ¼ inch as you work your way to the top. Press the overlaps tightly together. Stop wrapping the strips when there is 2½ inches of apple exposed at the top.

7. Place the apples in the baking pan. Pour the juice mixture into the cores, then wrap with the remaining 3-inch circles. Brush with egg mixture and top with the 2-inch circles.

8. Bake for 10 minutes, then reduce the temperature to 350°F and bake for an additional 40–60 minutes, or until the apples are tender when a knife is inserted. Cover loosely with foil if the crust gets too browned before the apples are tender. Cool on a rack for 20 minutes.

9. Dip the bottom half of apples into the topping, or brush the topping on the apples with a pastry brush. Attach the stems and leaves with more of the topping.

Chunky Candy Bar Pie

Makes one 10-inch single-crust pie

Looking for a treat to make with all that extra Halloween candy? Look no further. Many different candy flavors can happily come together in this pie, or you can use only your favorite flavor combinations. This pie is for peanut butter and chocolate lovers—it combines peanuts, peanut butter candies, and malted milk balls in a chocolate crust.

1. Preheat the oven to 450°F. Butter and flour a 10-inch pie pan.

2. Roll out the crust on a floured surface into a circle about ⅛ inch thick and 13 inches in diameter. Drape the dough over the pie pan, allowing the excess to hang over the rim. Press the dough into the bottom edges, and trim the excess to a ¼-inch overhang. Fold the overhang over the rim and decoratively crimp the edge. Prick the bottom with a fork. Top the crust with parchment paper and fill with pie

Medium batch (one disk)
Chocolate Cream Cheese Crust
(page 245)
8 ounces peanut-flavored
candy bars (about 6 large or
12 small), cut into ½-inch cubes
1 ½ cups malted milk balls
16 ounces cream cheese, at room
temperature
1 cup creamy peanut butter
¼ cup granulated sugar
2 large eggs
½ cup sour cream
1 cup semisweet chocolate chips
⅔ cup chopped unsalted peanuts

weights. Blind-bake for 7 minutes, then remove from the oven and cool on a rack. Reduce the temperature to 325°F.

3. Place half the candy into the crust. Combine the cream cheese, peanut butter, and sugar in a medium mixing bowl. Beat with an electric mixer on medium speed until smooth. Beat in the eggs, one at a time, then the sour cream. Fold in the remaining candy bars, ½ cup of the chocolate chips, and ⅓ cup of the peanuts. Bake for 30–40 minutes, or until set. Cool on a rack for 2 hours.

4. Melt the remaining chocolate chips in the top of a double boiler set over simmering water. Divide the melted chocolate in half and spread one half in a ring around the inside edge of the crust. Spoon the remainder into a pastry bag fitted with a small round tip and drizzle over the pie in crosshatched lines. Sprinkle the remaining chopped peanuts around the inside edge of the crust, over the chocolate. Cover the pie with plastic wrap and chill for 20 minutes to set before serving.

Pumpkin Ice Cream Tart

Makes one 11-inch tart

For many years, pumpkin ice cream was a seasonal treat. When it hit the supermarket shelves I would stock up for the year. I was always bummed if I ran out before the next year's supply was available. When I received an ice cream maker as a gift, I realized that I could make it—and all my favorite hard-to-find flavors—at home, from scratch. That's when I developed this recipe.

One of my favorite things to do with homemade ice cream is to serve it in a piecrust. It is much more festive than plain old scoops. This tasty crust is made with large waffle cones; sugar cones, the smaller version of waffle cones, work well, too.

1. Preheat the oven to 325°F. To make the crust, mix the crushed waffle cones and honey in a medium mixing bowl. Gradually add the butter and stir with a wooden spoon to moisten.

2. Butter an 11-inch tart pan. Spread the crust mixture into the pan ¼ cup at a time, starting with the bottom and working your way up the sides to create a ¼-inch-thick crust. Flatten the bottom with a pie plate. Bake for 7–10 minutes. Cool on a rack.

3. Soften the ice cream to a spreadable consistency. Spoon it into the piecrust, spreading until smooth. Cover with plastic wrap and freeze for 3 hours.

4. Spoon the whipped cream into a pastry bag fitted with a large star-shaped tip. Pipe cream stars in a large circle in the center of the pie and small stars around the edge. Break off a few pieces from the tops of the sugar cones and set the cones upside down on the center of the pie. Crush the pieces into small crumbs and sprinkle them on the tops of the small stars. Sprinkle the entire pie with cinnamon sugar. Serve immediately.

THANKSGIVING PIES

Perhaps more than any other American holiday, Thanksgiving is associated with pie. In fact, there are so many to choose from that most people start thinking about which pies to serve weeks ahead of time. Most classics are made from New World ingredients—pumpkins, pecans, sweet potatoes, and cranberries—transformed for modern tastes. But I couldn't resist including a savory turkey pot pie recipe here: make it if you want to serve a more casual holiday meal or if you need a tasty way to use up leftover turkey.

Pumpkin Pie

Makes one 11-inch single-crust pie

Thanksgiving is the major pie holiday in the United States—and although you could pick your favorite, to me it is a "make them all" day. But if you can only make just one, this is it. Evaporated milk is a thing of the past—this pie uses heavy cream and half-and-half. The cardamom will keep your guests wondering what it is that makes this pie taste a bit different but so good.

1. To make the filling, combine the eggs and sugars in a large mixing bowl. Beat with an electric mixer on medium speed until fluffy. Beat in the pumpkin, spices, and salt until blended. Stir in the cream and half-and-half until smooth. Set aside.

2. Preheat the oven to 450°F. Butter and flour an 11-inch pie pan. Roll out the large disk of dough on a floured surface into a circle about ⅛ inch thick and 14 inches in diameter. Drape over the pie pan, pressing the dough into the bottom edges. Trim the excess, then fold the dough over to form a thick edge flat against the top rim of the pan.

3. Roll out the small disk into a circle about ⅛ inch thick and 13 inches in diameter. Using a large straw, cut out about fifty ½-inch circles from the dough. Brush the edge of the crust with egg white and press the circles into the edge. Cut slits

---

Pumpkin Filling

4 large eggs

⅓ cup granulated sugar

⅓ cup firmly packed dark brown sugar

1 15-ounce can pumpkin purée (about 1¾ cups)

1 teaspoon ground ginger

1½ teaspoons ground cinnamon

½ teaspoon ground cloves

½ teaspoon ground allspice

½ teaspoon ground cardamom

⅛ teaspoon salt

1 cup heavy cream

½ cup half-and-half

Crust

*Medium batch (two disks, one
   three times larger than the other)
   Spiced Crust (page 243)*
*2 large egg whites, beaten with
   2 tablespoons water*

Topping

*2 cups Maple Whipped Cream
   (page 261)*

in the circles with the tip of a knife. Brush the circles and crust with egg white. Pour the filling into the crust.

4. Bake for 10 minutes, then reduce the temperature to 325°F and bake for an additional 45–50 minutes, or until a knife inserted in the center comes out clean. Cool on a rack. Serve at room temperature with maple whipped cream.

Variation

BANANA RUM PUMPKIN PIE: Reduce the pumpkin to 1½ cups. Add 2 mashed ripe bananas and 3 tablespoons dark rum to the filling at the same time as the pumpkin.

Filling

3 large eggs, beaten

½ cup firmly packed dark brown
    sugar

¼ cup maple syrup

¼ teaspoon salt

3 tablespoons unsalted butter,
    melted

1 teaspoon vanilla extract

1¼ cups chopped pecans

Crust

Large batch (two disks) Spiced
    Crust (page 243)

Topping

½ cup pecan halves

Bourbon Spiced
Whipped Cream

1½ cups heavy cream

1 tablespoon bourbon

½ teaspoon ground cinnamon

Pecan Pie Bars

Makes eight 3¾ x 2½-inch single-crust pies

For an informal holiday party, pie bars are a good choice. They are easy to pick up and eat without a plate and fork. I made these in a metal bar pan—intended for brownies, lemon bars, and other bar cookies—that has eight 3¾ x 2½-inch cavities. There are many different sizes of bar pans on the market, in both metal and silicone, but don't worry too much about finding exactly the same pan as I used. For smaller bars, just decrease the baking time; for larger bars, increase the baking time. Line metal pans with parchment to make it easy to lift out the bars.

1. Preheat the oven to 400°F. Line a bar pan with parchment paper, leaving a 2-inch overhang on both of the long sides.

2. To make the filling, combine the eggs, sugar, maple syrup, salt, butter, and vanilla in large mixing bowl. Beat with an electric mixer on medium speed until blended. Set aside.

3. Roll out each pastry disk on a floured surface into a rectangle about 12 inches long, 9 inches wide, and ⅛ inch thick. Using a pastry wheel or knife, cut each rectangle into four 4½ x 3-inch rectangles. Drape the rectangles over the compartments in the pan, allowing the excess to hang over the rim. Fold over the overhang and press it down so it is flush with the rim. Use a knife to cut decorative slits ¼ inch apart on the edge. Prick holes in the bottoms of the crusts with a fork. Line with parchment paper and fill with pie weights. Blind-bake for 7–10 minutes, or until lightly browned. Reduce the temperature to 325°F.

4. Remove the parchment and pie weights. Divide the chopped pecans among the crusts. Pour the filling mixture over the pecans, then arrange the pecan halves on top to create decorative patterns. Bake for an additional 30–40 minutes, or until set.

5. Cool on a rack to room temperature. Holding the parchment, lift the bars out of the pan. Peel off the paper.

6. To make the whipped cream, combine the heavy cream, bourbon, and cinnamon in a medium mixing bowl. Beat with an electric mixer on medium speed until soft peaks form and the cream is smooth and satiny; stop before it becomes stiff. Spoon on top of the pies or pour it into a separate bowl and serve it on the side.

Variations

CHOCOLATE PECAN BARS: Prepare the bars with a large batch of Chocolate Butter Crust (page 242). Add 3 ounces melted semisweet chocolate to the egg mixture. Top with chocolate curls.

BOURBON PECAN BARS: Replace the vanilla with 3 tablespoons bourbon.

Cashew Nut Pie

Makes one 11-inch single-crust pie

Bite into this pie and you'll discover an exotic nutty alternative to the tried-and-true peanut butter pies and pecan pies. This recipe also tastes great when made with almond butter and chopped almonds.

1 cup firmly packed dark brown sugar
½ cup cashew butter
3 large eggs
½ teaspoon salt
1 cup dark corn syrup
1 teaspoon vanilla extract
1¼ cups chopped cashews
Medium batch (one disk) Nut Butter Crust made with cashews (page 243)

1. Preheat the oven to 350°F. Butter and flour an 11-inch pie pan.

2. Combine the brown sugar and cashew butter in a medium mixing bowl. Beat with an electric mixer on medium speed until fluffy. Beat in the eggs, one at a time, for 1–2 minutes, until blended. Add the salt, corn syrup, vanilla, and 1 cup cashews.

3. Roll out the disk on a floured surface into a circle about ⅛ inch thick and 15 inches in diameter. Drape the dough over the pie pan, allowing the excess to hang over the rim. Press the dough into the bottom edges, and trim the excess to a ¼-inch overhang. Fold the overhang over the rim and decoratively crimp the edge. Prick the bottom with a fork. Top the crust with parchment paper and fill with pie weights. Blind-bake for 7–10 minutes, or until lightly browned. Remove the pie weights and parchment paper and cool on a rack.

Crust

Medium batch (two disks, one
   slightly larger than the other)
   Basic Butter Crust (page 242)
2 large eggs, beaten with 2
   tablespoons whole milk

Sweet Potato Filling

1 ½ pounds sweet potatoes (about
   2 medium), roasted until tender
   and cooled
½ cup granulated sugar
½ cup firmly packed light brown
   sugar
½ teaspoon salt
¼ teaspoon baking soda
½ teaspoon ground cinnamon
¼ teaspoon ground nutmeg
¼ teaspoon ground cloves
⅓ cup unsalted butter, melted
1 teaspoon vanilla extract
3 large eggs
½ cup whole milk
2 cups Marshmallow Meringue
   (page 259)

Pecan Topping

2 tablespoons unsalted butter
1 cup pecan halves
½ teaspoon ground cinnamon
1 tablespoon freshly squeezed
   lemon juice
1 tablespoon firmly packed light
   brown sugar

4. Pour the filling into the crust and bake for 40–50 minutes, or until the filling has set but is still a little gooey. Cool on a rack. Top with remaining cashews.

Roasted Sweet Potato Marshmallow Pie

Makes one 9-inch single-crust pie

From the first bite, this sweet potato pie will transport you to Thanksgiving in the South in the 1950s. Just make the crust and filling if you want to keep it simple, but if you want to serve the pie all gussied up, add appliqué circles to the edges and top it as directed below.

1. Butter and flour a 9-inch pie pan. Preheat the oven to 425°F.

2. Roll out the larger disk of dough on a floured surface into a circle about ⅛ inch thick and 12 inches in diameter. Drape the dough over the pie pan, allowing the excess to hang over the rim. Press the dough into the bottom edges, and trim the excess to a ¼-inch overhang. Fold the overhang over the rim and decoratively crimp the edge.

3. Roll out the second disk of dough into a circle about ⅛ inch thick and 10 inches in diameter. Cut out about thirty-six ¾-inch circles from the dough. Brush some of the egg mixture on the edge of the bottom crust and press the small circles onto it. Brush additional egg mixture on top of the circles. Line the crust with parchment paper and fill with pie weights. Blind-bake for 7–10 minutes, or until light golden. Remove the paper and weights and cool on a rack. Reduce the temperature to 375°F. Prepare a water bath (see page 34) and set the water bath in the oven.

4. To make the filling, scoop the potato out from the skin and transfer to a large bowl. Using a wooden spoon, mix in both sugars, salt, baking soda, cinnamon, nutmeg, and cloves. Using an electric mixer on medium speed, beat in the butter, vanilla, eggs, and milk.

5. Pour the mixture into the crust, being careful not to go over the edge. Set the pan into the water bath and bake for 45–55 minutes, or until the middle feels firm to the touch. Remove water bath and pie from the oven and cool in pan on a rack.

6. Preheat the broiler. Cover the edges of the crust with foil to prevent burning. Spread the marshmallow meringue in a circle in the center of the pie, leaving a 2-inch ring between the meringue and the crust. Place the pie on a baking sheet and broil for 1–2 minutes, or until the meringue is lightly browned. Keep a close watch, as it can burn quickly. (Alternatively, you can toast the meringue with a kitchen torch.)

7. To make the pecan topping, melt the butter in a skillet over medium heat. Add the pecans and cinnamon and sauté until lightly toasted. Remove from the heat and add lemon juice and brown sugar, mixing well. Spoon the topping onto the border between the meringue and the crust.

Cranberry Chocolate Cream Pie
Makes one 9-inch single-crust pie

If you can't get enough of the amazingly tart taste of cranberries, try them in this novel holiday pie.

1½ cups fresh cranberries
1 cup granulated sugar
½ cup water
2 teaspoons freshly squeezed lemon juice
1 packet (¼ ounce) unflavored gelatin
1 cup heavy cream
⅛ teaspoon salt
¾ cup dark chocolate (at least 60% cacao) shavings
Small batch (one disk) Chocolate Wafer Crust (page 243)

1. Preheat the oven to 325°F. Bake the crust for 8–10 minutes, or until it darkens. Cool in the pan for 10 minutes, then transfer to a rack to cool completely.

2. Combine the cranberries, ½ cup sugar, and ¼ cup water in a medium saucepan over medium-high heat. Boil for 7–10 minutes, or until the cranberries have popped and the mixture has thickened. Transfer to a food processor or blender and add the lemon juice. Process until smooth.

3. Combine the gelatin and remaining ¼ cup water in a small saucepan and let sit for 5 minutes to soften. Set over medium heat until the gelatin is dissolved and clear. Stir in the cranberry mixture.

4. Combine the cream, remaining ½ cup sugar, and salt in a medium mixing bowl. Beat with an electric mixer on medium speed until soft peaks form. Add the cranberry purée and ½ cup chocolate shavings and whip until smooth. Pour into the crust, smoothing the top with a spatula. Cover with plastic wrap and chill for 6 hours, or until firm.

5. Remove from the refrigerator for 30 minutes before serving. Top with the remaining chocolate shavings.

Variation

CRANBERRY ORANGE CREAM PIE: Prepare the pie in a small batch of Graham Cracker Cookie Crust (page 248). Omit the chocolate shavings. Add 1 teaspoon orange zest to the cranberry mixture. Top with candied oranges (page 230).

Turkey Pot Pie

Makes one 10-inch double-crust pie

This recipe shows that pie can also be the main attraction at a Thanksgiving meal. For a homey alternative to a big bird, this creamy savory pie may soon become a new tradition. If you can't give up the Thanksgiving bird, make this pot pie with leftover cooked turkey instead of the turkey breasts. Just shorten the baking time to 20–25 minutes so you don't overcook the meat.

1. To make the filling, combine the olive oil, ½ teaspoon thyme, ½ teaspoon sage, and ½ teaspoon paprika in a small bowl. Rub on the turkey and mushrooms to coat.

2. In a large skillet, sauté the turkey until it is crisp around the outside but still pink in the center (5–7 minutes). Add the mushrooms and sauté until softened (8–10 minutes).

3. Place the chicken broth, celery salt, pepper, and remaining thyme, sage, and paprika, and carrots in a medium saucepan and heat over medium-high heat. Bring to a boil and cook for 5–7 minutes, or until the carrots are softened. Remove the carrots from the broth and set aside.

2 tablespoons olive oil

1½ teaspoons fresh thyme

1½ teaspoons fresh sage

1 teaspoon paprika

2 pounds boneless skinless turkey
 breast, cut into cubes

6 ounces portobello mushrooms,
 sliced

1½ cups chicken broth

⅛ teaspoon celery salt

¼ teaspoon freshly ground black
 pepper

2 carrots, peeled and diced

3 tablespoons unsalted butter

1 medium onion, diced

2 celery stalks, diced

2 tablespoons all-purpose flour

½ cup heavy cream

1 batch (two disks) Herb Wheat
 Germ Crust made with thyme
 and sage (page 249)

1 large egg, beaten

2 teaspoons sesame seeds

4. Melt the butter in another medium saucepan over medium heat. Add the onion and celery and sauté about 5 minutes, or until tender but not browned. Sprinkle in the flour and cook, stirring, for 2 minutes.

5. Gradually add the chicken broth, then stir in the cream and simmer for 5 minutes, or until mixture thickens. Add more flour if necessary to thicken. Add the turkey, mushrooms, and carrots and mix well. Remove from heat.

6. Preheat the oven to 425°F. Butter and flour a 10-inch pie pan. Roll out one disk of dough on a lightly floured surface into a circle about ⅛ inch thick and 13 inches in diameter. Drape the dough over the pie pan, allowing the excess to hang over the rim. Press the dough into the bottom edges, and trim the excess to a ¼-inch overhang. Fold the overhang over the rim and press flat. Prick the bottom with a fork. Top the crust with parchment paper and fill with pie weights. Blind-bake for 10 minutes, or until the crust is light golden.

7. Remove the parchment and pie weights. Spoon the filling into the crust, pressing the mixture down to eliminate air pockets.

8. Roll out the second disk of dough into a circle about ⅛ inch thick and 12 inches in diameter. Cut vents into the center of the crust with a knife or a cookie cutter. Brush the edges of the bottom crust with some of the beaten egg and place the top crust over the filling. Press the edges firmly together to seal, then trim the excess and fold the crust to make a thick edge. Brush the remaining beaten egg over the crust. Sprinkle with sesame seeds. Bake for 30–40 minutes, or until golden. Serve hot.

Variation

SWEET AND SAVORY CHICKEN POT PIE: Replace the turkey with chicken. Replace the onion with ½ cup chopped leeks. Add ½ cup corn kernels, ¼ cup chopped dried apricots, and ¼ cup golden raisins in step 4.

Apple Cranberry Filling

Makes 7½ cups

9 Fuji apples, peeled and thinly
   sliced (about 5 cups)

3 Bartlett pears, peeled and thinly
   sliced (about 2 cups)

2 cups fresh cranberries

½ cup chopped walnuts

½ cup granulated sugar

½ cup firmly packed light brown
   sugar

½ teaspoon ground cinnamon

½ teaspoon ground ginger

3 tablespoons instant tapioca

2 tablespoons cold unsalted butter,
   cubed

Crust

*Large batch (two disks) Nut
   Butter Crust made with walnuts
   (page 243)*

1 large egg white, lightly beaten

Topping

¼ cup Cinnamon Sugar
   (page 258)

Baked Lady Apples

¼ cup chopped fresh cranberries

¼ cup chopped walnuts

¼ cup firmly packed light brown
   sugar

½ teaspoon ground cinnamon

7–8 lady apples (red or green),
   cored

Apple Cranberry Pie with Baked Lady Apples

Makes one 12-inch double-crust pie

There are so many choices for Thanksgiving pies that it's hard to pick just one. Mixed fruit pies are a good solution if you want to have all your favorite flavors in a single pie. And just in case you didn't know, here's a tip: the secret to a good apple pie is to add a few pears. To chop fresh cranberries for the lady apples, pulse them a few times in a food processor—it works wonders.

When transporting pies for the holidays, using disposable paper liners or foil pans means you won't have to leave your pan at the host's event. I prepared this pie in a paper liner; these tend to come in a wider range of sizes than foil pans. Just remove the pie and liner from the pan after it has cooled, place in a box or pie carrier, and go. Top with lady apples when ready to serve.

1. To make the filling, combine the apples, pears, cranberries, and walnuts in a large bowl.

2. Combine the sugars, cinnamon, ginger, and tapioca in a small bowl. Stir into the apple mixture; set aside.

3. Preheat the oven to 450°F. Line a 12-inch pie pan with a disposable paper liner. Roll out one disk of dough on a floured surface into a circle about ⅛ inch thick and 14 inches in diameter. Drape the circle over the pie pan, pressing it into the bottom edges and allowing the excess to hang over the rim. Brush the edge with some of the egg white. Spoon the filling into the crust, pressing down to eliminate air pockets. Top with the butter cubes.

4. Roll out the second disk into a circle about ⅛ inch thick and 14 inches in diameter. Using a knife or a cookie cutter, cut a 3-inch vent in the center. Place the crust over the filling, pressing the edges of both crusts firmly together to seal, then folding the edge toward the center. Crimp decoratively. Brush the remaining egg white over the entire top crust. Sprinkle with half the cinnamon sugar.

5. Bake for 10 minutes, then reduce the temperature to 350°F and bake for an additional 45–50 minutes, or until the apples are tender (test with a knife). Cover the crust with an edge shield if it begins to brown too much. Cool slightly in the pan on a rack.

6. To make the baked apples, combine the cranberries, walnuts, brown sugar, and cinnamon in a medium bowl. Press mixture into the cavities in each apple.

7. Fill an 8 x 8-inch baking dish with ½ inch water. Set the apples in the dish. Cover with aluminum foil and bake for 20–25 minutes, or until tender when pierced with a knife. If necessary, bake for an additional 10–15 minutes, adding more water if it evaporates. Spoon the juices in the pan over the apples, then place them around the vent on the pie. Sprinkle with remaining cinnamon sugar.

Variation

BRANDY APPLE CURRANT PIE: Replace the cranberries in the filling with ½ cup dried currants. After the filling is placed in the pie, drizzle with ¼ cup brandy.

LADY APPLES

Tiny lady apples, with their bright red or greenish coloring, show up at farmers markets right before Thanksgiving and are available through Christmas. Two to three inches in diameter, they only take two bites to eat. Leave the peel on; it gives the apple a semisweet, winey taste.

CHRISTMAS PIES

Yuletide pie? Certainly we expect to have cookies and fruitcake at Christmastime, but apple, pumpkin, and pecan pies can all make for tasty celebrating, too. If you're looking for a real taste of Christmas past, make the Mincemeat Pie—I've left out the meat and substituted fresh and dried fruits. For other modern interpretations of the ingredients, flavors, and colors of the holiday season, take a look at what I've done with orange, peppermint, gingerbread, eggnog, and "grasshopper"—this section has an array of playful pies and tarts that will get you into the spirit of the season.

Gingerbread Tarts

Makes twenty-four 2-inch tarts and twenty-four 2-inch cookies

If you like gingerbread cookies, this is the recipe for you. These gingerbread crusts, made from cookie dough, are filled with a great cranberry filling and make a fine, crowd-pleasing mini dessert for adults and kids alike. Have fun decorating the gingerbread men.

1. Butter and flour twenty-four 2-inch tart pans or twenty-four 2-inch muffin cups. Line a baking sheet with parchment paper.

2. To make the filling, heat the water, sugar, and cranberries in a medium saucepan over medium heat. Cook, stirring occasionally, for 7–10 minutes, or until the cranberries pop and the mixture thickens. Remove from the heat and stir in the orange zest. Cool for 15 minutes. Cover with plastic wrap and refrigerate for 1 hour, or until mixture thickens into a jelly-like consistency.

3. To make the crust, combine the flour, sugar, ginger, cinnamon, allspice, nutmeg, and salt in a large bowl. Cut in the butter with a pastry blender or your fingertips until the mixture resembles coarse meal.

4. Combine the egg yolks and molasses in a small bowl. Gradually add to the flour mixture until combined. Add the

Cranberry Filling

1 cup water
⅔ cup granulated sugar
12 ounces whole cranberries
½ teaspoon grated orange zest

Gingerbread Crust

3 cups all-purpose flour
½ cup firmly packed dark brown
  sugar
1½ tablespoons ground ginger
2 teaspoons ground cinnamon
1½ teaspoons ground allspice
½ teaspoon ground nutmeg
¼ teaspoon salt
1 cup (2 sticks) cold unsalted butter, cut into cubes
2 large egg yolks
⅓ cup unsulfured molasses
2 tablespoons cold water

Topping

⅓ cup Lemon Icing (page 261)
1 tablespoon red cinnamon candies
1 tablespoon silver dragées
1 teaspoon round white candies

water, a little at a time, until the dough sticks together. Add a little more, if necessary.

5. Divide the dough into two disks, one twice as large as the other. Wrap the smaller disk in plastic wrap and chill for 30 minutes. Divide the larger disk among the tart pans, pressing the dough into the bottoms and up the sides. Cover with plastic wrap and chill for 30 minutes.

6. Preheat the oven to 375°F. Roll out the smaller disk into a circle about ⅛ inch thick and 13 inches in diameter. Using a 2-inch-tall cookie cutter or a knife, cut out twenty-four gingerbread men. Place them on the baking sheet and bake for 7–10 minutes, or until browned around the edges. Transfer to a rack to cool completely. Once cooled, pipe with the icing and decorate with candies. Let the icing dry for 1 hour to harden.

7. Remove the crusts from the refrigerator and prick the bottoms with a fork. Line with parchment paper and fill with pie weights. Bake for 10 minutes, or until set. Remove the parchment and pie weights and bake for an additional 10–15 minutes, or until browned. Cool in the pans on a rack.

8. Fill each tart with 1–2 heaping tablespoons of filling. Press the feet of the gingerbread men into the filling to stand.

Variation

CHOCOLATE GINGERBREAD TARTS: Replace the cranberry filling with Chocolate Ganache (page 258).

Spiked Eggnog Pie

Makes one 9-inch single-crust pie

Transform the flavors of your favorite holiday drink into a creamy pie. If you prefer your eggnog "unspiked," you can replace the rum with 1 teaspoon of vanilla extract. For a playful presentation, prepare the pies in mugs, as you would prepare pies in jars (see page 106).

Crust

*Small batch (one disk) Spiced
    Crust (page 243)*

Eggnog Cream

¾ cup granulated sugar

¼ cup cornstarch

3 large egg yolks

3 cups eggnog

¼ cup golden rum

Topping

*2 cups Cinnamon Whipped
    Cream (page 261)*

8 maraschino cherries

*2 tablespoons Cinnamon Sugar
    (page 258)*

1. Preheat the oven to 425°F. Butter and flour a 9-inch pie pan.

2. Roll out the dough on a floured surface into a circle about
   ⅛ inch thick and 12 inches in diameter. Gently drape the
   crust over the pan and press it into the bottom, allowing
   the excess to hang over the rim. Trim the excess to a ¼-inch
   overhang. Fold the overhang over the rim and decoratively
   crimp the edge. Prick the bottom with a fork. Top the crust
   with parchment paper and fill with pie weights. Blind-bake
   for 10 minutes, or until the crust is partially baked. Remove
   the paper and weights and bake for additional 5–7 minutes.
   Remove from the oven and cool on a rack.

3. To make the eggnog cream, mix ¼ cup sugar and cornstarch
   in a heatproof medium bowl. Add the egg yolks and stir to
   form a paste, then stir in ½ cup eggnog.

4. Combine the remaining eggnog and sugar in a saucepan
   and bring to a boil over medium heat. Pour into the paste
   mixture and stir with a wooden spoon until smooth.

5. Pour this mixture into the saucepan and cook, stirring
   occasionally, over medium-low heat for 7–10 minutes, or
   until thick and smooth. If the mixture begins to boil, lower
   the heat. Remove from the heat and stir in the rum. Transfer
   to a bowl, cover with plastic wrap touching the surface, and
   chill for 2 hours, or until thickened.

6. Spread the cream in the crust. Spoon the whipped cream into a
   pastry bag fitted with a large star-shaped tip. Pipe the cream in a
   ring around the outside edge of the filling and in the center. Place
   cherries on the whipped cream. Sprinkle with cinnamon sugar.

Crust

1 batch (two disks, one twice as
  large as the other) Fluffy Orange
  Almond Crust (page 243),
  chilled for only 30 minutes
2 large egg whites, beaten with
  2 tablespoons heavy cream

Filling

3 cups orange marmalade

Orange Sauce

1 tablespoon unsalted butter
1 cup confectioners' sugar
½ cup orange juice
3 oranges, peeled, seeded, sliced,
  and puréed in a food processor

Orange Tarts

Make six 3½-inch tarts

Orange is the flavor of the season, and with both the sauce and marmalade
in this recipe, you get a double dose. This fluffy crust is very cake-like.

1. Preheat the oven to 425°F. Butter and flour six 3½-inch tart
   pans. Roll out the larger disk of dough on a floured work
   surface into a rectangle that is 15 inches long, 10 inches
   wide, and ⅛ inch thick. Using cookie cutters or a knife, cut
   six 5-inch circles out of the dough and place them gently
   into the pans, allowing the excess to hang over the rims.
   Press the dough into the bottom edges, and trim the excess
   to a ¼-inch overhang. Fold the overhang over the rims and
   press to make flat edges. Brush the bottoms of the crusts and
   the edges with some of the egg mixture.

2. Fill the crusts to the very tops with orange marmalade.

3. Roll out the smaller disk of dough on a floured work surface
   into a rectangle that is 12 inches long, 3½ inches wide,
   and ⅛ inch thick. Using a pastry wheel or a knife, cut the
   rectangle into twelve 1 x 3½-inch strips. Place two strips
   over the marmalade in each pan, overlapping them in a cross
   pattern, and press the edges to seal. Brush the strips with the
   remaining egg mixture.

4. Bake for 15 minutes, then reduce the temperature to 350°F
   and bake for an additional 20–30 minutes, or until the crust
   is golden. Cool on a rack until warm.

5. To make the orange sauce, combine the butter, sugar, and juice
   in the top of a double boiler set over simmering water. Cook
   over low heat until the butter and sugar are melted and the
   mixture has thickened. Remove from the heat and beat with an
   electric mixer on medium speed until smooth. Brush a thin coat
   of sauce on the tops of the pies.

6. Stir the puréed oranges into the remaining sauce and serve
   on the side, while still warm.

Candied Fruits

1 cup granulated sugar

½ cup water

2 tablespoons light corn syrup

Rind of 2 blood oranges, washed
and cut into very thin strips

2 unpeeled blood oranges, washed
and sliced into thin rounds

¼ cup fresh currants, washed

Crust

Small batch (one disk) Almond
Brown Sugar Crust (page 242)

Orange Mousse

3 large egg yolks

⅔ cup granulated sugar

1 packet (¼ ounce) unflavored
gelatin, dissolved in ¼ cup cold
water

⅓ cup freshly squeezed blood
orange juice

2 teaspoons grated orange zest

2 tablespoons confectioners' sugar

1 teaspoon cornstarch

½ teaspoon ground ginger

⅛ teaspoon salt

1½ cups heavy cream

Topping

2 cups Ginger Whipped Cream
(page 261)

Candied Blood Orange Currant Pie

Makes one 9-inch single-crust pie

Before the advent of refrigerated trucks and cross-country shipping, oranges were a rare delicacy, especially in the winter months. Perhaps for that reason, oranges are traditionally stuffed in Christmas stockings, alongside other desirable treats such as toys and candies. In this silky mousse pie, candied blood oranges and fresh currants—another traditional flavor of the season—make a tasty, edible garnish. I especially like the aesthetic of the currants, which remind me of bright holly berries. If you're a fan of orange and chocolate together, dip the sliced rind in melted chocolate (let the candied sugar set completely first). If you can't find blood oranges, use navel oranges.

1. To make the candied fruits, set a piece of parchment paper under a wire cooling rack. Combine the sugar, water, and corn syrup in a medium heavy-bottomed saucepan and boil until sugar is dissolved. Add the orange rind and slices and boil for 20 minutes, stirring occasionally. Remove from heat and use tongs to place the fruit on the rack. Toss the currants in the remaining juices and place on the cooling rack. Dry overnight.

2. Preheat the oven to 425°F. Butter and flour a 9-inch pie pan. Roll out the dough on a floured work surface into a circle about ⅛ inch thick and 12 inches in diameter. Drape the dough over the pie pan, allowing the excess to hang over the rim. Press the dough into the bottom edges, and trim the excess to a ¼-inch overhang. Fold the overhang over the rim and decoratively crimp the edge. Prick the bottom with a fork. Top the crust with parchment paper and fill with pie weights. Blind-bake for 10 minutes, or until the crust is partially baked. Remove the paper and weights and bake for additional 5–7 minutes, or until golden. Remove from the oven and cool on a rack.

3. To make the filling, combine the yolks and granulated sugar in the top of a double boiler set over simmering water and cook, stirring, for about 5 minutes, or until thickened. Add

the gelatin mixture, juice, and zest. Mix thoroughly. Transfer to a large bowl, cover with plastic wrap, and chill for 1 hour.

4. Combine the confectioners' sugar, cornstarch, ginger, salt, and ¼ cup cream in a small saucepan set over medium-low heat. Gradually bring to a boil and stir until the mixture thickens. Remove from heat and let cool to room temperature.

5. Beat the remaining cream in a chilled mixing bowl with an electric mixer on medium speed until soft peaks form. Add the cornstarch mixture and continue to beat until stiff peaks form.

6. Fold the cream into the gelatin mixture. Spread evenly into the crust, cover with plastic wrap touching the surface, and chill for 4–5 hours, or until firm.

7. When ready to serve, top with ginger whipped cream and the candied fruits.

Variation

CHOCOLATE-COVERED CANDIED ORANGE CURRANT MOUSSE PIE: Prepare the pie in a small batch of Chocolate Butter Crust (page 242). Dip orange slices, rind, and currants in ½ cup melted semisweet chocolate. Top the pie with dipped fruit and chocolate shavings.

Christmas Grasshopper Pie
Makes one 10-inch single-crust pie
Popular in the 1950s and '60s, grasshopper pie is pure midcentury nostalgia. The pie got its name from the popular cocktail of the time. My recipe includes both crème de menthe and crème de cacao; feel free to adjust the quantities (upward, naturally!) to taste. Prepare the marzipan decorations in advance, before you make the pie. They will remain moist and chewy—don't worry about them drying out.

1. Preheat the oven to 325°F. Bake the crust for 7–8 minutes, or until the bottom feels crisp. Cool in the pan for 10 minutes, then transfer to a rack to cool completely.

Crust

Medium batch Chocolate Wafer Crust (page 243), prepared in a 10-inch pie pan

Grasshopper Filling

1¾ cups whole milk

12 ounces miniature marshmallows or 12 ounces marshmallow crème

½ cup sour cream

3 tablespoons crème de menthe liqueur

3 tablespoons crème de cacao liqueur

4–5 drops green food coloring

Topping

2 cups Whipped Cream (page 261)

8 maraschino cherries

Holiday Marzipan Decorations (below)

2. To make the filling, heat the milk in the top of a double boiler set over simmering water until bubbles appear. Do not allow the milk to boil. Add about one-fourth of the marshmallows and stir until melted. Continue to add the marshmallows, a handful at a time, until melted. Add the sour cream and stir until thick and creamy.

3. Remove from the heat and stir in the liqueurs and food coloring. Stir until fully integrated.

4. Pour the filling into the crust, cover with plastic wrap, and freeze for 2–3 hours, or until firm. Remove from the freezer 30 minutes before serving.

5. Spoon the whipped cream into a pastry bag fitted with a large star-shaped tip. Pipe seven mounds of cream in a ring around the border of the pie, just inside the crust, and a larger mound in the center. Top each mound with a maraschino cherry. Place the marzipan decorations in between the mounds of cream.

HOLIDAY MARZIPAN DECORATIONS

½ cup Marzipan (page 259)

Green, red, and yellow food coloring

Confectioners' sugar for dusting

3 tablespoons confectioners' sugar, mixed with 1 teaspoon water

Color about ⅓ cup marzipan with green food coloring. Pull off a piece of the remaining marzipan, roll it into a ½-inch ball, and color it yellow. Color the remaining marzipan red. Divide the green marzipan into 6 equal pieces and roll them into balls. Roll out the red marzipan on a work surface covered with confectioners' sugar to a thickness of 1/16 inch. Using a cookie cutter, or working freehand with a knife, cut out ¾-inch flowers. Curl up the edges of the petals. Roll out the yellow marzipan to a thickness of 1/16 inch. Using a plastic coffee stirrer, or working freehand with a knife, cut out ⅛-inch dots. Attach the dots to the flowers and the flowers to the balls with the confectioners' sugar mixture.

½ cup chopped dried figs

½ cup golden raisins

½ cup dried cherries

½ cup chopped dried apricots

1 ounce chopped crystallized
    ginger

½ cup chopped walnuts

1 teaspoon grated lemon zest

1 teaspoon grated orange zest

4 Granny Smith apples, peeled,
    cored, and chopped into small
    cubes

⅓ cup brandy

¾ cup firmly packed light brown
    sugar

1 tablespoon cornstarch

½ teaspoon ground allspice

½ teaspoon ground cinnamon

¼ teaspoon ground cloves

¼ teaspoon ground nutmeg

Large batch (two disks) Spiced
    Crust (page 243)

2 large egg whites, lightly beaten

Cinnamon Sugar (page 258)

Mincemeat Pie

Makes one 9-inch double-crust pie

Mincemeat pie harks back to the Christmas celebrations of more than five hundred years ago, when pie doughs were not edible and were hard as ceramics. Their main function was to preserve spiced-meat main courses. Over time, pie dough became flakier and fruit more readily available, and pies became sweeter. Served today as a (meatless) Christmas dessert, mincemeat pie is also a good choice for giving. This recipe includes fresh apples and dried figs, raisins, and cherries. Feel free to experiment with your favorite fresh and dried fruits.

1. To make the filling, combine the figs, raisins, cherries, apricots, ginger, walnuts, and zests in the bowl of a food processor and pulse until finely minced. Transfer to a large bowl and stir in the apples and brandy. Let soak for 1 hour.

2. Preheat the oven to 425°F. Combine the brown sugar, cornstarch, allspice, cinnamon, cloves, and nutmeg in a small bowl. Add to the chopped fruit.

3. Roll out one of the pastry disks on a floured surface into a circle about ⅛ inch thick and 12 inches in diameter. Drape over the pie pan, pressing into the bottom and allowing the excess to hang over the rim. Spoon the filling into the crust, pressing the mixture down to eliminate air pockets.

4. Roll out the second disk of dough into a circle about ⅛ inch thick and 12 inches in diameter. Cut vents into the center with a knife or cookie cutter. Brush the edges of the bottom crust with some of the egg white and place the top crust over the filling. Trim the excess dough and fold the bottom edge over the edge of the top crust. Press the edges firmly together to seal. Refrigerate for 30 minutes.

5. Brush the remaining egg white over the top of the crust. Sprinkle with cinnamon sugar. Bake for 10–15 minutes, or until light golden. Reduce the temperature to 375°F and bake for an additional 40–50 minutes, or until lightly browned. Cover the crust with an edge shield if crust begins

to brown too much. Cool on a rack. Serve warm or at room temperature.

Variations

PEAR MINCEMEAT PIE: Replace the apples with Bartlett pears and the dried fruit with 2 cups combined dates, dried cranberries, and dried apricots.

TROPICAL MINCEMEAT PIE: Replace the dried fruit with 2 cups combined dried pineapple, dried mango, and dried papaya. Replace the brandy with dark rum.

BERRY MINCEMEAT PIE: Replace the dried fruit with 2 cups combined dried blueberries, dried strawberries, and dried cranberries.

White Chocolate Peppermint Mousse Pie with Pretzel Crust

Makes one 10-inch single-crust pie

This pie's main claim to fame is its sweet white chocolate combined with its salty pretzel crust. The peppermint gives it a seasonal flair.

Pretzel Crust

2 cups pretzel crumbs

2 tablespoons firmly packed light brown sugar

3 tablespoons unsalted butter, melted

Filling

1⅔ cups heavy cream

8 ounces white chocolate, chopped

2 tablespoons granulated sugar

½ teaspoon peppermint extract

Topping

½ cup white chocolate–covered pretzels

3 tablespoons crushed peppermint candies

1. Preheat the oven to 350°F. Butter and flour a 10-inch pie pan.

2. To make the crust, combine the pretzel crumbs and brown sugar in a large bowl. Add the butter. Press firmly into the pie pan, starting in the center and working your way up the sides. Bake for 7–10 minutes, or until crisp. Cool on a rack.

3. To make the filling, heat ⅔ cup cream in a small saucepan. Stir in the white chocolate until melted. Transfer to a large bowl and let cool for about 30 minutes, stirring occasionally.

4. Combine the remaining 1 cup cream, granulated sugar, and peppermint extract in a medium mixing bowl. Beat with an electric mixer on medium speed until stiff peaks form. Fold into the chocolate mixture until smooth. Gently spoon into the crust. Cover with plastic wrap and chill for 3 hours.

5. When ready to serve, top with white chocolate–covered pretzels and peppermint candies.

Chapter 6

Crusts, Fillings, and Toppings

Baking is playing, and one of the best ways to enjoy time in the kitchen is to bake a different crust every time you make a pie. This chapter is filled with an assortment of recipes to mix and match for that purpose. Use the same filling and swap out the crust for a new flavor and texture. Or, if you have already discovered your favorite crust, use this chapter to explore encasing different fillings and toppings to develop unexpected taste combinations. Have fun and happy eating.

A GUIDE TO CRUST SIZES

This list will show you whether the pie you want to make calls for a small, medium, large, or extra-large batch of crust. Note that this chart doesn't include crusts that are used in one size only; nor does it include crusts for which recipes are provided within the pie recipe itself (i.e., in chapters 2–5). If a pie recipe calls for two different crusts, the pie appears under the name of both crusts. If a pie recipe calls for crusts in two different sizes, the pie appears under both sizes.

Basic Butter Crust

SMALL

Banana Cream Pie with Candied Walnuts

Blackberry Buttermilk Pie

Boozy Buttermilk Pie

Buttermilk Pie with Peach Sauce

Caramel Banana Cream Pie

Coconut Cream Pie

Key Lime Coconut Cream Pie

Mango Coconut Cream Pie

MEDIUM

Apple Raisin Pie with Crumble Topping

Berry Granola Pie

Berry Pie with Nut Butter Crumble

Blackbird Pies

Cheddar Coconut Pies

Individual Deep-Dish Berry Pies

Panda Bento Box

Roasted Sweet Potato Marshmallow Pie

LARGE

Baked Caramel Apples

Classic Apple Pie

Concord Grape Pies

Individual Wedding Pies

Pie in a Jar

Rum Raisin Pudding with Piecrust Chips

EXTRA LARGE

Happy Birthday Nectarine Pie with Raspberry Sauce

Happy Pop-in-the-Oven Tarts

Wedding Pies

Almond Brown Sugar Crust (variation of Basic Butter Crust)

SMALL

Candied Blood Orange Currant Pie

Chocolate Butter Crust (variation of Basic Butter Crust)

SMALL

Chocolate-Covered Candied Orange Currant Mousse Pie

Panda Bento Box

MEDIUM

Berry Granola Pie

Berry Pie with Nut Butter Crumble

Cherry Chocolate Chip Cookie Pie

Crème Brûlée Tarts with Chocolate Dots

Individual Deep-Dish Berry Pies

Sour Cherry Crème Brûlée Tarts

White or Dark Chocolate Crème Brûlée Tarts

LARGE

Chocolate Cherry Pie

Chocolate Pecan Bars

EXTRA LARGE

Happy Pop-in-the-Oven Tarts

Chocolate Almond Butter Crust (variation of Basic Butter Crust)

SMALL

Chocolate Almond Tart

Coconut Lemon Crust
(variation of Basic Butter Crust)

MEDIUM

Piña Colada Cream Pies

Nut Butter Crust
(variation of Basic Butter Crust)

SMALL

Hazelnut Mocha Pie

MEDIUM

Apricot-Almond Skillet Pie

Cashew Nut Pie

LARGE

Apple Cranberry Pie with Baked Lady Apples

Brandy Apple Currant Pie

Pie Pops

Pineapple Macadamia Brown Sugar Slab Pie

Spiced Crust
(variation of Basic Butter Crust)

SMALL

Plain Eggnog Pie

Shoofly Pie

Spiked Eggnog Pie

MEDIUM

Banana Rum Pumpkin Pie

Pumpkin Pie

LARGE

Berry Mincemeat Pie

Bourbon Pecan Bars

Mincemeat Pie

Pear Mincemeat Pie

Pecan Pie Bars

Tropical Mincemeat Pie

Chocolate Wafer Crust

SMALL

Chocolate Chip Ice Cream Pie

Chocolate Peanut Butter Pie

Cookies-and-Cream Ice Cream Pie

Cranberry Chocolate Cream Pie

Crunchy Mississippi Mud Pie

MEDIUM

Barbecued-Fruit Ice Cream Tarts

Christmas Grasshopper Pie

Chocolate Chili Wafer Crust
(variation of Chocolate Wafer Crust)

SMALL

Chocolate Chili Hearts

Cornmeal Crust

SMALL

Butternut Squash Custard Pie with Tres Leches Sauce

Ginger Peach Pies with Cornmeal Crust

Peach Cinnamon Crumble Pie

LARGE

Ginger Peach Pies with Cornmeal Crust

Peach Basil Pie

Pie Pops

Cream Cheese Crust

LARGE

American Slab Pie with Star Pie Pops

Chocolate Pudding Pie with Chocolate-
  Covered Strawberries

Sour Cherry Pie

Sweet Cherry Pie with Cream Cheese Crust

Truffle Pies

Chocolate Cream Cheese Crust (variation of Cream Cheese Crust)

SMALL

Brownie Cream Cheese Pie

Chocolate Pudding Pie with Chocolate-Covered
  Strawberries

Marshmallow Brownie Pie

Raspberry Brownie Pie

MEDIUM

Chunky Candy Bar Pie

Mini Brownie Sundae Pies

LARGE

Truffle Pies

Mocha Cream Cheese Crust (variation of Cream Cheese Crust)

SMALL

Mocha Pie

Egg Crust

MEDIUM

Coconut Custard Pie

Guava Coconut Custard Pie with Meringue Topping

Orange Coconut Custard Pie

LARGE

Blueberry Ravioli

Flaky Crust

LARGE

Blueberry Pies

Ricotta Pie

Shaker Lemon Pie

Sour Cherry Pie

Chocolate Chip Crust (variation of Flaky Crust)

SMALL

Chocolate Banana Cream Pie

Gingersnap Crust

SMALL

Blueberry Ginger Tart with Gingersnap Crust and Cream
  Cheese Filling

Fig Mint Ice Cream Pie

LARGE

Blackberry Lemon Meringue Tarts with Gingersnap Crust

Graham Cracker Cookie Crust

SMALL

Cheesecake Pie with Marzipan Butterflies

Chilly Milk Chocolate S'more Pie

Cranberry Orange Cream Pie

Peach and Soy Ice Cream Pie

MEDIUM

Cherry Mascarpone Cream Petits Fours Pies

Mascarpone Cream Petits Fours Pies

Orange Mascarpone Cream Petits Fours Pies

Vanilla Mascarpone Cream Petits Fours Pies

Butterscotch Graham Cracker Cookie Crust (variation of Graham Cracker Cookie Crust)

SMALL

Brandied Butterscotch Pie

Plain Butterscotch Pie

Coconut Graham Cracker Cookie Crust (variation of Graham Cracker Cookie Crust)

SMALL

Banana Date Nut Ice Cream Pie

Peppermint Marshmallow Pie

Lemon Graham Cracker Cookie Crust (variation of Graham Cracker Cookie Crust)

SMALL

Strawberry Rhubarb Pie

Three-Citrus Chiffon Pie

Sesame Graham Cracker Cookie Crust (variation of Graham Cracker Cookie Crust)

SMALL

Peanut Butter and Jam Pie

Peanut Butter Banana Pie

Peanut Butter Marshmallow Pie

Sesame Peanut Butter and Jam Pie

Oatmeal Crust

SMALL

Fresh Strawberry Pie

Oatmeal Cookies-and-Cream Ice Cream Pie

LARGE

Baked Strawberry Pie

Raisin Friendship Pie with Oatmeal Crust

Shortbread Cookie Crust

MEDIUM

Key Lime Pies

Mango Key Lime Pies

Papaya Key Lime Pies

LARGE

Marshmallow Cookie Pies

Peanut Butter Marshmallow Cookie Pies

Basic Tart Crust

MEDIUM

Dark Chocolate Lavender Tart

LARGE

Blueberry Custard Tart

Mini Chocolate Blueberry Almond Cream Cheese Tarts

Cashew Tart Crust (variation of Basic Tart Crust)

LARGE

Plantain Cashew Custard Tart

Chocolate Walnut Tart Crust (variation of Basic Tart Crust)

LARGE

Chocolate Fig Ricotta Tart

Dried Fig Tart

Sweet Tart Crust

MEDIUM

Honey-Sweetened Apple Tart

LARGE

Chocolate Almond Cream Tarts

Chocolate Cherry Cream Tarts

Chocolate Cream Tarts

Pine Nut Tart

EXTRA LARGE

Fruit Tarts with Sweet Tart Shells

Almond Sweet Tart Crust (variation of Sweet Tart Crust)

MEDIUM

Deconstructed Cherry Pies

LARGE

Apricot Almond Tart with Marzipan Lattice Top

Cherry Almond Tart

Lavender Lemon Meringue Tarts

Meyer Lemon Meringue Tarts

Chocolate Sweet Tart Crust (variation of Sweet Tart Crust)

SMALL

Milk Chocolate Mint Tart

LARGE

Chocolate Rice Pudding Tarts

Rice Pudding Tarts

CRUSTS

Basic Butter Crust

	Small	Medium	Large	Extra large
All-purpose flour	1¼ cups	1¾ cups plus 2 tablespoons	2½ cups	3¾ cups
Granulated sugar	1 tablespoon	1½ tablespoons	2 tablespoons	3 tablespoons
Salt	Pinch	¼ teaspoon	½ teaspoon	½ teaspoon
Cold unsalted butter, cut into cubes	½ cup (1 stick)	¾ cup (6 tablespoons)	1 cup (2 sticks)	1½ cups (3 sticks)
Cold water	3 tablespoons	4¼ tablespoons	6 tablespoons	½ cup plus 1 tablespoon

1. Combine the flour, sugar, and salt in a large bowl.

2. Using a pastry blender or your fingertips, cut in the butter until the mixture resembles coarse meal. Add the water a little at a time, tossing with a fork until the dough sticks together. If necessary, add more water a little at a time.

3. Pat the dough into one or more flattened disks (whatever is called for in the recipe), wrap in plastic wrap, and chill for 30 minutes before proceeding as directed in the recipe.

Variations

ALMOND BROWN SUGAR CRUST: Make a small batch of Basic Butter Crust and replace the granulated sugar with brown sugar. Add 2 tablespoons ground almonds to the flour.

CHOCOLATE ALMOND BUTTER CRUST: Make a small batch of Basic Butter Crust and reduce the flour to 2⅓ cups. Add ¼ cup sifted Dutch-process cocoa powder, 2 tablespoons granulated sugar, and 3 tablespoons chopped almonds to the dry ingredients.

CHOCOLATE BUTTER CRUST: For a large batch, reduce the flour to 2⅓ cups. Add ¼ cup sifted Dutch-process cocoa powder and 2 additional tablespoons granulated sugar to the dry ingredients.

COCONUT LEMON CRUST: Make a medium batch of Basic Butter Crust and add 2 tablespoons desiccated coconut and ½ teaspoon grated lemon zest to the dry ingredients.

MOCHA BUTTER CRUST: For a large batch, reduce the flour to 2¼ cups. Add ¾ cup sifted Dutch-process cocoa powder and 1½ teaspoons ground espresso beans to the dry ingredients.

NUT BUTTER CRUST: For a large batch, add 3 tablespoons ground macadamia nuts, walnuts, cashews, pecans, hazelnuts, peanuts, or almonds to the flour.

SPICED CRUST: For a large batch, add ¼ teaspoon ground nutmeg, ¼ teaspoon ground ginger, ¼ teaspoon ground cardamom, and ½ teaspoon ground cinnamon to the dry ingredients.

Chocolate Wafer Crust

	Small	Medium
Crushed chocolate wafer cookies	2 cups	3 cups
Unsalted butter, melted	¼ cup	⅓ cup
Semisweet chocolate chips, melted	¾ cup	¾ cup

1. Toss the cookie crumbs and the butter in a large bowl until well coated.

2. Butter and flour the pan or pans called for in the recipe. Using your hands, press the crumb mixture onto the bottom and sides of the pan. The bottom, sides, and edge of the crust should be ¼ inch thick. Using your fingers, flatten the edge flush with the top of the pan. Freeze for 30 minutes.

3. Spread the melted chocolate over the cold crust and refrigerate for 20–30 minutes to set before proceeding as directed in the recipe.

Variation

CHOCOLATE CHILI WAFER CRUST: Make a small batch of Chocolate Wafer Crust and add ¼ teaspoon cayenne pepper and ⅛ teaspoon ground cinnamon to the cookie crumbs.

Cornmeal Crust

Medium-grind yellow or blue cornmeal can be used to make this crust. The peach nectar can be replaced with cold water or another kind of fruit juice to enhance the flavor of the filling—for example, you can use apple cider for an apple pie and cranberry juice for a cranberry pie.

	Small	Large
Unsalted butter, at room temperature	5 tablespoons	¾ cup
Shortening, at room temperature	¼ cup	⅓ cup
All-purpose flour	1 cup plus 3 tablespoons	2⅓ cups
Yellow or blue cornmeal	¼ cup	½ cup
Granulated sugar	1 tablespoon	2 tablespoons
Salt	Pinch	½ teaspoon
Cold peach nectar	4–5 tablespoons	8–10 tablespoons

1. Combine the butter and shortening in a medium mixing bowl. Beat with an electric mixer on medium speed for 30–60 seconds, or until blended. Cover and chill for 1 hour, then cut into small cubes.

2. Combine the flour, cornmeal, sugar, and salt in a large bowl. Using a pastry blender or your fingertips, cut in the fat until the mixture resembles coarse meal. Add the peach nectar a little at a time, tossing with a fork until the dough sticks together. If necessary, add more juice a little at a time.

3. Pat the dough into one or more flattened disks (whatever is called for in the recipe), wrap in plastic wrap, and chill for 1 hour before proceeding as directed in the recipe.

Cream Cheese Crust

This dough is sweet yet tangy, and is extra stretchy so it's easy to work with—but it won't be as flaky some other crusts. It is excellent for making detailed decorative crusts. To make it easy to distribute the butter and cream cheese evenly through the dough, mix them together first, then chill before adding them to the dry ingredients.

	Small	Medium	Large
Unsalted butter, at room temperature	¼ cup	6 tablespoons	½ cup
Cream cheese, at room temperature	2 ounces	3 ounces	4 ounces
All-purpose flour	1½ cups	2¼ cups	3 cups
Salt	Pinch	¼ teaspoon	½ teaspoon
Confectioners' sugar	1 tablespoon	1½ tablespoons	2 tablespoons
Cold water	¼ cup	⅓ cup	½ cup

1. Combine the butter and cream cheese in a medium mixing bowl. Beat with an electric mixer on medium speed for 30–60 seconds, or until smooth. Cover and chill for 30 minutes, then cut into small cubes.

2. Combine the flour, salt, and sugar in a large bowl. Using a pastry blender or your fingertips, cut in the fat until the mixture resembles coarse meal. Add the water a little at a time, tossing with a fork or your fingertips until the dough sticks together. If necessary, add more water a little at a time.

3. Pat the dough into one or more flattened disks (whatever is called for in the recipe), wrap in plastic wrap, and chill for 1 hour before proceeding as directed in the recipe.

Variations

CHOCOLATE CREAM CHEESE CRUST: For a large batch, reduce the flour to 2¾ cups. Add ⅔ cup sifted Dutch-process cocoa powder and 2 additional tablespoons confectioners' sugar to the dry ingredients.

MOCHA CREAM CHEESE CRUST: Make a small batch of Cream Cheese Crust and reduce the flour to 2¾ cups. Add ⅔ cup sifted Dutch-process cocoa powder to the dry ingredients. Grind 1 tablespoon instant coffee granules or 2 teaspoons coffee beans in a food processor until extremely fine and add to the dry ingredients.

Egg Crust

The egg in this crust binds the ingredients together and adds flavor and color. It is a little less flaky than other crusts, but the trade-off is worth it when you're looking for a crust that is easy yet tasty.

	Medium	**Large**
All-purpose flour	1½ cups	2¼ cups
Granulated sugar	1 tablespoon	1½ tablespoons
Salt	⅛ teaspoon	⅛ teaspoon
Cold unsalted butter, cut into cubes	6 tablespoons	½ cup (1 stick) plus 1 tablespoon
Egg yolk	1 large	2 medium
Cold water	6 tablespoons	8 tablespoons

1. Combine the flour, sugar, and salt in a large bowl.

2. Using a pastry blender or your fingertips, cut in the butter until the mixture resembles coarse meal.

3. In a small bowl, beat the yolk and the water together. Add the yolk mixture to the dough a little at a time, tossing with a fork until it sticks together. If necessary, add more cold water a little at a time.

4. Pat the dough into one or more flattened disks (whatever is called for in the recipe), wrap in plastic wrap, and chill for 1 hour before proceeding as directed in the recipe.

Flaky Crust

The rumor is true: shortening *does* make the flakiest crust. If flaky is your goal, this is the crust for you.

	Small	**Large**
All-purpose flour	1½ cups	3 cups
Salt	⅛ teaspoon	¼ teaspoon
Shortening	½ cup	1 cup
Cold water	3–4 tablespoons	7–8 tablespoons

1. Combine the flour and salt in a large bowl.

2. Using a pastry blender or your fingertips, cut in the shortening until the mixture resembles coarse meal. Add the water a little at a time, tossing with a fork until the dough sticks together. If necessary, add more water a little at a time.

3. Pat the dough into one or more flattened disks (whatever is called for in the recipe), wrap in plastic wrap, and chill for 1 hour before proceeding as directed in the recipe.

Variation

CHOCOLATE CHIP CRUST: Make a small batch of Flaky Crust and add ½ cup chopped semisweet chocolate chips to the dry ingredients.

Fluffy Crust

The baking powder in this recipe allows the dough to expand and puff out a bit while baking, thus filling in all the crust's imperfections! The result is a crust that has a delicious touch of cakeyness to it.

½ cup (1 stick) unsalted butter, at room temperature
½ cup granulated sugar
1 large egg
1½ teaspoons baking powder
½ teaspoon salt
1 teaspoon vanilla extract
1¾ cups all-purpose flour

1. Combine the butter and sugar in a medium mixing bowl. Beat with an electric mixer on medium speed until light and fluffy. Add the eggs, one at a time, and continue to beat for an additional 2 minutes.

2. Reduce the mixer speed to low and add the baking powder, salt, and vanilla. Gradually add the flour, 1 cup at a time, until it is fully incorporated.

3. Pat the dough into one or more flattened disks (whatever is called for in the recipe), wrap in plastic wrap, and chill for 2 hours before proceeding as directed in the recipe.

Variation

FLUFFY ORANGE ALMOND CRUST: Replace the vanilla extract with 1 teaspoon grated orange zest and ½ teaspoon almond extract.

Gingersnap Crust

1¾ cups gingersnap cookie crumbs
¼ cup granulated sugar
¼ cup unsalted butter, melted
½ teaspoon grated orange zest

1. Combine all ingredients in a large bowl.

2. Butter and flour the pan as directed in the recipe. Using your hands, press the crumb mixture onto the bottom and sides of the pan. The bottom, sides, and edge of the crust should be ¼ inch thick. Using your fingers, flatten the edge flush with the top of the pan. Freeze for 30 minutes.

3. Preheat the oven to 350°F. Bake for 6–8 minutes, or until the crust begins to darken. Cool on a rack.

Graham Cracker Cookie Crust

	Small	**Medium**
Graham cracker crumbs	1½ cups	2¼ cups
Granulated sugar	3 tablespoons	4½ tablespoons
Unsalted butter, melted	¼ cup	⅓ cup

1. Combine the graham cracker crumbs and sugar in a large bowl. Gradually add the butter to moisten.

2. Butter and flour the pan as directed in the recipe. Using your hands, press the crumb mixture onto the bottom and sides of the pan. The bottom, sides, and edge of the crust should be

¼ inch thick. Using your fingers, flatten the edge flush with the top of the pan. Freeze for 30 minutes.

3. Preheat the oven to 325°F. Bake for 7–10 minutes. Cool on a rack.

Variations

BUTTERSCOTCH GRAHAM CRACKER COOKIE CRUST: Make a small batch of Graham Cracker Cookie Crust and spread ½ cup melted butterscotch chips over the crust before freezing.

COCONUT GRAHAM CRACKER COOKIE CRUST: Make a small batch of Graham Cracker Cookie Crust but reduce the graham cracker crumbs to 1 cup. Add ⅓ cup desiccated or sweetened flaked coconut and an additional 1 tablespoon butter to the crumbs.

LEMON GRAHAM CRACKER COOKIE CRUST: Make a small batch of Graham Cracker Cookie Crust and add 1 tablespoon grated lemon zest to the crumbs.

SESAME GRAHAM CRACKER COOKIE CRUST: Make a small batch of Graham Cracker Cookie Crust and add 2 tablespoons sesame seeds to the crumbs.

Herb Wheat Germ Crust

2¼ cups all-purpose flour
¾ cup whole wheat flour
¼ cup untoasted wheat germ
½ teaspoon salt
1½ cups (3 sticks) cold unsalted butter, cut into cubes
1½ cups cold water
3 tablespoons chopped fresh herbs, such as rosemary, thyme, sage, dill, tarragon, or basil

1. Combine the flours, wheat germ, and salt in a large bowl.

2. Using a pastry blender or your fingertips, cut in the butter until the mixture resembles coarse meal. Add the water a little at a time, tossing with a fork or your fingertips until the dough sticks together. If necessary, add more a little at a time. The dough should be moist but only slightly sticky.

3. Pat the dough into one or more flattened disks (whatever is called for in the recipe), wrap in plastic wrap, and chill for 30 minutes before proceeding as directed in the recipe.

Meringue Crust

2 large egg whites

¼ teaspoon cream of tartar

¼ teaspoon salt

½ teaspoon vanilla extract

½ cup granulated sugar

Combine the egg whites, cream of tartar, and salt in a medium mixing bowl. Beat with an electric mixer on medium speed until soft peaks form. Add the vanilla, then slowly beat in sugar until very stiff and glossy. Proceed as directed in the recipe.

Oatmeal Crust

The crust has the flavor and crunchy texture of oatmeal cookies.

	Small	**Large**
Rolled oats (not instant)	¾ cup	2 cups
All-purpose flour	1 cup	1½ cups
Firmly packed light brown sugar	⅓ cup	¾ cup
Ground walnuts	⅛ cup	¼ cup
Baking soda	½ teaspoon	¾ teaspoon
Salt	Pinch	¼ teaspoon
Flax seed	1 tablespoon	2 tablespoons
Unsalted butter, melted	10 tablespoons (1¼ sticks)	1¼ cups (2½ sticks)

1. Combine the oats, flour, sugar, walnuts, baking soda, salt, and flax seed in a large bowl. Mix thoroughly. Gradually add one-third of the butter and stir to coat. Mix in the remaining butter, one-third at a time, until the dry mixture is completely coated and it sticks together.

2. Pat the dough into one or more flattened disks (whatever is called for in the recipe), wrap in plastic wrap, and chill for 1 hour before proceeding as directed in the recipe.

Olive Oil Crust

⅔ cup extra virgin olive oil

1¼ cups all-purpose flour

About ½ cup cold water

1¼ cups semolina

¼ teaspoon salt

1 teaspoon baking powder

1 large egg

1 tablespoon cider vinegar

1. Freeze the olive oil for 6–8 hours, or until thick.

2. Combine ¼ cup flour and ⅓ cup water in a small bowl and mix into a paste. Set aside.

3. Combine the remaining flour, semolina, salt, and baking powder in a food processor and pulse about 5 times to combine.

4. Add the olive oil, egg, and vinegar and pulse until the mixture resembles coarse meal. Add the reserved flour paste and pulse until mixture forms a ball. Add remaining water if necessary.

5. Pat the dough into one or more flattened disks (whatever is called for in the recipe), wrap in plastic wrap, and chill for 1 hour before proceeding as directed in the recipe.

Puff Pastry

3 cups all-purpose flour

1 cup cake flour

½ teaspoon salt

2 cups (4 sticks) cold unsalted butter, sliced into tablespoon-size pats

1⅓ cups ice water

1. Mix the flours and salt in a large bowl. Toss the butter in the flour mixture until coated. Break up the butter a little with your fingertips.

2. Form a well in the center of the dough. Gradually add the water and mix until the flour is slightly moistened.

3. Turn out the dough on a floured surface and knead 8–10 times, then gather into a ball. Flatten the dough into a rectangle.

4. Roll the dough into a 15-inch square. Fold into thirds horizontally, forming a 15 x 5-inch rectangle. Rotate the dough a quarter turn, then fold horizontally into thirds again to form a 5-inch square. Wrap in plastic wrap and chill for 30 minutes.

5. Repeat the rolling and folding process twice more, chilling for 30 minutes each time, before proceeding as directed in the recipe.

Shortbread Cookie Crust

	Small	**Medium**	**Large**
All-purpose flour	1½ cups	2¾ cups	3 cups
Salt	Pinch	¼ teaspoon	½ teaspoon
Unsalted butter, at room temperature	¾ cup (1½ sticks)	1 cup plus 2 tablespoons (2¼ sticks	1½ cups (3 sticks)
Confectioners' sugar	½ cup	¾ cup	1 cup
Vanilla extract	¾ teaspoon	1 teaspoon	1½ teaspoons

1. Combine the flour and salt in a medium bowl; set aside.

2. Combine the butter and confectioners' sugar in a large bowl. Beat with an electric mixer on medium speed until light. Beat in the vanilla.

3. With the mixer on low speed, gradually stir in the flour mixture.

4. Pat the dough into one or more flattened disks (whatever is called for in the recipe), wrap in plastic wrap, and chill for 30 minutes before proceeding as directed in the recipe.

Basic Tart Crust

	Medium	**Large**
Egg yolks	1 jumbo	2 large
Cold water	¼ cup	⅓ cup
Vanilla extract	1 teaspoon	1½ teaspoons
All-purpose flour	1¾ cups	2½ cups
Granulated sugar	¼ cup	⅓ cup
Salt	⅛ teaspoon	¼ teaspoon
Cold unsalted butter, cut into cubes	¾ cup (1½ sticks)	1 cup (2 sticks)

1. Combine the egg yolks, water, and vanilla in a small bowl; set aside.

2. Combine the flour, sugar, and salt in a large bowl. Using a pastry blender or your fingertips, cut in the butter until the mixture resembles coarse meal.

3. Gradually add the egg yolk mixture and stir with a fork until the dough gathers together.

4. Pat the dough into a ball and then into a flattened disk. Wrap in plastic wrap and chill for 30 minutes before proceeding as directed in the recipe.

Variations

CASHEW TART CRUST: For a large batch, reduce the flour to 2¼ cups. Add ½ cup ground cashews to the flour and a few additional drops cold water if necessary.

CHOCOLATE TART CRUST: For a large batch, reduce the flour to 2¼ cups. Add ½ cup Dutch-process cocoa powder and 2 tablespoons sugar to the dry ingredients. Add a few additional drops cold water if necessary.

CHOCOLATE WALNUT TART CRUST: For a large batch, reduce the flour to 2¼ cups. Add ½ cup Dutch-process cocoa powder, ½ cup ground walnuts, and an additional 2 tablespoons sugar to the dry ingredients. Add a few additional drops cold water if necessary.

Sweet Tart Crust

	Small	Medium	Large	Extra large
Egg yolks	2 medium	2 large	3 large	4 large
Vanilla extract	1 teaspoon	1½ teaspoons	2 teaspoons	1 tablespoon
Cold water	1¼ tablespoons	1¾–2 tablespoons	2½ tablespoons	3½–4 tablespoons
All-purpose flour	1¼ cups	1¾ cups plus 2 tablespoons	2½ cups	3¾ cups
Confectioners' sugar	⅓ cup	½ cup	⅔ cup	¾ cup
Salt	Pinch	⅛ teaspoon	¼ teaspoon	¼ teaspoon
Cold unsalted butter, cut into cubes	½ cup (1 stick)	¾ cup (1½ sticks)	1 cup (2 sticks)	1½ cups (3 sticks)

1. Combine the egg yolks, vanilla, and water in a small bowl; set aside.

2. Combine the flour, sugar, and salt in a large mixing bowl. Using a pastry blender or your fingertips, cut in the butter until the mixture resembles coarse meal. Add the egg yolk mixture, tossing with a fork until the dough sticks together. Using your hands, form the dough into a ball, then press it on a floured surface, kneading it a few times to make sure all the butter pieces are worked in.

3. Pat the dough into one or more flattened disks (whatever is called for in the recipe), wrap in plastic wrap, and chill for 1–2 hours before proceeding as directed in the recipe.

Variations

ALMOND SWEET TART CRUST: For a large batch, reduce the flour to 2¼ cups and add ¼ cup ground almonds to the flour mixture. Replace the vanilla extract with ¼ teaspoon almond extract.

CHOCOLATE SWEET TART CRUST: For a large batch, reduce the flour to 2¼ cups and add 1 cup sifted Dutch-process cocoa powder and 2 additional tablespoons sugar to the flour mixture.

FILLINGS

1 cup water

⅓ cup freshly squeezed lemon juice

1 packet (¼ ounce) unflavored gelatin

¾ cup granulated sugar

3¾ cups (30 ounces) cream cheese, at room temperature

1 tablespoon grated lemon zest

Cream Cheese Filling

Makes 4 cups

Make sure to add this very smooth and creamy filling to the shell right after it is mixed, before it has time to set.

1. Bring the water and lemon juice to a boil in a saucepan set over high heat. Reduce the heat to low. Stir in the gelatin and sugar until dissolved. Transfer to a large bowl and let cool for 10 minutes.

2. Combine the cream cheese and lemon zest in a large bowl. Add the gelatin mixture and beat with an electric mixer on medium speed until smooth. Spoon into the crust immediately. Cover and chill for 2 hours, or as directed in the recipe.

¼ cup unsalted butter

⅓ cup granulated sugar

2 large eggs

½ teaspoon grated lemon zest

½ cup freshly squeezed lemon juice

Lemon Curd

Makes 1¼ cups

Melt the butter in a saucepan. Add the sugar, eggs, lemon zest, and lemon juice and stir over medium heat until it forms a custard. Allow to cool, then pour into a bowl, cover with plastic wrap, and refrigerate for 3 hours. The curd will thicken while cooling.

Variation

KEY LIME CURD: Replace the lemon juice and zest with Key lime juice and zest.

¾ cup granulated sugar

6 tablespoons all-purpose flour

3 cups whole milk

3 large egg yolks

1 ½ tablespoons unsalted butter

1 tablespoon vanilla extract

Pastry Cream

Makes 3½ cups

This versatile, easy-to-make pastry cream can be used to fill baked tart shells or as a base for cream pies.

1. Combine the sugar and flour in a heavy, heatproof mixing bowl; set aside.

2. Heat the milk over low heat in a heavy saucepan until bubbles begin to appear. Do not let the milk boil. Remove the skin that forms on the surface of the milk. Slowly pour the milk into the sugar mixture, whisking constantly. Pour the mixture into the top of a double boiler set over simmering water and cook for about 10 minutes, or until the mixture lightly coats the back of a spoon.

3. Add egg yolks and cook, stirring constantly, for an additional 10 minutes, or until the mixture thickens and heavily coats the back of a spoon. Remove from heat and add the butter, stirring until melted. Stir in the vanilla.

4. Transfer to a bowl, cover with plastic wrap touching the surface, and chill for 2 hours.

Variations

ALMOND PASTRY CREAM: Add ⅓ cup ground almonds and 3 tablespoons amaretto liqueur along with the vanilla.

CHOCOLATE PASTRY CREAM: Add 4 ounces melted dark chocolate (at least 60% cacao) along with the vanilla.

Vanilla Ice Cream

Makes 4½ cups

6 large egg yolks

1 cup granulated sugar

⅛ teaspoon salt

2 cups heavy cream

1½ cups whole milk

1 tablespoon vanilla extract

1. Combine the egg yolks, sugar, and salt in a medium mixing bowl. Beat with an electric mixer on medium speed until the mixture forms ribbons when the beaters are lifted.

2. Combine the cream and milk in a medium saucepan over medium heat until just below the boiling point. Slowly

whisk in the egg mixture and cook, stirring constantly, about 5 minutes, or until the custard thickly coats the back of a wooden spoon.

3. Return the mixture to the mixing bowl and stir in the vanilla. Place the bowl inside a larger bowl half full of ice water and let cool, stirring occasionally. Cover and chill for 1 hour.

4. Transfer to an ice cream maker and freeze according to manufacturer's instructions.

Variations

CARAMEL ICE CREAM: Add ½ cup caramel ice cream topping or dulce de leche (available at most grocery stores) to the saucepan along with the cream and milk.

CHOCOLATE ICE CREAM: Add 2 ounces chopped semisweet chocolate to the saucepan along with the cream and milk. Make sure chocolate is melted completely before returning mixture to the bowl.

PUMPKIN ICE CREAM: Reduce the milk to 1 cup. Stir one 15-ounce can pumpkin purée, 1 teaspoon pumpkin pie spice, and 3 drops orange food coloring into the mixture when you set it over the ice water.

TOPPINGS

Candied Pecans

Makes 1 cup

1 large egg white
¼ cup granulated sugar
½ teaspoon ground nutmeg
½ teaspoon ground cinnamon
¼ teaspoon salt
1 cup pecan halves

1. Preheat the oven to 300°F. Butter a rimmed baking sheet or jelly-roll pan.

2. Using an electric mixer on medium speed, beat the egg white until foamy. Add the sugar, nutmeg, cinnamon, and salt. Continue to beat until the mixture is thick. Add the pecans and stir until coated. Spread on the baking sheet.

3. Bake nuts until golden brown, about 20–25 minutes, stirring occasionally. Cool completely on the baking sheet.

Chocolate Ganache

Makes 2⅔ cups

12 ounces white or dark chocolate (at least 60% cacao), chopped

1½ cups heavy cream

Place the chocolate in a heatproof bowl. Bring the cream to a boil in a small saucepan. Pour the cream over the chocolate and stir until the chocolate is melted. Let cool to room temperature. Store in the refrigerator for up to 2 days.

Cinnamon Sugar

Makes ¼ cup

1 teaspoon ground cinnamon

¼ cup granulated sugar

Combine the cinnamon and sugar in a small bowl. Store in a cool, dark place for up to 6 months.

Crumble Topping

Makes 2¾–3 cups

1½ cups rolled oats (not instant)

½ cup all-purpose flour

⅔ cup firmly packed light brown sugar

½ teaspoon salt

1 cup (2 sticks) cold unsalted butter, cut into cubes

Combine the oats, flour, brown sugar, and salt in a bowl. Using a pastry blender or your fingertips, cut in the butter until mixture resembles coarse meal. Proceed as directed in the recipe.

Variation

NUT BUTTER CRUMBLE: Replace ½ cup of the butter with ½ cup peanut butter, almond butter, or cashew butter.

Fondant

Makes 4 cups (about 2 pounds)

¼ cup water

1 packet (¼ ounce) unflavored gelatin

½ cup light corn syrup

1½ tablespoons glycerin

1½ tablespoons vanilla extract

2 pounds confectioners' sugar, plus more as needed

Food coloring (optional)

If it happens that this fondant recipe makes more than I need for a particular pie, I prepare more decorations than required and dry out the extra. I store them with my decorating ingredients and they are ready to go when I need a nicely decorated dessert in a hurry.

1. Combine the water and gelatin in a small saucepan. Heat for about 5 minutes, or until the gelatin is dissolved and clear. Remove from the heat and stir in the corn syrup, glycerin, and vanilla until blended.

2. Put the sugar in a very large bowl and make a well in the center. Pour the gelatin mixture into the well and mix with a wooden spoon until blended.

3. Dust a work surface with additional confectioners' sugar. Turn out the fondant and knead for about 5 minutes, or until smooth and pliable. If the mixture is sticky, add more confectioners' sugar until smooth. Wrap the fondant in plastic and let sit at room temperature for several hours, or overnight if possible. Do not refrigerate. The fondant will stay fresh at room temperature for up to 2 days. If you do not plan to use the fondant within 2 days, you can refrigerate it for up to 2 weeks.

4. When ready to use, knead in the food coloring as desired. Add more sugar if sticky or water if dry.

Hot Fudge
Makes 2¾ cups

⅔ cup (about 4 ounces) unsweet-ened chocolate, coarsely chopped

½ cup (1 stick) unsalted butter

½ teaspoon salt

3 cups granulated sugar

1 can (12 ounces) evaporated milk

In a double boiler set over simmering water, combine the chocolate, butter, and salt. Stir until chocolate is melted. Add the sugar ½ cup at a time, stirring after each addition until dissolved. Slowly add the evaporated milk until fully integrated. Cool as directed in the recipe. Store extra sauce in the refrigerator for up to 1 week.

Marshmallow Meringue
Makes 2 cups

3 large egg whites

⅛ teaspoon salt

1 jar (7 ounces) marshmallow crème

1. Combine the egg whites and salt in a medium mixing bowl. Beat with an electric mixer on medium speed until soft peaks form.

2. Gradually add the marshmallow crème, continuing to beat until stiff peaks form. Use as directed in recipe.

Marzipan

Makes 3¾ cups (about 1½ pounds)

Unlike fondant, marzipan doesn't keep—it's best to use it within 24 hours. But if you have more than you need for a recipe, the leftover marzipan can also be formed into shapes and eaten on its own as candy.

3 cups ground almonds
1½ cups confectioners' sugar, plus more for dusting
¾ cup superfine sugar
1½ teaspoons freshly squeezed lemon juice
1 teaspoon almond extract
1 large egg, beaten

1. Combine the almonds and both sugars in a mixing bowl and mix with a wooden spoon. Add the lemon juice and almond extract, then add enough of the egg to make a soft firm dough. Gather to form a ball.

2. Dust a work surface with additional confectioners' sugar. Turn out the marzipan and knead until smooth and pliable. Wrap in plastic wrap until ready to use.

Meringue Topping

Makes about 4 cups

Combine the egg whites, salt, cream of tartar, and vanilla in a large mixing bowl. Beat with an electric mixer on medium speed until soft peaks form. Beat in the sugar, a little at a time, until stiff but not dry. Do not overbeat.

4 large egg whites
⅛ teaspoon salt
⅛ teaspoon cream of tartar
½ teaspoon vanilla extract
6 tablespoons superfine sugar

Variation

ALMOND MERINGUE TOPPING: Substitute ½ teaspoon almond extract for the vanilla.

Vanilla Buttercream

Makes 2¼ cups

Combine the butter and vanilla in a large mixing bowl. Beat with an electric mixer on medium speed until fluffy, then add the sugar until blended. Gradually add the water until the buttercream reaches a spreadable consistency.

1⅓ cups (2 ⅔ sticks) unsalted butter, at room temperature
1 teaspoon vanilla extract
1½ cups confectioners' sugar
¼ cup cold water

Variation

ALMOND BUTTERCREAM: Substitute ½ teaspoon almond extract for the vanilla.

Vanilla Icing

Makes 1½ cups

> 3 cups confectioners' sugar, plus more if necessary
>
> 3 tablespoons warm water
>
> 2 teaspoons vanilla extract

Place the sugar in a medium bowl and gradually beat in the water until smooth. Beat in the vanilla. If necessary, add more sugar to stiffen.

Variations

ALMOND ICING: Replace the vanilla with 1 teaspoon almond extract.

CHERRY ICING: Replace the water with cherry juice.

LEMON ICING: Replace the vanilla with freshly squeezed lemon juice.

ORANGE ICING: Replace the water with orange juice.

Whipped Cream

Makes 3½–4 cups

> 2 cups heavy cream
>
> 1½ teaspoons vanilla extract
>
> 2 tablespoons granulated sugar

Beat the cream only until it forms soft peaks if you want to dollop it on top of or alongside your pie; beat it until it forms medium peaks if you want to transfer it to a pastry bag and use it for piping.

Combine all ingredients in a large mixing bowl. Beat with an electric mixer on medium speed until the cream reaches the desired consistency.

Variations

BRANDIED WHIPPED CREAM: Replace the vanilla with ¼ cup brandy.

CHOCOLATE WHIPPED CREAM: Add 3 tablespoons Dutch-process cocoa powder and 3 additional tablespoons of sugar to the mixture before beating.

CINNAMON WHIPPED CREAM: Mix 1 teaspoon ground cinnamon in with the sugar.

COCONUT LEMON WHIPPED CREAM: Chill a 13.5-ounce can of full-fat coconut milk. Skim off the thick cream that forms and fold it into the cream after beating. Replace the vanilla with 1½ teaspoons freshly squeezed lemon juice and add 1–2 drops yellow food coloring before beating.

GINGER WHIPPED CREAM: Fold 3 tablespoons chopped crystallized ginger into the cream after beating.

MAPLE WHIPPED CREAM: Add ½ cup grade A maple syrup to the cream after the soft peaks form.

METRIC EQUIVALENTS

Liquid Ingredients

This chart can also be used for small amounts of dry ingredients, like salt and baking powder.

U.S. quantity	Metric equivalent
¼ teaspoon	1 ml
½ teaspoon	2.5 ml
¾ teaspoon	4 ml
1 teaspoon	5 ml
1¼ teaspoons	6 ml
1½ teaspoons	7.5 ml
1¾ teaspoons	8.5 ml
2 teaspoons	10 ml
1 tablespoon	15 ml
2 tablespoons	30 ml
⅛ cup	30 ml
¼ cup (2 fluid ounces)	60 ml
⅓ cup	80 ml
½ cup (4 fluid ounces)	120 ml
⅔ cup	160 ml
¾ cup (6 fluid ounces)	180 ml
1 cup (8 fluid ounces)	240 ml
1½ cups (12 fluid ounces)	350 ml
2 cups (1 pint, or 16 fluid ounces)	475 ml
3 cups	700 ml
4 cups (1 quart)	950 ml (.95 liter)

Dry Ingredients

Ingredient	1 cup	¾ cup	⅔ cup	½ cup	⅓ cup	¼ cup	2 tablespoons
All-purpose flour	120 g	90 g	80 g	60 g	40 g	30 g	15 g
Brown sugar, firmly packed	180 g	135 g	120 g	90 g	60 g	45 g	23 g
Butter	240 g	180 g	160 g	120 g	80 g	60 g	30 g
Chopped fruits and vegetables	150 g	110 g	100 g	75 g	50 g	40 g	20 g
Chopped nuts	150 g	110 g	100 g	75 g	50 g	40 g	20 g
Confectioners' sugar	100 g	75 g	70 g	50 g	35 g	25 g	13 g
Cornmeal	160 g	120 g	100 g	80 g	50 g	40 g	20 g
Cornstarch	120 g	90 g	80 g	60 g	40 g	30 g	15 g
Granulated sugar	200 g	150 g	130 g	100 g	65 g	50 g	25 g
Ground nuts	120 g	90 g	80 g	60 g	40 g	30 g	15 g
Shortening	190 g	140 g	125 g	95 g	65 g	48 g	24 g

INDEX

Note: Page numbers in *italics* indicate recipes. Recipes titles by (var.) indicate variations of main recipes.